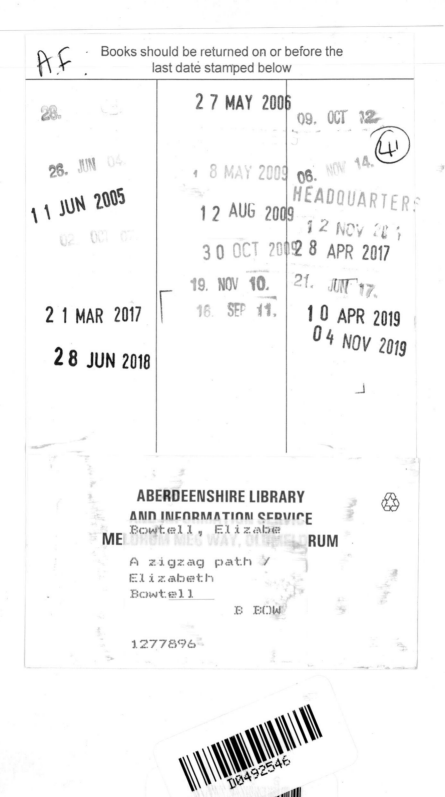

A.F.

Books should be returned on or before the
last date stamped below

28.

26. JUN 04.

1 1 JUN 2005

02 OCT

2 7 MAY 2006

1 8 MAY 2009

1 2 AUG 2009

3 0 OCT 2009

19. NOV 10.

16. SEP 11.

09. OCT 12

06. NOV 14.

④

HEADQUARTERS

1 2 NOV

2 8 APR 2017

21. JUN 17.

2 1 MAR 2017

2 8 JUN 2018

1 0 APR 2019

0 4 NOV 2019

D0492546

1277896

A ZIGZAG PATH

Also available in this series:

A ZigZag Path

Elizabeth Bowtell

ISIS
LARGE PRINT
Oxford

First published in Great Britain 2000
by Seagull Press

Published in Large Print 2002 by ISIS Publishing Ltd,
7 Centremead, Osney Mead, Oxford OX2 0ES
by arrangement with Elizabeth Bowtell

British Library Cataloguing in Publication Data
Bowtell, Elizabeth
  A zigzag path. – Large print ed. – (Isis reminiscence series)
  1. Bowtell, Elizabeth 2. Large type books 3. Cornwall
  (England) – Biography
  I. Title
  942.3'7'082'092

ISBN 0-7531-9716-2 (hb)
ISBN 0-7531-9717-0 (pb)

Printed and bound by Antony Rowe, Chippenham and Reading

ACKNOWLEDGEMENTS

My thanks go to Hugh Graham whose enthusiasm, professional expertise and generous help led to the publication of this book. I am grateful to all who have helped me, particularly to Neill Beasley for giving me the cover design and architectural drawings and to my daughter, Jill Bradon, for contributing many illustrations.

A Dedication

To Peter, our Children and Grandchildren

CONTENTS

CHAPTER ONE

2nd Class boy

In my mother's kitchen there was an eel that would not die. I tiptoed into the larder to inspect the jutting jaw and wicked teeth of the conger lying death-still on the cold grey slab. With a sudden wild convulsion, it started thrashing, snapping. I leapt back. "Come on out, Miss Betty," cried Myrtle, pulling me by the shoulder, as she and Mother went in, taking turns to smite the eel with a rolling pin. Neither Mother nor Myrtle, a strong Cornishwoman, were easily beaten, but the eel's flat brown eyes glared balefully at them, apparently unaffected by blows that would have slain a shark.

Even through the shut larder door, the thuds and wallops were unbearable, yet rather like the noise Myrtle made plumping up the pillows when she made our beds.

Fleeing to the garden, to my refuge in the bay tree, thumps still echoed in my head. Again and again I'd struggled vainly to climb to the top, so that I could brag to my brother, Peter. Being four years older and cumbersome, he would have snapped the branches, but I was lithe and this was one thing I could do better

1

than him; but I was already seven years old and the more I grew, the harder the ascent.

In 1930, girls wore cotton dresses, not shorts or jeans. My climbing resulted in scratched legs, dirty smudges, and the risk of a torn dress. As I climbed, bruised leaves released gusts of exotic scent, more pungent than anything from Myrtle's kitchen, where a single bay-leaf was enough to flavour a whole simmering casserole. I never knew what became of that eel, but we never ate it. I don't know how Father came to have it. Usually he brought home creatures he had shot; very dead.

Father was a Land Agent. He managed the vast estate of Prideaux Place, in Padstow, supervising the Home-Farm and the many tenanted farms and houses spread over a wide area of North Cornwall.

Our home was "Fentonluna", which belonged to the estate, and Father's office adjoined the house. At his roll-top desk and a free-standing drawing board, he made architectural drawings for alterations and improvements, using fine pens with black, red and green Indian ink on pale blue glazed linen sheets.

A path led from his office through the Shrubbery to Prideaux Place, carpeted in spring with yellow-trumpeted daffodils, double white narcissi and sweet-smelling jonquils. As the first flowering faded, the pheasant-eyes followed on, with bright orange cups in white single flowers.

New-born fawns sometimes lay in the grass near the fence, so well-camouflaged and lying so still that once

Mother almost stepped on one; in fright, it leapt into the folds of her skirt.

Fourteen generations of the Prideaux-Brune family have lived in Prideaux Place. There was already a Prideaux there in the reign of Queen Elizabeth I. The house has not suffered the "improvements" defacing other great houses. Completed in 1592, Prideaux Place has three castellated bays forming the traditional Elizabethan "E".

Father often took Peter with him on his rounds and I yearned to go too. Disappointment ran deep, but false pride and fear of rebuff stopped me asking directly; I longed to be *invited*. In truth, I was jealous and it was Father's affection I craved, but I was knocking on the door of an empty house. I reasoned that if I were more like a boy, my chances of pleasing him would increase. Wrong. Many years elapsed before I realised that girls get on far better by being girls, rather than second-class boys.

One red-letter day I did go. I was astonished how such big families crushed into the tiny cottages, with low ceilings and small dark rooms. Father was well over six feet tall and had to duck to get through the doorways. Reaching outlying farms often meant driving along rough tracks, with a gate to be opened and closed between each field.

I wanted to be the one allowed to stand on the running board between gates, hair flying in the wind; it felt very daring. I hoped for better luck when Peter went away to school, but by then I had a governess and a schoolroom.

Occasionally I was in demand when Father went rabbit-shooting, with Peter-dog at his heels. Peter-dog, a black and white brindled spaniel, went everywhere with him, with no time for anyone else. If Father went off without him, he'd sit in the road all day, facing up towards Prideaux Place (known locally as Place), refusing to budge until his master returned.

Clearly if I wanted to be treated as a boy, no invitation from Father could be spurned, so rabbit-shooting I went. I shut my eyes tight when he fired, to avoid that last agonised leap. I had to carry home the warm furry corpses, which exuded blood and urine that ran down my bare legs into my white socks.

I also carried the ferrets, ready to put down burrows to flush the rabbits out. Father reached into the bag, grasping a ferret behind the head to stop it turning to bite. Fortunately my hands weren't strong enough for that job.

Back in the kitchen, Myrtle decapitated and skinned the bodies. I could not watch. Neither could I eat rabbit; not then, not since. Father almost turned me into a vegetarian. Faced with rabbit, a sheep's eye or starvation, it would be a hard choice. One day, when we were visiting an elderly lady, rabbit was served at lunch. "I'll be sick," I whispered to Mother. "Eat it," she hissed. I did. I was.

I could manage to help Myrtle pluck pheasants. I did not like handling them, but the beauty of their perfectly marked feathers marginally offset the repellence of the naked flesh. Myrtle was my friend and I spent a lot of time in her kitchen. Born in Delabole, she lived all her long life in Padstow and was nearly a hundred when she died. I doubt if she ever went further than Wadebridge. She was a sturdy woman, her short black hair gradually turning whiter, her dark eyes sparkling when her face creased with laughter.

Using brushes and blacklead polish, she made the kitchen range shine and kept its fire glowing by regularly raking out ash and topping-up from a hod of coal. As well as cooking, she put the flat-irons on it to heat. The ironing was done on the pine table, covered with an old blanket. To test the heat of an iron, she spat on it, judging its heat by the sizzle. As one iron cooled, it went back on the stove and she picked up the next one. With no synthetics to melt, the only risk was scorching and she avoided that by ironing fragile fabrics through brown paper.

Before Myrtle came to us as cook/general, we had Ida. Mother suffered for years from warts on her hands. All known remedies were tried in vain.

One day, Ida said: "If I were a gypsy, I'd wish them away." Ida was no gypsy, she was a local Padstow girl, but the warts vanished and never returned.

Much of our life centred on Place activities. The old coach-house and the yard stood next to the house, also reached from the road under a stone bridge, past a pair of tall pillars, each topped with a lidded stone urn. The sturdy slate-roofed stone buildings formed a square.

Immediately inside, on the left, lived the resident bull. He had a byre with a pocket-handkerchief yard, surrounded by a high wall — a sadly small area for so large a creature, but he had to be confined, so he couldn't get up speed to charge the cowman. By standing on an upturned pail, I could reach over to scratch his forehead, but even with a wall between us, I still felt a frisson of fear. He had mean little eyes.

When time came for him to go away, two men led him by a pole through his nose-ring. As he ambled down Fentonluna Lane, I watched from the safety of a favourite place, high-up on the slate slab that topped the wall between our house and the garden gate. He walked placidly down the hill, round the harbour and along to the station, showing no agitation, perhaps indifferent because of his myopic eyes.

The cowman also looked after a herd of brown cows that shared the Paddock with the deer — there were no black and white Friesians or blond Charolais in those days. At milking time, he and his dog fetched them across the road. The silly creatures always jostled and barged as they came through the gate, not because of any pecking order. Perhaps it jollied up their boring lives a little, making a change from all the hours head-down munching grass. Dogs and horses can be trained, but whoever heard of a biddable cow?

They trooped into their stalls, waiting patiently for hand-milking. Luckily my hands were too small to be effective, as they towered over me when I sat on a milking stool. One kick would have sent me and the bucket flying.

The adjoining dairy was always scrubbed spotless and smelling sweetly of fresh milk. To make butter, milk was put in wide shallow slate-edged settling dishes and left to stand until the cream had risen to the top.

A plug was then removed and the residue drained out. Cream was scraped from the sides and the butter-making process continued. No milk, cream or butter has ever equalled what we enjoyed then.

Father was very proud of a new electric cream separator, gleaming with stainless steel and scarlet paint, powered by a generator housed in its own building. The throbbing machine alarmed me greatly. Constant parental admonition to be careful was superfluous, for I half-expected it to reach out and grab me.

At home, the milkman called twice daily, the milk in tall churns on a two-wheeled cart pulled by a pony who knew the round so well that he stopped at each house unbidden. Myrtle took out white china jugs to be filled by long-handled half-pint and pint dippers. Protected by muslin covers weighted with blue beads sewn round the edges, the jugs kept cool on the slate slab in the larder. We had no refrigerator.

One day, Mother pointed out a mottled blue bowl in a shop window, insisting, despite my puzzlement, that it was made from milk. It made no sense to me. Little did I know that materials would be developed into the all-embracing modern plastics industry.

Shooting parties were a regular feature of the Prideaux Place calendar. Webber, the Gamekeeper, looked after the Pheasantry, out at Crugmeer, a plantation of pines giving it shelter from the westerly gales.

He reared stocks of pheasants for the annual shoots. His weather-beaten face matched the brown tweed cap, waistcoat, jacket, breeches and knee-high leather leggings that he always wore, winter and summer. He also looked after the dogs at the nearby Kennels. There were pointers, retrievers, a pair of spaniels and a terrier, each highly trained for its hunting role.

The pointers would stand stock-still, one paw raised, a straight line from muzzle to tail-tip, pointing straight at a fallen bird, so that a retriever could go to bring it gently back in its soft mouth.

Peter-dog once fell over a cliff and survived. Webber wrapped him in orange Thermogen wool and nursed him back to health. He was a patient man, but he pronounced Peter-dog to be "the most HIGORANT dog I've ever known."

After a big shoot, the birds were brought back to Place yard and hoisted to the long attic above the milking barn. Tied together in pairs, they hung in rows on poles slung from the ceiling. The total of brace shot was entered in a heavy leather-bound ledger. Some of the bag was given away locally, the rest went by train to market in London.

At home in the evening, it was my self-important job to sit on a box at the back door to pay the beaters. Heaps of sixpences, shillings, florins and half-crowns were ranged along the windowsill to pay each man. I would not leave, even to have my supper, until all were paid.

"Thank you, Miss Betty" they all said, as they replaced caps so courteously removed on arrival. (Although christened "Elizabeth", somehow "Betty" had crept in. Mother felt guilty and spotted a chance make amends later. I became Elizabeth again to all but Peter, who still called me Little'Un.)

Another errand, equally prized, was to deliver the weekly wages. A responsible eight-year-old, I set off alone up Fentonluna Lane to Place, carrying a leather bag with the labelled wage packets. Most of the men would be around the yard, but some searching could be needed to find the gardeners. The flower gardens lay behind the house, not seen from its main rooms, which look out over the Paddock to a glimpse of blue water in the Estuary beyond.

Making my round, I liked to keep the carpenter till last. I was always welcome in his workshop, with its resinous smell of fresh-cut wood. Perching on a stool, I watched him sawing, golden sawdust building soft pyramids on the stone floor. Crisp curly shavings followed the plane, as it hissed over the wood with steady rhythm. Watching how he worked gave me a useful grounding in the use of tools.

When I was bigger, my grandfather taught me how to use them myself. The workshop must once have been the harness room for the adjoining coach-house, now a garage. Buttressed pillars divided three pairs of tall black doors. Above each shallow-pointed arch, an open quatrefoil window let in light and air, wire-meshed to keep out birds. The workshop got its light from two more, with a mullioned window beneath.

The deer were counted and culled annually. On the appointed day, men from the estate formed a line beating across the Paddock to a hollow, where the deer had to run in single file. Father and Webber could then pick off the ones to be shot. I hated the whole business, but I was caught in my second-class-boy trap again.

Being left behind on such an important day was even worse than being there. I coped by getting on the farthest end of the beaters' line and shutting my eyes at the worst bits. I heard the shots but did not have to see deer stumble and fall. I sensed the fear and panic that gripped the herd and felt treacherous at even being present at the slaughter of the gentle soft-eyed creatures.

Occasionally house guests were invited to join the guns. Once a prized buck, a present from the King at Windsor, was accidentally shot. Father had to break the embarrassing news to Colonel Prideaux-Brune. Doubtless, some visitor was never invited again.

Thankfully I was not there the day one doe was not shot cleanly. She attempted to jump the spiked iron railings, gashing herself horribly. It was amazing that she struggled over, as the railings are four-feet high, set on top of a steep bank that adds another four-feet. Father stormed home in a fury, got the car and chased for miles before he and Webber caught up and put her out of her agony. Blood and hair stuck to the spikes until finally rain washed the railings clean.

Shortly after one of these days, I went up to the yard with a message. Going into a barn, I found two men skinning a doe. She was tied by the feet and slung over a pole hanging from a rafter. Recoiling from this shock, I was appalled to find a row of upright heads by my feet, all neatly sawn through at the neck. I almost tripped over one as I fled.

Much later, when middle-aged, I saw venison on the menu in Germany. I thought it would be a nice change, but after only one mouthful I was revolted and had to send it back uneaten. How strange that although I cannot face rabbit or venison, I enjoy beef. Yet I knew every cow by name, even better than the deer.

Perhaps the intervening abattoir made the matter less personal.

CHAPTER TWO

Sibling Squabbles

Pundits say character is formed by the age of four, which is just as well for me. That best of reference books, the family photo album, reveals a radiant child. Smiles, laughter and shining eyes are plain to see. I was only a baby when we first came to Padstow. As I grew through childhood, two factors crept in to cloud the sunny beam a shade. In the 1920-30's, it did not occur to middle-class parents to send their children to the local village school, so I had no children of my own age to play with.

My other problem was that Peter became a little overbearing. We were fine when we were busy together, but if he had nothing better to do, he had the knack of teasing me to the point of hysteria, then leaving me to take any blame. Four years younger, I was an easy target. I was told to be serene like Pam, our cousin, but she was only one year younger and tall for her age, so he seldom picked on her. For the rest of her life, Pam remembered her terror when Peter chased her, to drop a frog down her neck. Equally vivid, the time he pushed her to the floor, pinioned her arms with his knees, and tickled her ribs until she was utterly desperate. Finally her hysterical screams made him stop, in case a grown-up heard.

I was his usual victim for this torture. I knew no way of standing up to him. If I was accused of sulking, no wonder. But I knew I was not sulky or difficult and resented having this false reputation foisted on me. No one ever stopped him teasing me. Never. Just once would have made all the difference. I still do not understand his motivation. He showed no other sign of cruelty. He did not pull wings off flies.

He went to Padstow Infants' School briefly, then went to live with our grandparents in Bromley during term-time, attending Carn Brea school, in Sundridge Avenue, a few hundred yards from their home at "Hurst". Perhaps Granny saw him replacing her only son, who had died very young. Peter's every whim was indulged by her and three doting aunts.

In term time, I had respite from his teasing and relaxed. A friend of Mother's said: "I expect you are looking forward to having your brother back for the holidays." She was shocked by my vehement "No, I'm not."

We were equally bright, but I never won a verbal argument. When stumped, he'd always assert: "Of course it's true. I read it in *The Modern Boy*," a boy's newspaper. Maybe he was bluffing. I should have challenged him: "Show me!" Instead, I weakly allowed myself to be intimidated. Even in our teenage years he never outgrew these habits. He could not pass behind my chair without jabbing me under the armpits to make me jump.

After I grew up, I worried whether I had been at fault. I asked Aunt Stella, Mother's twin, for her view. She agreed he should have been stopped. It was some consolation, but left me pondering why no one had interceded on my behalf.

When we first came to Padstow, an extension was being added for us at Fentonluna, so until all was ready, we lived in another of the estate's houses, "Bella Vista" at Trevone. Sometimes we went to Harlyn Bay, Mother Ivey's, Booby's, Constantine, or Treyarnon, but Trevone remained favourite. The beach had a sweep of firm crisp sand, the rock pools invited inspection for creatures left by the receding tide. The beach was shallow, so the tide's lengthy advance provided children with excellent surfing. Although the waves were seldom large enough to support adults, with my light weight I got long runs.

A cave out beyond the low-water mark ran deep under the cliffs, so the field above was forbidden territory without adult escort. A round blow-hole, some twenty feet across, dropped sheer to the cave beneath. The crashing waves echoed eerily upwards, booming and hissing as the water advanced and retreated.

From behind the bay a fresh-water stream ran through a field down to the beach. Cows came to drink, their hooves churning the mud. Their many cowpats were a hazard to our feet, but encouraged the growth of giant kingcups, like thick-set buttercups with glossy golden flowers over an inch across. The hollow stems grew eighteen inches high, with dark green leaves. Taller still grew the wild iris we called "flags", their stiff broad leaves and stout stems bearing yellow flowers. They were unscented, but even if they had been, the fragrance would have been swamped by the smell of cow dung.

The stream provided ideal conditions for the complicated systems of dams, tunnels and bridges we constructed. "Sandcastle" is an inadequate term for the engineering works we created but our work was made more difficult by the blunt wooden spades we used. It was a wet and messy business, so if not wearing a swimsuit, my cotton dress had to be kept dry by stuffing the skirt into waterproof rompers, with elastic round the legs, pushed up to thigh level. From a front bib, braces went over the shoulders, crossed at the back and buttoned on to the waist. I hated rompers because I disliked the smell and feel of rubber. According to Mother, I'd even screamed if a rubber duck was put in my bath.

The Trevone idyll was shattered one famous day. I was working with a red metal spade, borrowed from another child, building the world's finest castle. Peter tried to take it away from me. All my accumulated rage boiled over. Swinging the spade, I gashed his shin to the bone with one hysterical whack. Blood, howls, chaos. Beach things hastily bundled up. Back to the car. Peter, the self-righteous wounded victim, being pampered and petted. I was in deep disgrace.

"Go to your room, and stay there," Mother instructed. A trial of strength followed. For days I was pressed to apologise, but I'd drawn my personal "line in the sand" with that metal spade and nothing was going to make me say I was sorry.

I wasn't then. I'm unrepentant still.

In spite of the way he sometimes behaved, Peter was, in truth, very fond of me. He called me "Little 'Un" until I grew up, and sometimes later. It would have been better if we'd had an even hand above us.

His adult life foundered on the twin rocks of pomposity and the certainty he was always right. His superiors, both in the army during the war and afterwards in civilian life, were always wrong; never him. In the end this killed him. His shock at being made redundant, before redundancy was heard of, and being unable to get another job as the potential captain of industry he saw himself to be, brought on the fatal coronaries which took his life at 42.

I was devastated. Despite our childhood tiffs, I was bereft and miss him still.

When I became too old for a nanny, but too young to be sent away to school, Miss Webb arrived, as my governess. She was young and pretty, with dark eyes and wavy hair. She made lessons a pleasure and we were happy together. She was my friend as well as my teacher and I would have been a lonely scrap without her, but still nothing could make up for the lack of children of my own age.

A surprise present arrived for me from Mr. LeBlanc-Smith, an elderly gentleman who lived next door. He'd made a little wooden stool, with "BETTY" carved into the top. This generous gesture could have led to a mutually welcome friendship, for we were both lonely in our different ways. There was nothing sinister in the gift but my parents decided the most suitable response was a laboriously written thank-you note pushed through his letter box. The stool is battered now after years of service, but still helps me get things just out of reach.

Miss Webb and I often walked through St. Saviour's, over Stile and down to St. George's Well. Though much smaller than Trevone, it had all the right ingredients . . . sea, sand, rock-pools and stream, though no surfing. We swam from May until November, quite used to cold water. I do not remember learning to swim, it came as naturally as walking.

Swimming rules were strict: never go out of your depth, swim parallel to the shore and not straight out, do not swim for an hour after a meal. Above all, only go in on an incoming tide, for the currents were strong. Every summer, visitors ignored warnings and either drowned or were rescued by some local who risked his own life for their folly. Sometimes we walked inland through the narrow lanes, with high banks and slate walls giving shelter from the westerly gales. In spring, the banks had flowers in profusion, but Miss Webb was a town girl and did not know all their names. Cowslips, pink and white campion, buttercups, bright blue periwinkles and violets grew among the grasses. In May, pink, red or white valerian sprang in great clusters from crevices in the walls, places where it seemed impossible they could find enough soil or water to survive.

Every Easter we made an expedition to pick primroses for Granny Clay (Mother's mother) in Bromley. The primroses in our wood were so profuse we had to watch where we trod, for fear of crushing them. Steep banks fell down to a stream tumbling over mossy rocks where large boulders created seats and an ideal picnic table. Cupping our hands, we drank the sparkling water. Our first task was to line a tin with damp moss. The primroses were tied with wool into bunches, leaves round the outside, laid head to tail inside the box. When full, we added a final layer of moss before closing the lid.

We had to rush home in time to catch the evening post. We wrapped our parcel in brown paper, tied with string. The flowers always arrived the following morning and Granny wrote that they still smelled as fresh as when we'd picked them.

Polzeath was the best beach for surfing but, lying on the opposite side of the Estuary from Padstow, it was too far to walk from Rock ferry, carrying our boards, so our visits had to coincide with Father's golf at St. Enodoc. Then we could surf until he collected us in the car.

It was at Polzeath Mother came a surfing cropper. She was good at sports. Before her marriage she'd played tennis for Kent, hockey for England and now played golf for Cornwall, but surfing was not her forte. She never got the knack of timing her runs. Trailing our boards, we waded out, ducking under incoming breakers, until we were nearly out of our depth. Then we turned, on tiptoe, boards poised, looking over our shoulders for the perfect moment to launch and settle to a creaming run back to the water's edge. On this occasion, Mother let the front of her board dip. It nose-dived to the bottom and broke as she somersaulted over it. She suffered fearsome bruising across her stomach, but luckily had no internal injury.

Father never came to the beach with us. He was such a tall thin man that maybe he felt the cold and never went in the water. Perhaps he had scars from his war wounds he did not wish to show. Whatever the reason, he never joined the picnics Myrtle made for us. All was packed in a wicker hamper, sandwiches wrapped in greaseproof paper, with vacuum flasks of hot drinks to warm us after long spells in the cold sea.

My surfboard was wooden, about twelve inches wide and shoulder height, Peter's was proportionately bigger. One winter, I painted mine orange, with my initials forming a black and white monogram and black and white stripes round the edge. Peter painted his royal blue, with a coat-of-arms copied from Father's signet ring, in yellow. We drew admiring glances on the beach the next summer.

If the car was available, we sometimes went to Treyarnon. There the attraction was not the sea, for it was a dangerous place to swim, but a huge deep pool left high in the rocks when the tide went out. A rock outcrop made a perfect diving platform. The water was stinging-cold. Sizeable fish often got stranded until the next tide came and washed them out.

One day at Treyarnon, when Pam was with us, we heard a dog barking, obviously in distress. Wearing

19

plimsolls, we were nimble over the rocks and, following the sound, found a bedraggled white Sealyham stranded on a rock shelf, rising water already lapping her feet. Left much longer, she'd have been swept away, dashed against the rocks and drowned. She was difficult to reach, but between us we managed to grasp her and inched back to safety. After that, whenever she spotted us she'd come racing across the beach to greet us. After much licking and tail-wagging, she trotted back. We never met her owner.

CHAPTER THREE

Home Port

The finest approach to Padstow was by train. For the last few miles after Wadebridge, the line ran beside the water, where the River Camel broadened to form the Estuary. In contrast to the stark grandeur of Bodmin Moor's granite outcrops, the landscape softened, the land on each side rising gently, farms tucked into sheltered valleys.

The tide-line provided good feeding for wading birds. A tall grey heron might be standing statue-still or stalking the shallows patiently, alert to seize its prey with a lightning strike of its yellow dagger-sharp bill. Curlew waded delicately, probing mud with long curving beaks. At high tide, they went inland, returning punctually as the water receded to uncover the mud. With its unmistakable two-note cry, the curlew seems to call its own name. Sandpipers fussed busily about, always restless, heads bobbing as they ran along the water margins.

As the Estuary spreads to a mile wide, it swings north, suddenly revealing a sweep of water right out to the Atlantic. At the mouth, the twin headlands of Stepper and Pentire appear to be opposite each other, the island of Newland midway between. That is how I always think of them, although the map contradicts me.

As suddenly as the vista opened, it closed again, the train clattering over the Iron Bridge, view obscured by a lattice of girders. Passing Dennis Hill, topped with the Obelisk marking Queen Victoria's Jubilee, the train slowed down as it ran to its terminus in Padstow Station. Emphasizing its final stop, a turntable, like a big full-stop, stood waiting for the engine to be unhitched and swung round to face the opposite way, ready to pull its carriages back to London.

To prevent collisions on the single track between Wadebridge and Padstow, no train could proceed without the "Tablet" from the man in the signalbox. To prevent dropping it between them, the Tablet was in a leather purse fixed to an iron hoop. As the train steamed slowly past, the driver stretched out of his cab to receive it, thrusting his arm through the hoop held out by the signalman, leaving no scope for butter-fingers.

Gangs of navvies, working with picks and shovels, completed the line in time for Padstow Station's ceremonial opening and the arrival of the first London and South Western train on March 23rd, 1899.

On the great day, the platform canopy was decked with bunting. The eighteen-strong Padstow Town Band stood ready, smartly turned out in military-style blue uniforms. Their jackets sported epaulettes, seven brass buttons and whitened webbing belts, all topped with pillbox hats, held in place by chinstraps, exactly aligned at the angle of maximum jauntiness.

Local worthies, with a handsome show of side-whiskers, moustaches and beards, waited on the new platform. They wore top hats or bowlers, flowers sprouting from their buttonholes. When the inaugural five-coach train steamed into the station, the sun was shining. Cheers of the crowds and the hissing of the engine almost drowned the music of the band.

Padstow's sheltered position, tucked into the elbow of the Camel Estuary, had ensured its importance as a port on the north Cornish coast for decades, well protected from the great Atlantic storms. The main function of the new railway was to transport freight passing through the busy little port, marking a turning point in the town's development. The 1893 timetable advertises Pockett's Bristol Channel Steam Packet Co. Ltd., with regular sailings between Bristol, Swansea, Padstow and Wadebridge. A poster names their ships as Velindra, Rio Formoso and Collier, a tramp steamer, her name suggesting she brought coal from the Welsh mines.

The Stepper Point Slate Quarry employed 30 men. A red flag flew on blasting days. I was fascinated by the interval between seeing the puff of dust and hearing the report. Mundane adult explanations did not dampen my interest. On clear days, if I was out near Stile, I could see the explosions and count out: "Puff-one-two-three-Bang!"

Because the quarry lacked a decent road, stone was carried away by sea. Much of the output was taken into Padstow by barge for off-loading on to lorries destined for the fast-expanding road network. The age of the

23

motor car had arrived. Stone for other markets went by cargo ships, loaded at the quarry's small quay.

By the turn of the century, Padstow's old harbour was too small to handle the growing fishing trade. Padstow's role as a fishing port blossomed, growing in importance to rival Lowestoft, Grimsby and Brixham.

A new harbour for the visiting fishing fleets was needed. The work began in June, 1911. Teams of men dug with shovels, filling metal tubs craned away as fast as they were filled. A year later the New Harbour was completed. Fleets of trawlers came each year for the herring season, tying up in rows across the harbour.

The catch was swung ashore in dripping baskets, then packed in wooden boxes and barrels, kept fresh with ice made in the factory on the north side of the old harbour. The fish was auctioned immediately in the open-sided shed alongside and then despatched by waiting train to London's Billingsgate Market.

To me, the train functioned exclusively for taking fish and pheasants to market, Peter to school and both of us, with Mother, to visit our grand-parents. That it stopped elsewhere for other people was irrelevant. It was the Padstow Train, it said so on the board at Paddington.

During the herring season, trawlers from other fishing ports came into Padstow. From a vantage point on top of Chapel Stile, I could see them as dots when they rounded Stepper Point and headed up the Estuary. As they came into range, I picked out the port registration numbers and their names. Boats from

Lowestoft were LT, those from Brixham BM and so on. Padstow had only one of its own, the PW3 Adclc.

Some boats had a dog on board, usually a small terrier. Keen to get into harbour, they scampered about, trying to find a spot where they were tall enough to see ahead. Crews came to know me, calling greetings and waving. Every boat was entered in my red notebook and ticked off as they came in each season. In the mornings, I begged to be taken down to the harbour to see who else had come in overnight. Given the chance, I'd have been there all-day, every-day. There was so much to see, so many sights and smells, strange accents from other parts of the country, scarcely intelligible to my southern ears.

Eventually the trawlers sailed away and I put my notebook aside for another year, hoping any missing names had not foundered. One of the Yarmouth boats, "Smiling Thru" was broken-up on the Trevone rocks.

Occasionally, Breton boats called. Instead of flat tweed caps, the Frenchmen wore black berets and clattered as they walked on wooden clogs over leather-heeled socks. The French onion man came regularly, pushing an old black bicycle laden with plaited strings of fine onions. Getting a lift over on one of the French fishing boats, he brought a big stock, then went out daily to sell.

During the period between the World Wars, fleets of herring trawlers, owned by rival companies, were based in the main fishing ports, from Aberdeen in the North, down the East Coast at Hull, Grimsby, Lowestoft and Yarmouth. At Lowestoft alone, the fleet was 250 strong. The boats were of similar design, some 104ft in length overall, with 20ft beam and a moulded depth of 10ft. A mast forward of the fish-holds served the hoists, gallows and fairleads for unloading the baskets, powered by steam-driven winches. An aft mast carried a small brown gaff-rigged canvas sail, used to conserve fuel when power was not needed — and for emergency in case of engine breakdown. Powered by steam, the coal furnaces posed a constant fire hazard as the boats tossed about in wild weather.

No mention was ever made of the conditions in which the eight-man crew lived. They must have been cold, wet and cramped. At sea, any food would be welcome, but it must surely have been awful.

Trawling for herring is an all-or-nothing game as the fish swim in dense shoals for self-protection. Always on the move, they cruise in constant search for the minute animals and plants forming their diet. In their turn, they are hunted by predators. If chased to the surface by hungry whales, seals or porpoises, voracious seagulls swoop down to carry them off.

These disturbances are what a skipper seeks, using his skill and experience to put down a trawl without accidentally trapping a mammal, whose thrashing would ruin his expensive gear. The enclosed bridge was set high, giving him the best possible vision as he constantly scanned the sea. He spent long hours on the bridge, for it was his sole responsibility to find and land the fish. He was paid a small wage, the bulk of his earnings coming from a profits share, which he split with his crew.

For fishermen, speed of handling was all-important for the catch deteriorates swiftly. Deckhands used the return trip for gutting cod. Years of this chore could strain a man's wrist to the point where he could no longer straighten it. There was no RSI compensation in those day. Risks were part of every fisherman's life. The waste was chucked overboard, providing feasts for the accompanying squadrons of gulls. It bothers me to see them scavenging refuse tips instead of soaring over the sea. I used to imitate their call. (Still can; better not.) I truly believed I was communicating. I remained silent when grown-ups were around, gull-talk was too private for them to hear.

My harbour visits were frowned on because I always came back with fleas. I had to stand on a big white towel, while Mother gingerly removed my clothes. Myrtle stood ready to pounce with a cake of damp soap. No flea could jump far enough or fast enough to avoid Myrtle's unerring aim. Finally I was dressed in fresh clothes. Myrtle lifted the fleas from the soap with a fingernail and flushed them down the lavatory.

I didn't question it at the time, but it occurs to me it was much more likely the fleas came from Peter-dog's spring crop.

Smoking is a traditional method of preserving fish. On the outer wall of Padstow New Harbour, a tall wooden smoke-house was built for curing kippers. Each herring season brought a team of lasses from the North to carry out this work. Wearing black aprons over full dark skirts, black shawls over their heads and shoulders, and shod in wooden clogs, they were a race

27

apart from the local women. They clustered together, haughty and superior.

Herring had to be prepared for smoking and this hard work was done by expert local women, who could gut 30 fish per minute. Their pay was tenpence a barrel and 26 barrels a good day's work. The skin on their hands was severely affected by salt, their only remedy to plunge their hands into oatmeal.

In the smoke house, prepared herrings were racked over smoke from oak-dust fires. When the curing was complete, the kippers were packed in wooden boxes and dispatched by train with the fresh fish to Billingsgate. Bloaters were also smoked herrings, but soaked in brine and not split open before being cured. They were a popular Yarmouth speciality, as was the bloater paste made from them.

In addition to Padstow's freight trade, the Railway Management envisaged an expanding passenger business. They built the South Western Hotel, later known as the Metropole. Fortunately, they sited it a little way up the hill from the station, where it was out of sight from the older part of the town, because its massive five-storey grey bulk and self-important style did not sit comfortably with the smaller scale of Padstow.

I cannot think its many rooms were often filled, despite patronage by Edward, Prince of Wales. From the hotel, he was ferried across to Rock, to play golf at St. Enodoc, resplendent in the flamboyant checked plus-fours he made so fashionable. One morning, on Langford's Quay with my nanny, his motor boat passed close by. With pointing finger and voice piping clear over the water I asked, "Is that the Prince of Wales?" He smiled and waved, so I waved back. My poor nanny was overwhelmed with embarrassment and too overcome to essay the customary curtsey to royalty. Blushingly she hustled me away.

Padstow's rhythm was governed by the tide. The Doom Bar was a spit of golden sand running up the middle of the Estuary, only just covered at high tide. Inbound vessels had to keep to the deep-water channel. A ship grounded on Doom Bar at high tide could quickly break her back.

Mermaids frequented the area off Polzeath and Greenaway, luring unwary sailors into danger. The Doom Bar was created by an angry mermaid after a young man shot at her with an arrow. She had her revenge by casting a handful of sand into the sea. Over the years, her Doom Bar grew inexorably, claiming many victims. On the morning of November 12, 1911, two vessels foundered. The first was a two-masted French brigantine, "The Angèle". The tide was too low for the lifeboat to get alongside and despite strenuous efforts, the stricken crew were lost.

Before the exhausted lifeboat crew had time to recover, they were called out again, pulling the ten-oared lifeboat "Arab" to rescue the crew of the "Island Mail", stuck fast on the Bar. This time they were successful. Fighting through punishing breakers, they saved all the crew. The fortitude and skill of the crew were recognised by the award of the R.N.L.I Silver Medal to Coxswain Baker.

On March 2, 1932, the Doom Bar took its last sailing vessel, the "Marie Regina", a French three-masted topsail schooner. As the tide went out, she was stranded, dying on her side. With no hope of recovery, she was sold for £5.00 to six Padstow men. On a rising tide, a gale blew her under Tregirls cliffs. There she was stripped of fixtures and fittings and broken up for her valuable timbers. The spoils were loaded into the barge "Beaumaris", towed to Padstow and auctioned on Langfords Quay. Arthur Reveley, Bill Orchard, Norman England, Oscar Martyn, Jim and Harry Benton must have been well pleased with the profits from their speculation.

The growth of Doom Bar began to threaten the fishing industry, heart of the town's prosperity. Dredging could not cope with the speed at which the sand built up. A project to build another pier outside the existing old harbour wall was proposed, with the hope it might alter currents and clear the Estuary. Father considered that it was more likely to exacerbate the problem and events proved him right.

The wall served no useful purpose, beyond providing a landing place for the Rock ferry at low tide. Until then it had used the boat-builders' small harbour if there was insufficient water to get further in. Had the German bomb which fell in the town during the war hit the new wall, it might have caused the Estuary to revert to its former state. No one was brave enough to admit the error of building it and no one has had the courage to blow it up.

The old harbour was the heart of the town. Roughly square, it had a road round the north, west and south sides. The Harbourmaster's office, on North Quay, controlled every aspect of port activity. Nothing moved without his consent. On West Quay, The Long Lugger was the focal meeting-place for retired men. The sixteen-seater wooden bench, built against a stone wall, was where they gathered to pass contented hours, reminiscing about earlier exploits and exchanging local gossip.

A three-masted ship, the "Isabella", was permanently moored in the centre of the harbour, rising on each tide, only to sink back to the mud as the water ebbed. Having dug herself a trench for the keel, she was spared the indignity of toppling onto her side. She appeared to have neither owner nor crew. The only people to board her were young men who swam out, clambered up and dived off. In 1938, she was finally towed further up the Estuary and beached at Cant Creek. The harbour looks bare without her.

Fierce water-polo matches against visiting teams were fought, cheered on by vociferous supporters. It looked a ferocious game. While some of the team busily passed the ball, trying for shots at goal, the rest seemed fully occupied trying to drown their opponents by shoving heads under water and holding them there. The water was too murky to see what skullduggery went on below the surface, but it cannot have been too bad, for each team ended with the original number of players. I was keen to watch more, but matches were not deemed fit spectacles for genteel young ladies.

Although built for trawlers, New Harbour occasionally sheltered more exotic vessels. Once a submarine came in and Father took Peter and me on board. The cramped interior was packed with alarming pipes, handles and dials. I was scared of accidentally touching something, causing some dire calamity.

Once a flying boat came in. Its engine had seized and it landed on the sea some fifteen miles north of Trevose Head. Luckily the sea was calm.

The steamer Skeloon went to help and towed it gently in, the wing-tips just clearing the harbour walls. It was a Southampton S1232 biplane, with twin four-bladed propellers, wings linked by struts and a float suspended under each lower wing. The tail carried three fins.

When repaired, it was towed out tail-first and, using the Estuary as a runway, Flying Officer F.R. Worthington took off and returned to his base at Mount Batten Air Station, Plymouth.

In its early days, air travel was the focus of keen public interest. Records were constantly being set up, only to be speedily surpassed. Flight in a flying boat was the height of fashion for those who could afford the luxury. Imperial Airways' Queen of the Skies carried 24 passengers in great style. They could have a gourmet meal, snooze in bunks or observe the passing scenery as they strolled round the promenade deck, all while cruising for up to 800 miles at 165mph.

Nevertheless aircraft over Padstow were a rare sight. When the R100 airship sailed serenely overhead, all the town ran outside to gaze skywards. Not long after, while its sister ship, the R101, was flying over France, its unstable hydrogen exploded and it crashed, killing forty-eight of its 54 passengers. Pictures in the newspapers showed the crumpled burned-out wreckage. Everyone was shocked.

Alan Cobham's Flying Circus paid a visit to the disused First World War airfield at Crugmeer. Father took Peter and they had a brief flight in a single-engined biplane. I'd have enjoyed that. Mother told me a very dashing lady owned a private plane which she landed and took-off from a field at Treyarnon. I never witnessed this wonder, but gazed in awe at the empty field. In total, I'd seen one flying boat in the harbour, one airship overhead, a Cobham's biplane in the distance and one empty field at Treyarnon — the sum total of my knowledge of things aeronautical.

CHAPTER
FOUR

Saved by Lifebuoy

My little red book logged visits from trawlers with "Sunlight" in the name — "Ocean Sunlight" and "Sunlight Princess" were two. Several had "Lifebuoy" added — "Ocean Lifebuoy" was one I recall. I knew nothing then of the story behind the names. In 1917, William Hesketh Lever, first Lord Leverhulme, bought the Hebridean islands of Lewis and Harris. Some income for the islanders came from producing traditional Harris tweeds, using the strong wool of the hardy local sheep. Spinning and weaving were done by the women working in their own cottages. Untreated wool was harsh. To render it pliable hanks of spun yarn were immersed in urine, each croft having a barrel at the door, topped up by the whole family.

Most of the men were fishermen, who found the distance from the islands an insurmountable obstacle to selling their catch on the mainland. To resolve this difficulty, Lord Leverhulme founded "MacFisheries" to provide a direct retail market, selling fish "fresh from sea to slab". By Christmas, 1919, one hundred High Street MacFisheries were open — 360 were doing brisk business two years later.

Lever Brothers was a solid firm, with worldwide sales of their famous soaps. Hefty slabs of yellow "Sunlight" were found in kitchens around the world. "Lifebuoy", its pungent smell suggesting antiseptic, reigned like Neptune in most bathrooms — a sovereign cure for B.O. — underarm deodorants had not then been invented.

Supported by such a company, MacFisheries had the financial muscle to grow at great speed, becoming associated with 48 other companies, ranging from the Aberdeen Steam Trawling Company in the northeast of Scotland to the Helford Oysterage in the Duchy of Cornwall.

In under four years, Lever Brothers were well-established in the business of catching, salting, smoking, canning and selling fish and fish products. The MacFisheries chain expanded well beyond the original concept as trade in fresh fish was seasonal and subject to shortages when storms kept fleets in port. Other lines were needed to balance the stock, so poultry and game businesses were acquired. The start of the shooting season on 12th August heralded the arrival of pheasant and grouse, as well as hare and rabbit. The autumn trade built up to turkeys and geese for Christmas.

The layout of all the shops was identical and instantly recognisable by the shopping public. The company's logo — deriving from Scotland's national flag — featured prominently either side of "MacFisheries" on the fascia board above the shop. Within a border of blue and white concentric circles, a bold white X floated upon a mid-blue ground, with a plump fish in each segment. The famous symbol appeared on every price ticket, bill and bag.

The shop front was open to the street and the weather, delivering an advertising odour to the whole High Street. A framed advertisement for T.Wall and Sons, prominent with a royal coat-of-arms, conveyed the thought that MacFisheries offered the same sausages gracing breakfast tables at Buckingham Palace and Balmoral.

Poultry and game hung from high rails running across the shop, rabbits and hares by their feet, sometimes with miniature buckets under their noses, and pheasant and grouse by their necks. The all-important central feature was the white marble slab, as wide as the total width of the shop allowed, usually fifty square feet, leaving an aisle on each side. At the front, close to the pavement, the slab was 2ft high, sloping to 3ft, providing the solid canvas for a still-life of fish laid out with artistic flourish, commanding the attention of passers-by.

The moment a potential customer paused, an alert salesman stepped forward. Wearing white overalls, striped blue aprons and straw boaters, they worked in the aisles either side of the slab. Selected fish were taken to a bench at the back for trimming, weighing and wrapping. Then, insulated in newspaper, purchases were placed in a paper bag boasting the MacFisheries name and company logo.

High at the back, in a little office reminiscent of a trawler's bridge, a female cashier handled change —

the salesmen's hands smelled of fish, and, in any case, for much of the year were far too cold to handle fiddly coins.

The company gave much attention to advertising. Rebuilding the fishing industry after the First World War was a struggle because the public thought fish expensive. The British Trawlers' Federation launched an "Eat More Fish" advertising campaign. MacFisheries staff were unimpressed and countered with more sparky suggestions — "Turn Your Attention to Tench — Hooray for Ray — Pop in for a Popular Pollack — Say it with Sole."

MacFisheries most important speciality was their "Kiltie Kipper", featured in many of their advertisements. A promotional campaign being planned for the South African market prompted a wag to suggest — "Kiltie Kippers, vot you tink — keep dem long — and vot a stink."

The branches courted local customers assiduously, distributing about 250 circulars a week to existing and new account customers. Many of the leaflets were dropped off by delivery boys on tradesman's bicycles, MacFisheries displayed prominently upon a plate hanging below the crossbar.

A branch in South East London received this postcard with an order from a customer: "Please send me early by 10-30 Wednesday tomorrow morning 20th Thursday a nice fresh lobster — would you kindly remove anything that needs doing and smash claw etc., for me please — 1/6d — otherwise if 1/9d. better and larger send instead Friday morning a salmon head please — three herrings and a whiting, two soft roes — by 11am for certain. Saturday morning 10-30 if possible as you see we dine at 12-45 always and there are others besides myself and puts my landlady out if things are not early — a nice roasting chicken please, very tender and a good breast particularly as I am very seedy. I will send money on Friday by boy. Kindly settle all and send receipt and change. With thanks I know you will send me a good lobster and chicken and salmon."

Two 1929 issues of the house journal, "MacMatters — by the Staff for the Staff", convey a picture of the company ethos and of the social climate in which it operated so successfully.

An article in the magazine by an author hiding behind the initials M.K. reveals his high opinion of himself as the guru of advertising. After heavy-handed attempts at levity, he ends with: "You cannot run an Empire on trivialities like kippers," said Jix recently, and, however momentous a kipper may be at breakfast, one cannot but agree with him — speaking Imperially. But it would have been another matter had he said "Kiltie Kippers." No one would feel inclined to dispute that statement. For who could call Kilties trivialities? There is nothing trivial about them. On the contrary, theirs is an important and vital place in our national life — they make it possible for us to wear that happy "morning face" — and their appetising odour is spreading from continent to continent. Perhaps on them one could not actually run an Empire, but — Imperially eating — how much smoother would the wheels of Empire run, greased each morning with the oil of Kiltie Kippers!"

If M.K.'s tongue ever strayed into his cheek, it was only to chase an errant fish bone.

Padstow did not have, and did not need, a MacFisheries — fish were bought directly from local fishermen and Prideaux Place was a generous source of game.

CHAPTER
FIVE

Congregating at
St. Petroc's

On Sundays, we went to church. A short cut between Fentonluna and the church went via Marble Arch, an alley going under houses and down a flight of steps into Church Road. We always sat in the same pew. Once, Peter-dog came tail-wagging up the aisle to find his master during the middle of morning service. He'd have settled quietly but Father removed him. Tiptoeing in heavy leather shoes on a stone floor is impossible, but the congregation loyally Pretended Not To Notice. Only the choirboys tittered.

I wish my education had included something of St. Petroc's history. Only those with academic interest in the past did any research into the origins and stories of earlier times. There was no tourist industry, visitors to the church were few and locals took their church for granted. St. Petroc's origins lay in the sixth century, when Petroc and a few monks left their monastery in Ireland to spread Christianity. Driven by tide and wind, they were swept into the Camel Estuary where Petroc established an important Celtic monastery on

40

the site of the present church, with cells for monks, a library, school, infirmary and a farm. He was said to have converted the Celtic King Constantine to Christianity, after rescuing a deer which the king was hunting. The name lives on in nearby Constantine Bay. As Saint Petroc, he is the patron saint of Padstow.

In the SW corner of the church, stands an impressive monument to Sir Nicholas Prideaux, wearing Jacobean armour, who built Prideaux Place in the 16th century. There are other memorials to his successors in the Prideaux-Brune family. The parish was in their gift, with patronage to appoint and pay the vicar. The link broke when the estate passed to a Roman Catholic member of the family and a new Roman Catholic church was built, across the road from the entrance gates to Prideaux Place.

One who may have taken an interest was Charles Dickens, who often came to stay at Rosehill with Mr and Mrs H. F. Marley. When Dickens was writing "A Christmas Carol", he needed a name for the chain-rattling ghost of Scrooge's erstwhile partner, so he used the name of his Padstow friend and "Jacob Marley" was created.

Such historical gems would have gone straight over my young head. For me, Sunday meant *Best Clothes*, my favourite outfit a harebell-blue and yellow floral silk dress, its round "Peter Pan" collar and puffed sleeves bound with blue and pearl buttons down the front. Over this, I wore a natural linen coat. Black shoes with single bar and button went with long white silk socks, held up by elastic garters. Best of all, I wore a broad-brimmed Leghorn straw hat, trimmed with blue cornflowers, red poppies and white marguerites on a black velvet band. No second-class boy on Sundays.

This finery was not available in local shops, so was bought when we went to stay with my Grandparents in Bromley. I cannot think why we were not taken to London. There were two cars standing idle in the garage and Wilkins, the chauffeur, would have been delighted to have somewhere to drive.

Instead, a telephone call was made to Marshall & Snelgrove, requesting a selection to be sent "On Approval". I waited impatiently for their dark red van to deliver a box, black with multi-coloured flowers all over it. The dresses came out from layers of rustling tissue paper, to be tried on and paraded. The final choice made, the rest were carefully packed away in the box again, to be collected by the van and returned to the store.

Peter's "Sunday Best" was a navy-blue sailor suit. The tunic, with three white stripes round the square collar, was worn over long trousers. To go out, he wore a reefer and a round cap, like the Royal Navy, who then did not put on white cap tops until the first of May. In summer his suit was white cotton with dark blue collar stripes.

Our main shopping centre was Truro. Mother borrowed the car sometimes to go there for Ladies' Golf Union meetings. I liked to go with her and wait in the car, parked by the Cathedral. There I could watch, through a nearby window, a woman working at a knitting machine, making the excellent quality knitted suits so popular with Mother and her friends.

Truro was my concept of a big city. My first experience of London threw up more questions than answers.

We went along Oxford Street, the pavements thronged.

Q. Why Oxford? Did it go to Oxford?

Q. Why such crowds? What is happening? Where are they all going?

At the end of Oxford Street stood a great Memorial Arch.

Q. Why is it called Marble Arch after our little alley in Padstow?

Standard winter wear for me was a comfortable and practical outfit, comprising a saxe-blue wool pleated jersey skirt, attached to a cotton bodice. Over this, a matching jumper, the ensemble completed with matching knickers. Photographs of me at that time usually show a modish few inches of knicker-leg drooping down and, as a smart accessory, a bandage around at least one knee, resulting from a recurring accident. French cricket often sent our ball over the hedge, into the road, where there was nothing much to stop it bouncing down the steep hill to the harbour. I would foolishly dash off in pursuit, only to flounder out of control and crash down, severely grazing a knee every time.

Both my parents were good golfers and played at St. Enodoc. There were two ways of getting there. By road, it meant driving to Wadebridge, crossing the bridge over the Camel, returning along the other side. When Father played, that was his route. When we went with Mother, we went by ferry, an open motorboat run by Jack England, a picture-book seaman, tanned face, bright blue eyes, sun-bleached hair and gold earrings.

He handled his boat with such skill it looked easy, but the water could be rough and the currents strong. Sometimes, when there were few passengers, he would let Peter or me steer the boat and bring it alongside the harbour steps. The fact that he treated me equally with my brother was deeply satisfying. I could handle the ferry as well as he could.

On the Padstow side, passengers boarded by walking down the harbour steps and stepping aboard. Landing on the Rock side was more sporting. A plank, some 10ins wide and 8ft long, had a notch at one end, with a rope loop attached. The loop was hitched over the bow of the boat and the other end rested on the sand. It was up, over and straight down the plank, as a wave receded. Any hesitation invited the plank to wobble and any hope of landing dry-shod vanished in a flash.

In the summer, when there were visitors, this provided good entertainment. The young and pretty girls usually had the good sense to giggle, look helpless and get carried ashore. There was a lesson for me, right in front of my eyes, but I did not have the wit to see it.

The climb to the golf club was long and upwards through slippery silvery dunes. Returning, we tried to spot the ferry from the crest and judge our descent accordingly. If it had just left Padstow, no need to hurry, but if was nearly across, we'd hurtle down the dunes, wildly, "Wait, Jack, please wait, we're coming." He always pretended not to hear us but would never have willingly left us behind. For our part, we could never bank on this, and were honour-bound to throw ourselves, panting and grateful, into the boat.

St.Enodoc was a splendid golf course then, but not for the faint-hearted. At several difficult holes, there was no easy option. If you were not prepared to keep your head down and hit hard, the obstacles became insuperable. The Himalayas were the most daunting. A steep sand dune blocked any view of the green. You had to play up to its foot, then loft the ball over the top. Then you walked round to see if you'd pitched on to the green.

Years later, at boarding school, we went to tea at the Vicarage. On the wall was a photograph of the vicar playing golf. It showed very little of the background, but "That's the Himalayas!" I exclaimed. The vicar nodded approval, but everyone else thought I had gone potty.

The clubhouse was a wooden pavilion, above the eighteenth green, which lay in a horseshoe-shaped grassy amphitheatre. Myrtle always provided us with great pasties, wrapped in greaseproof paper and white damask napkins. They were still warm when we ate them, watching players finishing their rounds on the green below.

The main course was no place for children, but there was also a relatively flat nine-hole artisans' course. Peter and I learned there. We had children's clubs, beautifully balanced, passed from family to family as they became outgrown. The Club professional, Randall, made hickory shafted clubs. I still have one, made originally for Mother. Unlike any modern club but it's uncommonly handy round the green.

I sometimes walked round with Mother, being allowed to play a few shots. From her, I learned rules and the strict etiquette of the game. St. Enodoc is an excellent course, the setting alongside the Estuary with its view out to Stepper Point, incomparable. At Brea Hill, the course turns inland, passing the curious little St. Enodoc Church, with its crooked steeple. At one time, the church was entirely engulfed in sand and for many years lay buried and forgotten. One day, a cow kicked the top of the steeple. The church was gradually dug out and, for a while, the congregation had to enter via the roof and descend a ladder into the nave. The top of the steeple was left crooked, in memory of the cow that had kicked the church back to life. It is now the burial place of the late John Betjeman, Poet Laureate.

The springy seaside turf was a joy to walk on and ideal for a golf course, its sandy soil draining well. Wild flowers abounded, with thrift, lady's slipper and wild violets. I remember the green of the turf, the blue of the sky, the sunshine, the larks trilling overhead and the sight and the sound of the sea.

I thought it a treat to go in the car sometimes with Father to St. Enodoc. We often stopped in Rock at a bungalow where two sisters, Benjie and Dollie Norman, lived. They were both good players and one of them partnered Mother in the Cornish Ladies' Team. I particularly liked their Old English Sheepdog because we were failures with pets. Peter-dog did not rate as a pet, he was Father's gun-dog. I had two apathetic Angora rabbits, Benjie and June. They lived in a hutch in the yard. Their smelly straw needed regular changing, they had to be fed and their thick coats got impossibly matted. I thought they might be happier if they had better quarters. After much pleading, a hutch with a chicken-wire run was erected on the lawn. I thought that they would gambol about and enjoy the grass, but they skulked in the hutch and were banished back to the yard. When I found them both dead, I wasn't sorry to lose them.

We had a Exmoor-type pony, called Brownie. He was meant for Peter to ride. The trouble was that Brownie lived in a field more than walking distance from the house and was virtually impossible to catch. The album has a photo of him saddled and on a leading-rein, with Peter on his back, but I have no memory of him being ridden regularly. By the time I was big enough, and dying to ride, poor Brownie had developed some sort of foot-rot, and vanished from our lives.

A grey and white fluffy kitten was more promising, but only lasted a few days. Cynthia, Philip and Roly Prideaux-Brune were playing rounders with us in the garden. A ball went into the flowerbed. Before I could shout a warning, lanky Cynthia leapt into a clump of montbretia, her big foot landing splat on the kitten, killing it outright.

Our butterfly-hunting was not consciously cruel. Before chemicals and pesticides decimated numbers, it was normal to build up a collection of the many varieties that were so plentiful in the Cornish climate. We had red admirals, tortoiseshells, fritillaries, blues, yellows, and whites, all with exquisite markings on their velvety wings. Collecting butterflies was thought no different from collecting foreign stamps. Our butterfly nets were about twelve inches in diameter. When we ran and caught one, we took great care not to damage it. If we already had one of that variety, we let it fly away unharmed. Otherwise, it was popped into a wide-necked glass jar, with a cork stopper. They were killed with some sort of ether, but how we did it, without knocking ourselves out, I have no idea. Each new specimen was gently transferred to the collection in a glass-fronted case, its wings pinned out on a cork mount to show off its delicate beauty.

Birds-nesting was equally popular. We learned where to search for nests of different species. We climbed trees, parted bushes, or scanned the ground and only ever took one egg from a clutch, taking care not to disturb the nest. We only selected eggs to augment our collection.

Peter and I always worked happily together when we were actively doing things. It was only when he was bored that he resorted to teasing me.

CHAPTER
SIX

Fishing in the Bush

Every year, we made a tedious journey to stay with Father's parents in Northern Ireland — by train to London then on to Scotland for the ferry crossing from Stranraer to Larne. At Kings Cross, a porter piled our luggage on his barrow, led us to the train and installed us in reserved seats, stowing cases on the rack above.

We didn't reserve the whole compartment, but Peter and I developed a system to keep it to ourselves. First line of defence was pulling faces through the window. Any traveller missing that signal and sliding the compartment door open was greeted with a hissed "Measles". If that didn't work and anyone came in and sat down, they could be evicted with the unfailing formula: "I'm going to be sick."

Soon after the train started, the guard put up our table. At one end, two brass lugs dropped into notches on each side of the carriage door. The other end was supported by a hinged leg. It filled the space between the seats and we could spread out our books and crayons, and settle down for the long journey. Meals in the restaurant car were too expensive for us, so we had sandwiches wrapped in greaseproof paper. As the day crept on, they became less appetising. The egg ones started to smell and the strawberry jam soaked into the bread, which curled up at the edges. Sadly, we were out of range of Myrtle's pasties.

By the time we reached Stranraer it was evening. From the ferry's deck, I watched in awe as the scarlet sun sank behind black hills, setting sky and sea ablaze. Slowly the brilliance faded, through all shades of flame, lemon, magenta and turquoise.

Padstow faces east. The semi-circular hill behind the town, with its sheltering band of trees, not only affords protection from westerly gales, but obscures the setting sun, so the annual splendour of the Stranraer sunsets made a spectacular and memorable sight.

We stayed on deck watching the loading activity until just before sailing, when the ship's farewell blast reverberated through my ears to the soles of my feet. After that first shattering sound, I was always apprehensive, waiting for the fearsome blast. I have no recollections of the crossing, probably being asleep in a cabin, snug and smug, while Mother coped with Peter being sea-sick. No wonder Father never chose to travel with us. He always arrived a day or so later.

Stranocum House was far too big for two people, but Grandpa Ford-Hutchinson had inherited it from his father and it never occurred to him to live anywhere else. It suited Grey Grannie's extravagant style better than it suited his country vicar's slender stipend.

We children knew our grandparents as "Grandpa Fordie" and "Grey Grannie". Grown-ups called Grannie, "Mamie". I can't remember now why we called her "Grey". Not from her hair, for that was pure white, worn swept up into a small bun on top. A handsome woman, tall and upright, she walked with a stately gait, her toes turning slightly out. If she had been made to walk with a pile of books on her head when a child, it had certainly worked.

A long skirt and loose jacket over a high-necked white blouse softened her angular frame. Round her throat, she always wore a black velvet band with a pearl brooch. She dominated her mild husband, who had about him a slightly apologetic air for not being a bishop. Frail, with thin mousy hair, a pale complexion and grey short-sighted eyes, he wore little gold-rimmed glasses, with thick pebble-lenses — even with these aids his sight was still poor.

From the lodge gates, a long drive ended in a broad sweep of gravel outside a white two-storey house topped by a hipped roof of grey slate. A square bay jutted forward from the centre of the facade, the windows in matching pairs on either side. The only break in the symmetry of the design was the surprising position of the front door, not where one would have expected in the middle of the bay, but tucked into the left side. A large sash window graced the centre.

The simplicity of the whole was enlivened by four slender-stemmed lidded urns, topping the corners of the bay. It was the building's only ornamentation, placed there by someone with inspired judgement, grace-notes on an elegant building. Seen out of context, they might have adorned an exotic oriental palace.

51

The main rooms were high, light and pleasant, with deep sash windows looking out over lawns and meadows down to the river. In the dining-room, a rope pulley worked a lift to bring food up from the kitchen. The joy of this novelty was only tinged with regret that it was not quite big enough for even a small girl to curl up inside. I don't remember seeing the kitchen, but a photograph shows basement windows on the side of the house where the ground fell away to the river. I only know that when we pulled the rope, great dishes of food arrived. I wish I had a rope like that in my house.

A two-storey wing, built on a smaller scale, ran back from the main building, forming an "L". On the ground floor, a number of small rooms opened off a single passage. Grandpa spent much of his time in his study there.

Next door was the gun room, where we were taught the strict discipline of handling guns. Half as much admonition would have sufficed for me, as I suspected that a gun had a life of its own and would turn round and shoot me, even without a cartridge in it, if I transgressed the rules. (Even now, when my grandchildren brandish plastic guns, it is all I can do not to shout "DON'T POINT")

Despite my nervousness, I liked helping to clean the guns. Their quality made them a pleasure to handle, with elegant decoration chased into the metalwork and the silken smoothness of the wooden stock. They had their own particular smell of steel and oily cotton-wadding, with traces of gun-powder. They were designed for killing but they were still beautiful objects.

Grandpa had a rickety car, known as a "tourer". This meant that in summer, rain or shine, the hood was folded down. We were never there in winter for the ceremonial raising of the hood.

On an early visit to her new "in-laws", during the time of the Sinn Fein troubles of the 1920's, Mother's gentle father-in-law invited her to come with him in the car, bringing Peter, a new baby, wrapped in his shawl. He later mentioned he'd wanted to transport a box of ammunition and thought it would allay any suspicion if she and baby were with him. The box was under her seat. The Protestants needed ammunition, so that they could fire in the air to scare off marauding Sein Fein bands, who might come at night, perhaps to burn a haystack or set light to a barn.

Another day, he asked Mother to go with him, patting her arm, saying "You do eyes for me, dear". This was a little safety precaution he took, on account of his bad eyesight, but she did not fully appreciate the importance of her role until he veered off the road, on to the grass verge, up one side of a heap of road-menders' stone, down the other and back on the road again. Since he seldom exceeded 25mph and there was scarcely any traffic, he never came to any harm.

In those days, parents had inexorable standards about what could be said "in front of the children". Consequently I did not realise at the time why we seldom went in the car with him. Behind the scenes, Mother was constantly manoeuvring to save us from automotive death. Mother's wiles were usually successful, so when we went in the car, Father drove.

Later I had the same problem with my unroadworthy Mother-in-Law.

We seldom ventured outside the triangle of Portstewart-Ballycastle-Ballymoney. I never saw where "the Mountains of Mourne Sweep Down to the Sea".

A favourite trip was to the Giant's Causeway, eight miles from Portrush, a truly amazing place. The Causeway is a low promontory running out to sea, formed by close-packed vertical pentagonal and hexagonal columns of black basaltic rock. Other groupings form the Giant's Loom, the Giant's Organ and the Lady's Fan. Beyond is the 400ft Pleaskin Head, a double tier of lofty columns, separated by a band of ochre. Altogether there are 40,000 pillars, covering half a mile. Nearby is Spanish Bay, where an Armada ship foundered.

Earnest geologists would have us believe the causeway was formed by cooling lava, but any local will tell you it's the creation of Finn M'Coul, or Fingal, who bridged the channel between Ireland and Scotland so Giants could pass between Antrim and Staffa.

I doubt whether Grandpa had any vocation to be a clergyman, but it had long been a custom to put the first son in the army, the second in the church. This practical plan kept the eldest son occupied until his father died. He would then relinquish his commission and take over the estate. With bad eyesight and poor physique, Grandpa would never have made a soldier, so he swapped roles with his younger brother, George, who became a Colonel in the Connaught Rangers. When Uncle George retired, he had a large house built near Stranocum, called Rangerford. Aunt Isabel, their sister, lived near at Willford, a house built by her father, William.

The River Bush runs through Stranocum grounds. Flowing north-west, it enters the sea by Portballintrae. On its way, it services Bushmills Whiskey Distillery, claimed to be the oldest in the world.

Father and Peter spent hours fishing for salmon and trout. In Cornwall, we had no suitable river for fly-fishing. At first, I was fobbed-off with a garden cane and a bent pin, but my indignation somehow resulted in me being given a proper rod of my own. I loved the coloured feathers of the flies, which I kept in a leather-bound wallet.

I could cast as well as Peter, but he was the hero who caught a salmon. I failed to see why this was lauded as such a great event. If a salmon chanced to take his bait, all he had to do was pull it out of the water to die. I was jealous of all the congratulations heaped upon him.

The balance of the rod in my hand and the whirring of the reel as it ran out were a pleasure, but I was not keen to actually catch fish. I hated to watch a graceful fish die, the hook wrenched brutally from its mouth. Once a fish was killed by someone else, I could handle it without a qualm, so long as I did not look it in the eye. It was the pathetic ever-weakening thrashing about as it expired and the barbed hook I hated. I went fishing because I did not want to be left behind and because I loved the tranquillity of the clear water, dappled by the trees above.

Outbuildings surrounded a yard at the back of the house. In one corner, a donkey walked delicately round and round an everlasting circle, attached to a radial arm that worked the pump for water, or was it electricity? He lived in a hay barn, sharing it with feral cats that clawed and spat. Efforts to ride the donkey were a failure. The animal was not used to anyone on its back. Grown-ups fussed us to be careful because donkeys kick sideways, the rider was held by an arm, and the donkey wouldn't budge.

One side of the yard was taken up with a long open-sided barn with an inspection pit for repairing the underside of the car. It was in regular use. Father rigged up a gallery where he taught Peter to shoot. Mother did not realise how quickly he was becoming proficient. When he wanted to show off his skill, he asked what he should aim at. Never thinking he could hit a haystack, she rashly waved her hand at a bird in a tree. He fired and a robin fell dead.

From the bedroom windows, Father took pot-shots at pigeons, kitchen garden predators. Whilst it was obligatory for boys to learn to shoot, mercifully it was not expected of girls. The thought of the loud report and the kicking recoil against my shoulder alarmed me. I tackled many things in my efforts to keep up with Peter, but shooting was beyond me.

A little way from the house, a high brick wall enclosed the flower and vegetable garden. Stepping through the door was magical. A lavender-edged stone-flagged path led between herbaceous borders filled with poppies, phlox, lupins, delphiniums and cornflowers . . . the flowers jostled in untidy profusion, their scents mingling and filling the air. A stone sundial stood half way along the path. Beyond, the flowers gave way to vegetables. Espaliered fruit trees and rambling roses sprawled over the sheltering walls. It was all a gloriously untidy riot of colour, scent and flavour. Everything thrived. Despite the pigeons, there was far more than one household could consume, so Grannie took basketfuls around the cottages, in her element as Lady Bountiful.

Another local smell contrasted with the sweetness of the walled garden. From ditches beside the roads rose the acrid reek of flax for the local linen trade. After harvesting, it was left soaking in the ditches until the outer part of the stem rotted away, leaving the fine strong core for weaving.

The annual village fete took place in the grounds. A photo shows me playing hoop-la, with Father standing by, hoops hanging from his arm, obviously in charge of the sideshow. It is my only photo showing him "playing".

After two weeks at Stranocum, Father would leave. We packed and followed, reversing the long haul back to Padstow. In that era, fathers were not expected to help with bringing up their children.

Grey Grannie once stayed at "Hurst". It was the first time I saw a grown-up blatantly cheating. We played croquet and if she mis-hit a ball, she blithely said "Oh dear! I struck it on the side!" — and hit it again before anyone could move. Nor was she above giving the ball a little help with the toe of her shoe. Whatever else we children did or did not do, cheating was unthinkable. The family tried to laugh it off, but Pam and I were shocked. Perhaps Grey Grannie was embarrassed that her croquet was not up to our standard.

After Grandpa's death, Stranocum was inherited by Father's elder brother, Roger. When he and his eccentric wife Alice, took over, with their five sons, the main rooms were closed and the family lived in the back wing. Mamie was dumped in a boarding house in Portrush. The tenanted farms that had once provided an income, had long since been sold. There was no money left.

During the Second World War, the whole place was requisitioned by the Government to house refugees from Gibraltar. The family took a bungalow near Portrush. After the war, Stranocum was bought as a private house for a while, but when my niece went to look at it in the 1980's, it was standing empty, the gravel drive almost vanished under rank grass. Some windows were smashed, roof tiles were missing. Ireland abounds in such places, sadly mouldering away. If real peace ever comes to the Province, it may be too late to rescue many houses for the tourist industry which would surely burgeon.

In 1946, Mother and I went to visit Mamie. She clung to her dignity, in spite of the pitiful way she eked out an existence in a bed-sitting room. We went with her for a shopping expedition in Ballymoney, where the local department store gave her a welcome fit for a duchess. It was infinitely sad to witness the play-acting, as she selected a new hat for some grand occasion which would never occur. Her extravagance seemed undimmed. Everyone must have known her penury, but maintained the facade of affluence. She had a brief hour when she could fancy herself living back in happier times.

She wanted to buy me a hat as well and it took all my tact to refuse without hurting her feelings. Some days later, I could have done with a hat, as I was unexpectedly enrolled as godmother to a cousin's daughter. Hats in church were obligatory. The war had taught us all to improvise, so I concocted a hat from a scarf and a sanitary towel. It was much admired and taken as the "dernier cri" in fashion, as my last job was in Paris.

When we left, Mamie was anxious we should take with us something she was leaving Mother in her will. Two big tea-chests were brought out of store. These contained a collection of fine Waterford glass and two tea services, one of which was said to be particularly valuable. Before trying to get these back with us to Bromley, we suggested opening them to check on the packing, but Mamie was affronted at the very idea. They had been packed and stored by a reputable local firm and that was good enough.

Our return journey was a real nightmare, coinciding with crates of Christmas turkeys being loaded on the ferry. When we finally got home the wonderful packing turned out to be a few flimsy sheets of paper and damp wisps of straw. Every piece of the Waterford was smashed. Part of one tea service survived, a showy pattern with flowers on a cobalt blue ground, liberally gilded. The other set was delicate porcelain — with little rustic scenes in grey. All were cracked, so I threw them in the dustbin. I now know that, in my ignorance, I threw away a tea service which could have graced a museum. My years with the RAF had taught me much, but nothing about antique treasures.

CHAPTER
SEVEN

A long shadow

The boom of the maroon going up to call out the lifeboat crew shook the whole of Padstow awake. My bedroom window overlooked Fentonluna Lane, where usually only an occasional footfall broke the silence. Kneeling shivering on my window-seat, I had a grandstand view of the excitement, men pounding up the hill, rushing past the house, on their way to see the boat launched from the Lifeboat Station, two miles away at Cove.

There were few cars in the town, so Father and Dr. Shervill always took the crew, Father in his rugged Renault, the doctor in his saloon. The only people living at Cove were Coastguards and Trinity House pilots who guided ships in and out of the Estuary. By the time the crew arrived, they and their wives had already dragged "Arab" out and part-way down the ramp, with fresh food and drink stowed on board, ready for launching. The town stayed gripped in anxious tension until boat and crew safely returned.

Once they were away for several days, called to help a ship off Hartland Point. Father took me to join the watchers waiting on the cliff-top, straining through binoculars for sight of the lifeboat returning. Eventually, it was thought to be seen, but it was hard to be sure, as it appeared for an instant on the crest of a wave and then vanished again into a trough.

Slowly, slowly, it was recognised and the word passed back to the town. Concern mounted until they were safely in and it was known no men had been lost. It had proved a false alarm this time, but the dangers were the same.

The Lifeboat Station had the advantage of a launching ramp leading straight into deep water. This was a great improvement over beach launchings that relied on a team of horses dragging the boat out stern-first on a wheeled trolley. With men astride the leaders, the horses went out through the breakers then swung in an arc until the boat floated free, bow pointing out to sea, when ten oarsmen took up their rowing rhythm. The strength and stamina needed to pull the long heavy oars for hours on end called for men of iron. When conditions allowed, they could step two masts and hoist small sails, but the great seas and gales made any progress hazardous.

The "Arab" was the second boat of that name stationed at Padstow. She was 35ft long and built to self-right after a capsize. Padstow also kept a reserve boat because more than one ship might need help on such a dangerous coast.

In 1929, the arrival of the twin-screwed RNLB Princess Mary marked a great step forward in design. She was 61ft long, with a 15ft beam and capable of more than 9 knots. After being moored in Padstow for everyone to see and admire, she took up station at Cove. She could be launched directly into the water, the crew already aboard.

There was talk of Peter and I being allowed a little trip, perhaps in recognition of Father's service driving crews. Of course I wanted to go, such a privilege was not to be missed. But I had never been further than to Rock by ferry and the prospect of the plunge down the ramp and the great splash as the bow hit the water left question marks in my mind. In the event, it was decided we could go, but with a sedate start from the Quay. I echoed Peter's disappointment, but was secretly a bit relieved. Maybe he was bluffing too.

The helmsman stood near the stern, protected by the roof of the hatch leading below. Behind his shoulders, a semi-circular wooden rail on brass supports kept him from being washed overboard when waves broke over the deck. Peter and I had to stand on upturned buckets to see ahead.

I wondered whether I would be allowed to try my hand at steering, in my usual twitter of not wanting to be left out, but apprehensive of the task ahead. As on the Rock ferry, it was taken for granted I would be treated as a grown-up man. No doubt there were smiles and winks behind me and strong hands alert to take over if I needed help, but the opportunity made one small girl ecstatically happy.

It was calm in the Estuary, but once past Stepper Point the waves in the open sea round Newland seemed huge, but I was too excited to mind. We were near enough to the island to see its colony of puffins.

We seldom saw them on the mainland. There is something odd about a puffin. Its orange legs and black body with white breast are orthodox, but where other birds have heads with beaks, the puffin has a face with a surprised expression. The black eyes are set in white oval bowls, like owls. The great triangular orange bill looks so unreal that one half-expects to see a piece of elastic round the back of the head, like a false nose from a Christmas cracker.

The island is also an ideal place for colonies of cormorants and shags, where they can build nests of seaweed undisturbed. When they fly fast and low over the water, their long necks thrust forward, they always seem bound on some urgent pre-occupying mission.

Not for them the idle gliding on thermals gulls enjoy. Off duty, stock-still on a post or rock, the cormorant does not flicker, unless it is to stretch out its wings to dry, still a petrified statue on a pedestal. It gives the impression of an aged cleric, shoulders hunched, in rusty black, pondering his next sermon. A pince-nez on the beak would not look out of place.

Although the shag is smaller and more lightly built, unless they are together, it takes an expert eye to tell them apart. Both are strong swimmers. They may submerge with scarcely a ripple, or jump clear of the surface before plunging, swimming fast under water and reappearing some distance away, often with fish in their beaks.

* * *

I had little knowledge of the Great War, but it cast a long shadow. I had seen photographs of my parents' wedding, with Father in the uniform of an army officer. He never spoke of it, perhaps seeking to bury memories of the horrors at Gallipoli. There were no War books or memorabilia in the house. Television had not yet been invented and I had never seen a film.

Each November, on Armistice Day, long before it became Remembrance Sunday, we walked along St Saviour's Lane and the top path to the War Memorial, by Chapel Stile. The main procession from the town came up the lower path from the harbour, led by the Town Band. As we stood round singing: "O hear us when we cry to Thee, for those in peril on the sea", it was the crews of the lifeboat and the trawlers that were in my mind.

Standing there, high above the Estuary, there is a sense of the earth's puny size compared with the vastness of the skies. In November, the sky was often filled with clouds driven scudding by the wind. It tugged at the Vicar's surplice and whipped the Standards of the British Legion.

The Memorial is a 20ft high granite Celtic cross, mounted on a triple-stepped base. It was unveiled by Mrs Richard Bates in 1922. Its carved inscription reads . . .

1914-1919
to
The Glory of God
In honoured memory of
THE MEN OF PADSTOW
who gave their lives in
The Great War
also
in grateful appreciation
of the services
of those who returned

56 names are inscribed. Some of the same family names appear more than once. I doubt if there is a finer Memorial site anywhere. It commands a panorama from the mouth of the Estuary, swinging east over Trebetherick, Brea Hill, the sand dunes of Rock and up the Camel until it turns out of sight on its way to Wadebridge. As the eye roves on, it comes round to the Iron Bridge, Queen Victoria's Jubilee Obelisk silhouetted against the sky and back to Padstow. The old harbour is hidden by a jumble of slate roofs but the trawler dock, the railway station and the glowering Metropole stand out clearly.

Years later, at boarding school in Bexhill-on-Sea, my turn came to carry the Girl Guides' Standard on Armistice Day and I found how hard it was to keep it steady in the wind. The War Memorial on the flat Promenade by the dull grey English Channel was a world away from Cornwall, but as we sang the hymn "Eternal Father strong to save . . . ", I was instantly transported back to Padstow. Tears trickled down my face, but I could not let go of the Standard to grope for a handkerchief. I had to snivel.

Every town and village in the land has its War Memorial, recording the names of those who fell in the "War to End All Wars". No words can describe the depth of grief and apprehension felt by bereaved families when, only twenty years on, they faced the inexorable slide into another World War. Those who had already lost husbands and brothers watched as their sons joined-up and marched away.

At the outbreak of the First World War in 1914, no-one had an inkling of the appalling toll of casualties it would bring as the British army slogged it out with the German army in Flanders. So small a distance lay between them. Each army operated from a maze of muddy trenches, only separated from each other by barbed wire and the bare "no man's land" of cratered mud, where once wild poppies had blossomed in green fields.

There the infantry lived, ate, slept and often died. To attack, young subalterns led their men "over the top" of the trench. Clutching their rifles, they ran blindly forward, their numbers dwindling as men fell.

There were too few doctors and nurses available to cope with the flood of casualties. The Red Cross saw the need to recruit women who, with minimal training, could undertake some of the simpler tasks, freeing regular nurses for where their skills were most needed. They were known as VADs — Voluntary Aid Detachment.

Military hospitals worked with rigid discipline. With cross-infection always a threat, wards were constantly scrubbed with carbolic. Every morning, the ward had to be spick and span, with all floors spotless, all bedside lockers cleaned. Even the beds had to stand to attention, their castors facing forward, ready for Matron's inspection.

As the VADs were unpaid, most volunteers came from middle-class families. They were young women from sheltered backgrounds, with little experience of the outside world. The minimum age was eighteen. Until the war, the eighteenth birthday was when girls "put their hair up". Only then could their long schoolgirl hair be swept up on top, in the fashion of adults, signalling goodbye to the classroom.

As the war went on, the flow of casualties in Flanders became a torrent. More and more nurses were needed, closer to the battlefields. From the front lines, stretcher bearers carried wounded to Field Dressing Stations. From there they went by ambulance to Casualty Clearing Stations, often laid out in rows in the open until they could be taken in. The ambulances had to off-load speedily and return for more.

When the casualties' needs had been assessed and urgent treatment given, their stretchers were loaded on racks inside ill-sprung ambulances and taken to one of the sixty Base Hospitals in Belgium and France. Each ambulance had a woman driver and a nurse. In spite of painted Red Crosses, ambulances frequently went through enemy bombardment.

Young nurses faced the task of getting men out of their mud and blood-caked uniforms, cleaning their wounds with swabs of stinging Lysol. Sometimes they carried away amputated limbs for burning. Many jobs got delegated to the VADs, so that the trained nurses could take on more tasks from the overworked doctors.

VADs saw dreadful sights, smelled stomach-churning stenches, heard men moaning in pain and crying out in their nightmares and tried to ignore the swearing. When septic wounds turned to gangrene, the best and only cure was to pack the open wound with maggots, who would eat away the rotten flesh, leaving it clean for treatment and healing. On duty VADs steeled themselves to appear calm, giving no hint of their own distress.

When rated fit, men returned to the Front. The rest went by hospital-trains to a Channel port. Back in "Blighty", hospital-trains took them to one of the many military hospitals and convalescent homes set up in mansions, schools or any other large building which could be made to serve.

Occasionally a soldier at the Front, driven to the end of his tether, would deliberately shoot himself in the foot. With an injured foot, he could not wear his boots, so could not march. This wound was rated "a Blighty one", ensuring return to England. A damaged foot was preferable to another moment in the hell of the trenches. (Curiously, "to shoot oneself in the foot" has become a term used to describe an accidental folly, rather than a deliberate act to prevent an even worse fate.)

My Mother, with her twin sister Stella, nursed in an Officers' Convalescent Home in Chislehurst, not far from their home. Muriel, the eldest sister, went as a VAD to Egypt, where she drove ambulances, rode motorbikes and served on Hospital Ships, two of which were torpedoed. The first time, off the Isle of Wight, she got away in a lifeboat. The second, off Alexandria, she was picked from the water, which fortunately was warm as she had Rubella at the time. She claimed she'd caught it off a letter sent from England by one of her sisters, who had the rash when she wrote.

She was engaged to a Royal Flying Corps pilot, Peter MacLean, but he was killed. Peter must have been a popular name. Had he survived, I would have had a Peter uncle, as well as brother and husband, a dog and the budgerigar.

CHAPTER
EIGHT

Scaring the French, scaring me!

Wherever rituals of unknown origin are carried on, tourist publicity will almost certainly claim them to be based upon "Ancient Fertility Rites". If there's little known history, who can argue?

However the origin of Padstow's May Day celebration can be traced to two sources — the siege of Calais, and the Celtic religion, older than Christianity.

The French Invaders came to plunder in May, 1346, thinking it would be easy to help themselves to the wealth of Padstow. King Edward had Calais under siege and the fishermen and shopkeepers, craftsmen and farmers of the Cornish port had built and manned two ships to help their king's blockade.

The French fleet, knowing that Padstow lay unprotected, seized the opportunity to sail into Padstow's Estuary thinking to rape and pillage — but they'd not reckoned on the formidable Ursula Birdwood. "Fetch your red cloaks and scarlet petticoats", she told the women of the town, "and meet me at Stepper Point!"

"And bring the 'Obby 'Oss, dancer-in of the May," she demanded as an afterthought. If Ursula was a witch she was a white witch, and if she could cast spells, they were of the ancient kind but to work her magic against the French she thought the 'Obby 'Oss could help.

Every May Day, the Padstow Hobby-Horses dance and twirl progressing through the streets on thin twin legs, their black canvas bodies flapping, their heads conical, pointed and menacing as witches' hats.

Ursula knew the magic of the 'Oss, originating in a Celtic religion, was a potent symbol of fertility and renewal, powerful enough to drive out the chill of winter and herald in the warmth of spring.

The French were invading with swords as sharp as winter icicles, their faces as cruel as February winds. There was nothing but a handful of women to save the town. "Perhaps," Ursula thought, "the magic of the 'Oss might be strong enough to drive the French away."

By the time Ursula Birdwood and her friends reached the headland at Stepper Point, the French ships had anchored in a crescent across the bay.

Ursula lit the beacon fire and the ceremony began. If the women were frightened they sang the fear out of their throats . . . if their legs were shaking, the trembling ceased as soon as they whirled into the May Day dance.

In a voice, resonant with defiance, Ursula Birdwood began to intone the familiar words, and soon her friends took up the cadence . . .

Unite and unite and let us unite
For Summer is acome unto day . . .

A drum took up the beat, a jogging, regular beat, like that of a horse trotting over broken ground . . .

And whither are we going we will all unite
In the merry morning of May!

Next they sang the Night Song, and then the Day Song again, even richer with magic . . .

O where is St George
O where is he O?
He is out in his long-boat all on the salt sea O
Up flies the kite and down falls the lark O . . .

Out on the Estuary the French saw the flicker of the red cloaks and petticoats as the whirling figures were silhouetted against the flames. Then, indistinct amongst the moving figures, another shape struck stark fear into their superstitious souls — a huge, flapping black creature, twisting and leaping amongst the women, a tireless figure, frightening and malevolent.

"Le Diable, peut-être?" they cried.

Had the English called up the Devil? Was he working some dreadful ritual on that headland to sink their ships? Would he enlist Neptune to cause a storm to crush their hulls, sending the mariners to watery graves?

From time to time Ursula screamed "Oss, Oss!"

And from the whirling dervishes a demonic response — "Wee Oss!"

It was too much! The French Fleet cut its cables in haste and sailed away, watched by Ursula Birdwood, standing on the edge of Stepper Point, one hand grasping the tail of the nodding, whirling leaping effigy that was Padstow's 'Oss.

Padstow's 'Obby 'Oss certainly scared the French. It also scared and fascinated me. Every May Day morning the town remembers its deliverance. Padstow is festooned with bunting and green garlands. Excitement builds to 11.00 when Red 'Oss, accompanied by its Teazer, emerges from the Golden Lion to be welcomed by a cheering crowd singing the May Day Song . . .

Unite and unite and let us all unite
For Summer is acome unto day
And whither we are going, we will all unite
In the merry morning of May.

Half an hour later, Blue 'Oss comes through the iron gateway next to Prior's, tobacconist and barber. Each 'Oss, goaded by its attendant Teazer, represents the eternal conflict between good and evil and takes a different route round the town.

Until the Great War, there was only one 'Oss. In 1919, a second was created, perhaps to represent St. George's triumph over Kaiser Wilhelm. The second 'Oss was first known as the Peace 'Oss, then White 'Oss and eventually Blue 'Oss.

Appropriately coloured ribbons are attached to the horses' jaws, continuously snapped open and shut by the "carrier" to reveal fearsome sets of teeth. No wonder the French fled. To a small girl, the 'Oss was threatening even though I knew there was only a man underneath because I could see his feet.

Each 'Oss has a tall black conical hat topped by a plume. The masks are fearsome — wild eyes ringed in red, blood-red beaky red noses with red oblong mouths, surrounded by grey beards. A hoop, five feet in diameter, holds a skirt of shiny black canvas taut at shoulder height, from where it falls to the ground. Protruding from the front is the small Oss' head, the neck about two feet long, with a mane of black hair.

The black wooden head, with red eyes, has a forelock of white hair.

Red 'Oss arrives at Prideaux Place in the morning, Blue 'Oss in the afternoon. Both are invited into the house for refreshments and beer. The current chatelaine, Elizabeth Prideaux-Brune, takes over the Teazer's club and does a fine dance.

The 'Oss is accompanied by a band of drummers and accordionists, all playing the May Day Song as they parade through the streets. Some are dressed in white, wearing sashes of red or blue, proclaiming their equine allegiance, a few wear white-topped caps decked with fresh flowers.

The numbers of those wearing white has grown greatly during recent years, because most townsfolk can now afford to buy the costumes. Before the great wars, only half a dozen whites made up each team.

Sometimes the 'Oss sinks to the ground as though dying. To revive it the crowd sings this plaintive verse:

O! where is St.George,
O where is he O?
He is out in his long-boat all on the salt sea O.
Up flies the kite and down falls the lark O.
And Ursula Birdwood she had an old ewe O
And she died in her own Park O!

As soon as this musical plea concludes, the 'Oss leaps up again, and, as the song shifts from minor to major key, the dance continues with renewed energy. From time to time the procession stops outside the home of well known residents, when the crowd gleefully seizes the opportunity to sing specially written verses, poking fun at the notables' expense.

Arise Mr . . . , I know you well afine,
For Summer is acome unto day.
You've a shilling in your pocket and I wish it
were in mine,
In the merry morning of May.

Coins are thrown from upstairs windows, collected for local charities. As each 'Oss progresses, the skirts are flipped up now and again to entrap pretty girls from the crowd. As the 'Oss feints and darts towards the crowd, girls shriek. In such narrow streets, they are hemmed in. When one is caught, she emerges with soot smudges on her blushing face — and reputedly will have a baby within the year. Others maintain she's protected from evil for a year.

I knew nothing about that, but was terrified of being caught. I hid behind an adult, heart thumping, peeping until I could see the vanishing tail of the 'Oss — danger passed. The buoyant mood of the crowd was infectious, making it a day for adventure, not timid safety.

All day the dances continue, the procession winding its way through crowded streets, up and down steep hills. Because the cumbersome costume of each 'Oss weighs heavily, even on strong men's shoulders, the "carriers" are changed regularly.

I was at home, tucked up and asleep long before the Padstow men and women returned to their beds.

By that time Red 'Oss was in his stable behind the Golden Lion, Blue 'Oss in his behind Prior's shop. There they rest until the next May 1st.

The following morning the roisterers are nursing sore feet, sore shoulders — particularly those that have been carrying the 'Oss — and sore heads. Nevertheless by noon the garlands and bunting have come down, and the town's life returns to normal.

Before the media fanned publicity, May Day was for the people of Padstow and the surrounding villages. Now crowds come from afar, camcorders whirring . . .

. . . Ursula Birdwood and her red cloaked women danced to scare away intruders. Today their successors dance to entice them in.

CHAPTER
NINE

A rotten Christmas present

It was time I started "proper" school. That September, at the start of the school year, Mother took Peter and me to stay with Grandparents Clay at "Hurst". Their extended family comprised their daughters Muriel, twins Vera (Mother) and Stella, and Kathleen. Their grandchildren were Pam (Stella's daughter), Peter and me . . .

I was to join Pam at Kinnaird Park School. Lonely days with only Miss Webb, whom I loved, were now behind me. I spent hours admiring my school uniform . . . white shirt, with navy, green and white striped tie, navy serge box-pleated tunic with braid girdle, worn knotted like a tie, and an emerald green heavy-knit cardigan. Long grey stockings were a novelty; keeping them up caused technical problems, solved by the liberty bodice. This inaptly named garment was made from white cotton-knit fabric, with shoulder straps and buttons down the front. Four elastic suspenders fastened to the hem, two back and two front, held my stockings up. Such a fuss! All this finery was topped with a big emerald green felt Tam O'Shanter, badge at the front, worn with the fullness pulled down at the back.

I was so tanned from Cornish outdoor life my classmates thought me foreign. India was suggested. My brown hair, hazel eyes and freckles had never seemed odd until I was dropped into the middle of pale urban children. Unused to playmates, I found it hard to relate to the girls in my form at first. During lesson breaks and at meals, I wanted to be with Pam and her friends, but she was three years older and according to school hierarchy it would have been an unbridled liberty to converse with someone so senior, so I settled in with my new contemporaries and breezed through the work.

The school was known by its initials, K.P. The school song ended with a rousing last line proclaiming — falsely as it turned out — "Always K P." The site, and that of Carn Brea, Peter's school, were sold later when re-development values outshone meagre school returns.

KP was run by two headmistresses, also known by their initials. JAL was the public face. She smiled insincerely at the mothers, was coy with fathers, made favourites among the girls and had a sarcastic tongue for those insufficiently sycophantic. She wore a parody of the school uniform, navy serge skirt, white shirt with school tie, a tailored jacket matching the colour of the girls' cardigans.

MEF was the reverse; quiet, kind, scholarly and an inspiring teacher of History and English to the senior forms. On Speech Day, she looked very well in her academic gown, with MA hood. JAL looked silly in her outfit. She had no academic qualifications.

Thanks to MEF, the school had some excellent teachers. English lessons taught us the building blocks of our eccentric language. We dissected sentences . . . nouns, verbs, adverbs, adjectives, pronouns — all were carefully scrutinised. We parsed, précised, avoided split infinitives, writing different from, not different to. We also knew enormity did not mean enormous. Our lessons were interesting, never dull.

We learned to spell, working through lists of difficult words. Regular competitions involved all girls from eleven upwards. A list of 200 words read at a brisk speed allows little dithering and the results showed that a young "natural" can achieve better results than many of her seniors. Top spellers joined the teams in inter-school championships, which I enjoyed.

When our art mistress swooped in under full sail, she taught us to use our eyes and observe accurately. The classroom casement window-frames were all painted from the same pot of paint, but we had to draw them first, studying how the light fell.

Looked at in this way, we saw that perhaps only one facet was pure white, the rest varying shades of grey. Each gradation had to be assessed and numbers pencilled in. Only then could we dip our brushes into the paint and begin. Our maths mistress was equally methodical in teaching arithmetic, algebra and geometry. She wore the same navy serge skirt year-in, year-out, the seat getting thinner and shinier each term. We all expected to witness the inevitable when it split right across, but it didn't while I was there. When she stepped on to the dais, she'd lean forward to clump her books down on the desktop.

One morning we balanced the front legs of her desk on the very edge of the platform. She came in, didn't bat an eyelid, pulled the desk back from the edge and got on with the lesson — giving not one sign she'd detected our small ambush. She was an excellent teacher, so the solutions to geometrical theorems seemed self-evident to me. At my next school, when my exam paper was marked 99% I could not see where I'd lost the elusive 1%. I asked politely for an explanation, but was told "Nobody is perfect." Such petty meanness rankled.

All her life, Pam has remembered an unmerited spiteful remark made during a scripture class. At the end of the parable of the wise and the foolish virgins, the mistress added: "Pamela, you would be one of the foolish ones." Poor Pam was most upset. Not only would her lamp have been filled to the brim, she'd have shared her oil with anybody in need.

When I lived in Cornwall I was healthy and do not recall having so much as a cold. At school, I was the victim of every passing germ, enduring endless sore throats and colds. I was said to be "outgrowing my strength" because I'd shot up to be the tallest in my class, although two years younger than some. To my furious indignation, JAL took it into her head I was malingering. The ultimate insult was being offered a whipped cream walnut for every week I completed at school — I didn't even like the sickly things. I did myself no good by showing anger, but I couldn't hide it. In any case, I hated being away, I *liked* school.

Measles was miserable, coinciding with my birthday. I lay in a darkened room, with a raging temperature. Whooping-cough was worse. Struggling to breathe, I got into cycles of "cough-whoop-be-sick-faint". It frightened me and Mother watching me. Modern vaccines have done much to eradicate the illness, so dangerous to young children.

Grandaddy made a bird-table and hung it outside my window, so I could watch the tits, finches, robins and other birds that flocked to the feast put out for them.

Every term, a chart was put up in our form-room. Good work gold stars were stuck beside the names of fortunate girls. Another girl and I were locked in keen contention, so each time I returned from sickness, she'd taken the lead and I had to struggle to catch up. The Gold Star system was badly flawed because it was discouraging for those who worked to the best of their ability, but never sparkled.

Absence from school made me miss the qualifying heats for Sports Day. Athletics played no regular part in the curriculum, so we just launched ourselves off at speed once a year. I was amazed when JAL, all unctuous magnanimity, said I could enter two events, the long jump and the obstacle race. I had never tried long jumping, so copied the others and hurled myself into the sandpit. Propelled by adrenalin, I covered a very respectable distance.

All obstacle race competitors belted off together over the first few hazards, then each lane had its individual set of sacks, hoops etc. Nothing had been put out for me. I was left stranded in mid-course, without obstacles to overcome. I walked off, scarlet in humiliation.

The finale of these Olympian afternoons was the Relay. Every pupil took part, from tearful tiny tots to seventeen-year-olds, embarrassed by wobbling breasts. We lined up in two teams. The youngest led off, overawed and unsure. They ran to the "turners", JAL and MEF, were twirled round and sent back to touch the next runner. As the size of the runners increased, so the turners backed away, leaving the senior girls unhindered in their final dash for glory.

All would have gone smoothly had it not been for the Scotcher sisters. To keep the handicap equal one Scotcher was assigned to each team. Both had difficulty running forwards. Their knees pumped furiously, but forward motion was minimal. Only the combined willpower of their team-mates and cheers of encouragement from all the parents got them over the course. They were not twins, so when the younger one "ran", the other team streaked ahead only to slow down again when the sister went.

The winning team received enamel brooches in green, white and navy school colours. Since a competition was held to find a new design each year, girls starting in the kindergarten could end in the sixth form jangling like a Suffolk Punch at a ploughing match.

Because there was so little space around the school, tennis and hockey was played on fields rented from local clubs. Crocodiles of bicycles, two abreast, weaved their way to and fro. Both clubs were nearer home than school, but I wasn't allowed to ride straight home. I had pedal all the way back to school, turn round and pedal home again.

Drama was MEF's province. The stage comprised a series of broad steps running the full width of the hall. They offered arresting tableaux possibilities. My first role was that of a Bong Tree in "The Owl and the Pussycat". I became a tree by putting my green cardigan on back-to-front, raising arms to screen my face and waving them about like a tree in a storm.

MEF's brother wrote a musical for the school. I have no idea what it was about. Although the story-line was a trifle weak, the music deserved a wider audience. Pam, by now a busty thirteen-year-old, was draped in grey tulle and wafted about, with seven others similarly clad, averring they were "little grey clouds in the twilight". I was one of a band of huntsmen, the effect of hunting-pink jackets and white breeches being somewhat diminished by having to wear wellies. We sang: "We're off to the hunt, Tally-ho!" repeated many times. Admittedly we were rather small huntsmen, but I do believe we could have handled more ambitious lyrics.

I soon had plenty of friends. We all lived near one another and could walk or cycle to each other's homes. In our family, the main summer activity was tennis. In winter, Mother organised badminton, two days a week, by invitation only. This really catered for Peter and Pam's age group, but I was included. All wore pristine white. One boy, who always turned up in grubby flannels, was frowned on. Had he not had two very clean older sisters, he'd have been dropped from the invitation list. Summer and winter, our bathroom windowsill usually had a row of shoes drying after an application of Blanco.

Our enterprising Girl Guide Company met twice weekly during the holidays, allowing plenty of time for ambitious projects. I was keen and liked my navy uniform, with leather belt, complete with dangling hank of cord and knife. Long black cotton stockings and a felt hat with the Guide Trefoil on the front completed the ensemble.

We learned First-Aid. We splinted "broken" arms. We improvised splints for broken legs, ready to carry the casualty away on a hurdle, always assumed to be readily at hand. We bandaged heads, ankles, knees. We gave artificial respiration. We administered pretend hot sweet tea. After a simple test, the First-Aid proficiency badge was awarded. Most of what we did would now be thought inappropriate, if not downright dangerous.

My haul of proficiency badges grew, worn in pairs, sewn down the left sleeve. I got my Second Class badge, worn above a pocket, but insuperable obstacles blocked the coveted First Class. The knots, first aid, nature-study were not difficult, but the syllabus also included simple cookery and child care. The only cooking I ever did was making sticky toffee in a pan on a gas ring. We only went into the kitchen once a year, on Boxing Day, when the maids were given the day off together, when they left cold meals for us. Being the youngest, I knew nothing about Child Care nor did I know a baby who would let me change its nappy or feed it from a bottle.

We learned to tie reef knots, clove hitches, bowlines as well as round-turn-and-two-half-hitches. All these have been useful, but I still await the day when my skill with a sheepshank proves invaluable. This shortens rope when both ends are already attached. So far, those with the rope have always had the wit to pull it taut before fixing the second end.

In those days girls of ten or eleven could wander safely on their own, unworried by threats of assault, abduction, rape or murder. It worries me that little children in Primary School are now being taught to be suspicious of grown-ups, trusting no one. This teaching seems too high an insurance premium to pay against an attack, no more probable than being struck by lightning. In any case, one small child squeaking "No" will not deter a determined predator.

We were friends with one set of neighbours, two boys and two girls. Our copper beech and their big trees were the Eigers of our tree-climbing. If our tennis court was wet, we shared their hard court. The family on the other side also had a girl of my age, but we were not allowed to talk to her. No reason for this was ever plainly stated. When I was grown up I learned why. The windows on one side of their house faced the windows of our upstairs pantry and the maids' bedrooms. The grown-up brother had been exposing himself, putting our maids into an awful flutter.

Americans lived in a house further down the road. Their family even wore cotton dresses in winter because they had central heating in every room. We had an ancient gas-fired radiator in the hall, another on the first-floor landing. The elder girl, Nancy, was in my form. She suffered from "blanching of the brain", which caused her to "freeze" in whatever position she happened to be in. Once, in Prayers, the rest of the school sat down cross-legged on the floor, but she was left standing, eyes open but glazed. After a few moments, the attack passed and she was normal again. It happened once when she had climbed to the top of a rope in the gym. Rigid, she slid to the bottom.

I hated having to go to school wearing home-made cotton shirts with ill-fitting collars because most girls wore silk. It was the same with my summer uniform. Dresses could be of blue/white or green/white stripes, with the stripes going in any direction. A dazzling variety of vertical, horizontal and diagonal stripes appeared, but I still felt mine were inferior.

Mother did her best, but she was no good at dressmaking. Knowing why she had to do it, I had to pretend satisfaction with her efforts.

My serious envy focused on the girls who did tap-dancing in scarlet tap-dancing shoes with satin bows. Sadly, tap-dancing was an "extra". I did not do "extras". On every Christmas and birthday present list I wrote "tap shoes". Finally I got and cherished the shoes, wore them until they were too small for my growing feet, but still refused to throw them away. I never got the classes.

An "extras" exception was made for piano lessons. Perhaps because Pam played quite well it was thought fair I should have the same chance. I was never consulted. Piano lessons for me were a waste of precious money, for not only had I no talent, but with two fingers of my left hand not working properly, I was an indifferent pianist.

An end-of-term concert was given to an audience of doting parents.

Everyone who had lessons had to take part. By the time my turn came I was almost fainting with panic. I tottered to the piano, put my music on the stand and sat down, but my eyes did not focus. In a blur, I played the opening bars, then the closing bars and bolted off the stage, unaware that I'd missed all the middle. JAL was livid, certain I'd done it on purpose. I would not have dared. End of piano lessons.

The annual Prize-Giving was tedious for all but the most senior girls. We sat cross-legged on the floor for hours, while they all trooped up to get their trophies. In my last term there, I was dozing in quiet boredom, when the shock of hearing my name jerked me to my feet. I'd won the Needlework Cup!

When I left Padstow for my first term at school, the novelty of it all carried me happily through to the school holidays. Every year, we spent Family Christmas at "Hurst". This was to be no different. Father was to join us on Christmas Eve. The Christmas routine scarcely changed from year to year.

We always made paper-chains to decorate the nursery. We always decorated the dining-room with holly, a sprig over each picture. More sprigs were tucked in the carved oak frame of the six-foot-wide mirror over the sideboard. Being the lightest, I was allowed to take off my shoes and climb on the sideboard, stretching on tiptoe to reach the top. In the hall, I had to be brave. I was nervous of the stuffed stag's head, with glass eyes, above the drawing-room door and the elk's head over the dining-room door. Both needed holly in their antlers. Deep breath, sprint up the stepladder, shove on the holly and leap down. Over the morning-room door, the woolly bison's scalp with horns was not so bad because it had no eyes.

Grandaddy's death coincided with the departure of these relics. After years of scuttling underneath it was a relief to be without them. I never heard of any big-game hunters in the family, so suppose they were fashionable decor items. The final Christmas touch was a bunch of mistletoe dangling from the centre light bracket in the hall and a hoard of a sixpence and silver threepenny-bits put in the key cupboard to reward carol singers. The first choir each season got the sixpence.

We all helped prepare the dining-room table. A handle inserted in the end wound the table apart in the middle, so that extra leaves could be dropped in and a white damask cloth spread. Referring to Mrs Beeton's chapter headed "napkins", we folded the starched damask into elaborate shapes. We had plenty of choice. She offered The Bishop, Boar's Head, Boats,

Cockscomb, Collegian, Fan, Flat Sachet, Mitre, Palm, Lily and Cactus, Pyramid, Rose and Star, Sachet, Slipper and Vase.

A two-foot high silver statue of Diana, the Huntress, formed the centre-piece. The previous day, she'd been lifted out of her brass-bound casket to be cleaned and polished. She stood on a round mirror base, with a wide border of silver leaves. Engraved glass dishes were fitted, filled with fruit and nuts. To finish, crackers were criss-crossed round Diana's feet.

The places were laid with cutlery, glasses and cut-glass finger-bowls. Four silver candlesticks stood ready for lighting. After a last look round to check everything, the door was closed. Christmas was the only day of the year wine was served; always hock. The rest of the year, Grandaddy had his whisky from a locked three-decanter tantalus on the sideboard. Others might have a thimble of sherry on occasion. Granny reckoned that a raw egg whisked into a glass of sherry was a potent tonic for frailty.

Our Christmas Day started early, exploring the contents of pillow cases left overnight at the foot of our beds. At mid-morning, we all trooped to church, sang carols, and walked home again. Auntie Dee and Auntie Helen, Granny's spinster cousins, were fetched from Upper Norwood, where they lived in genteel poverty. Auntie Dee seemed hardly real. She was extremely prim, wraith-thin, poker-straight, with bloodless skin like crumpled tissue paper. Pale eyes peered short-sightedly through tiny metal-rimmed spectacles. She dressed in rusty black, her sparse hair drawn up into a skimpy bun. Outdoors, she wore a wide-brimmed black hat, its deep crown pierced with hat-pins. Her thin neck looked too brittle to support the weight. Her quavering voice was scarcely audible. She did not really sit on a chair, but perched bird-like on its edge, never touching the back. It was impossible to imagine her naked in a bath with hair hanging down, let alone any other vulgar calls of nature. Yet she must have been young once, perhaps very pretty, before the process of dessication crept upon her. How sad.

Auntie Helen was younger, more real. When Auntie Dee died, Auntie Helen moved to a flat in a small block, near "Hurst". She was terrified of thunderstorms. In the Norwood house, she'd hidden in the cupboard under the stairs, but the flat offered no such refuge. When a storm threatened, one of the family had to dash round to keep her company until the danger passed.

The gong sounded at 1 o'clock to call us for lunch. Granny and Grandaddy led the way. It was the only day he did not do the carving. Stella was left-handed and stood shoulder-to-shoulder with Mother, her right-handed twin, each with a carving knife, each carving one side of the turkey. It speeded up the process most efficiently.

The afternoon was spent exchanging and opening presents; an important occasion for Peter, Pam and me, because we only got presents at Christmas and birthdays. Pam and I were fortunate in May birthdays, splitting the year, but poor Peter's fell only four days before Christmas.

On Christmas evening, we were joined by the headmaster of Carn Brea School, Mr Marshall and his wife. We seldom saw them during the rest of the year, but he was essential for the success of the evening parlour games, throwing himself whole-heartedly into charades, jollying everyone along.

The grand finale was always the Drawing Game, with Granny stationed in the morning-room with the list of objects to be drawn. One team went in the dining-room, the other in the drawing-room. Team captains were given the first item to draw and whoever identified it dashed back to Granny, whispered the answer and was given the next thing on the list. Much colliding in doorways. The team that included Auntie Kate had a problem. She panicked and came back twittering "Can't draw, can't draw", seemingly unable to make even a mark on the paper. I think Granny surreptitiously crossed one item off the list for her team, to level things up.

The day before Christmas Eve we put up the ping-pong table, not then dignified by the term "table-tennis," to serve as a present-wrapping worktop. Surrounded by rolls of coloured-paper, string and labels, we began wrapping our presents. I soon sensed something was wrong, because Mother and Peter were missing. Slipping away, I went up to our bedroom and found them both in tears. I'd never seen a grown-up crying.

Tearfully I was told Father would not be joining us. He'd left. We'd never see him again. Nor would we return to our home in Padstow.

CHAPTER
TEN

Just in time

Instantly the first ten years seemed wiped from the slate of my life. Father's absence posed many questions, few answers. Why had he gone? Was it my fault? Emotional shock brought disturbing memories to the surface and I thought of the day Pam and I had been playing with a red rubber ball. I bounced it once too often just as we were about to have lunch and it plopped into the stew. Father had been cross, more so when I giggled. Such incidents raced through my shocked little brain — a possible explanation for his departure?

I only knew that in future, Father's name was never to be mentioned. His existence was never to be discussed, even with Pam, my cousin, his niece. Pam's father had died when she was a baby. That I could understand. I had no idea fathers vanished for other reasons. The concept of divorce was beyond me.

The Family was essentially pragmatic, talking of what they *did*, not what they *felt*. By the end of the previous summer, the increasingly frosty atmosphere between my parents must have been apparent, but I'd not been aware. Grey Grannie had made the long journey from Stranocum to try to dissuade her son from breaking up the family. I'd heard their raised voices arguing.

Looking back, we'd been seeing less and less of Father. He'd become withdrawn, terse and short-tempered. He'd never joined in our games, read stories or come to the beach. He'd been unable to give or receive affection. I understand now my parents should never have married. They'd met at the military hospital where Mother and Stella were VADs. Frederick Ford-Hutchinson and Basil Redfern were fellow-officers during the 1914-18 War.

Before the war, Fred and Basil had been sheep-farming in New Zealand. They'd joined up and come to Europe with the ANZACs (Australian and New Zealand Army Corps.) After the disastrous Gallipoli campaign, they returned to the same hospital to convalesce. Fred was severely shell-shocked and was left with a piece of shrapnel embedded in his skull.

Vera and Stella made up a foursome with Fred and Basil. Basil and Stella fell in love and married. Pam was born and they would all have lived happily ever after, had Basil not ill-advisedly played tennis in the hot sun with a carbuncle on his neck. The poison spread through his body and he died. Stella returned to live at "Hurst" with Pam, then two.

Many years later, Pam heard the next chapter from our eldest aunt, Muriel. She said that after the marriage of Basil and Stella, my grandfather still had Muriel, Vera and Kathleen at home — and a dearth of possible husbands. Many middle-class young men had been instantly promoted subaltern, and were inevitably the first to fall when they led their men "over the top" from British trenches towards the German lines.

Perhaps these thoughts had been in Grandfather's mind when he took Frederick round the garden and asked him bluntly: "When are you going to marry Vera?" Fred, poor man, was railroaded into marriage. He was too chivalrous to run. Vera and Stella were not identical twins, Vera always dominant, Stella more gentle. Basil and Stella were ideally matched, Frederick and Vera not.

In later years, I realised how Mother was embarrassed by even the mildest display of public affection. I am thankful she did not live to see the explicit sex in programmes on today's television. She told me she had been traumatically shocked by a flasher who followed her from school one day. For a prim girl with no brothers, I daresay it was a surprise.

Mother was devastated by her divorce. She'd been content with Padstow life. She had friends, played golf and badminton and enjoyed the beach. She had no wish to live on her parents' charity.

It came as a jolting shock to me when, after I was grown-up, I learned Father had not just "left". I had a stepmother! He'd married one of the Miss Norman sisters at Rock, who'd had the Old English Sheepdog I'd been so fond of.

The significance of the little visits — so I could see the dog — dawned on me. I realised I had unwittingly contributed to the calamity, recalling with cold clarity, the icy silence in the car one day, when Father had been driving us all back from St. Enodoc. I'd innocently asked why we were not stopping at the Misses Norman bungalow as usual.

I saw Father only twice again. The first was when Peter introduced him to Pina, his Sicilian wife, and his one-year-old son, Tony. I was summoned to tea at their house in Bickley. It was awful. Pina spoke little English, Tony whinged in his high-chair, Father was desperately nervous, despite the waft of whisky I caught on his breath. It was a deeply painful episode. I resented my brother dragging me into the re-union and contributed little to make the occasion less difficult for us all. Loyalty to Mother had always made me feel my brother's continued contact with Father a betrayal.

Years later, while washing-up one Friday morning after Peter, my husband, had left for work, and the children had gone to school, I suddenly felt compelled to see Father without delay. I'd not thought of him for years; now it seemed urgent we should meet. I very rarely bothered Peter at his office, but this would not wait. The dear man understood, telephoned Father, and we visited the following day. I was nervous as we drove down, but with Peter's support, knew I would manage. We found Father living in a horrible 1930's bungalow in Ferndown, Dorset.

"Stepmother," I could not accept that, was the hard little brown nut I remembered. She kept very quiet. We told Father about his grand-children and our life. I felt desperately sorry for him. He and I went into another room, both near to tears. "We should have done this years ago," I blurted, hugging him. Now together, a burden fell away. Sadness was etched in every line of his gaunt face. Divorce and remarriage had clearly not brought him happiness. He'd lost his family, job, the way of life he'd enjoyed. I'm sure Colonel Prideaux-Brune did not sack him, but after such a major local scandal, his position would have been untenable.

He'd been unable to secure a similar position on another estate. He had no income, could not afford to play golf, his Purdeys had been sold.

There was nothing more for either of us to say. I felt thankful we'd made our peace at last, dreadfully sad it had taken more than 30 years to discover he really loved me.

I was just in time. A few weeks later, he died.

CHAPTER
ELEVEN

Three more mouths to feed

In 1933, when Mother, Peter and I came to live at "Hurst", we joined the Family, giving Grandaddy three more mouths to feed. The organisation of the household followed a set pattern. Each daughter and granddaughter had a role. I shared with Pam the daily task of helping Granny dress. When one of us was called, she was already sitting at her dressing table, clad in short-sleeved woollen combinations and a long petticoat. We never saw her legs, as they were wrapped in crepe bandages hidden under black cotton stockings. Pam thought she suffered from a malady known as "whiteleg". Her black shoes had two bars, buttoned over the instep.

Our job was to put on a back-buttoning lace-trimmed camisole, then another of fine net, with a boned stand-up collar. Over this went a dress of her personal design. Made of dark cloth, it dropped to her ankles, its deep V-neck revealing the lace-trimmed camisole beneath. She had a round pad of auburn hair kept from her youth. It went on top of her head and the remaining thin tresses swept up and over, the final construction secured with a fine hairnet. To give her hair more "body", we wound it round curling-tongs, heated over a flame of methylated-spirit. Its smell mingled with that of singeing hair.

I wonder when she began to dress as an old lady. Pam and I knew her no other way. In later years, we worked out that she cannot have been much more than fifty in a photo of her on the beach at Trevone, sitting in a chair, her girls grouped around. She is dressed from top to toe in black, wearing a black straw hat secured by hatpins. Grandaddy is beside her, wearing a lightweight suit with waistcoat, stiff-collared shirt, tie and panama hat. The height of informality was when he wore a linen jacket in the privacy of his own garden.

Granny's toilette complete, we escorted her downstairs to take her place at the end of the table, presiding over the teapot and coffee brewing in the Cona machine. Water went in the bottom glass globe and as the flame below brought it to the boil, the water leaped up a pipe to the coffee grounds above, gurgled for a bit, then subsided through a filter to the globe below, ready for pouring. I didn't like the bitter taste of coffee, but loved the performance of making it and the powerful aroma given off by meths and ground coffee.

At the other end of the table, Grandaddy dished out scrambled, poached or fried eggs and bacon from a covered silver dish, kept warm by hot water in a tank below the base. Lamb's kidneys on fried bread swimming in butter were a Sunday treat during winter months.

After breakfast, Granny took her place in an armchair by the dining room fire, attended by her youngest daughter Kathleen. The cook came in and meals from her limited culinary repertoire were settled for the day. Ordering food and supervision of the kitchen were Kathleen's province. She would unlock the storeroom to top-up jars kept in the kitchen. Orders were telephoned to shops and delivered daily.

Granny moved to the drawing room in the afternoon, when the fire there was lit, perhaps to be joined by Grandaddy, who'd been attending to his affairs in the morning room. He had a huge, specially-constructed armchair, so comfortable he was apt to nod off, his trumpeting snores drowning our conversation, but Granny would never allow him to be disturbed, let alone mocked.

When the cook left, Nelly was promoted from housemaid to take her place. She had no training beyond that gleaned from her predecessor. Her puddings were limited to fruit-pies, treacle pudding, trifle, castle puddings, steamed sponge and a staple known as "shape" — an unappetising mauvish-pink blancmange, made in a mould and turned out gently onto a dish to quiver and subside.

The family got through a prodigious amount of food. Cooked breakfast at 8a.m. was followed by coffee and biscuits at 11a.m. At 1 o'clock there was a two-course lunch. Tea was at 4 o'clock when the parlourmaid carried in a folding table, clicking down legs to set it beside Granny's chair. It bore a heavy silver tea-tray, silver teapot, milk jug, sugar bowl, slop basin and a tall fluted kettle, kept hot by a flame in the stand beneath. Another set of legs was spread to take the round Benares brass tray, laden with buttered bread, sandwiches and cakes. An additional cake stand held reserves.

At 7.15p.m., the first gong sounded, announcing it was time to change for dinner. Little tunes could be played on the gong's six notes, using two drumsticks with leather-covered ends, xylophone-style.

The sisters' evening uniforms were long black crepe skirts, blouses and velvet "bridge coats;" this useful garment was an edge-to-edge jacket made from dark silk velvet; one sister wore blue, another plum, bottle green and the fourth black. A second gong at 7.30p.m. signalled dinner was ready and they sat down to a three-course meal. No wonder they were all so heavy and Grandaddy so portly.

We children had a high tea in the nursery.

In Granny's eyes, Kathleen, her youngest daughter, could do no wrong, but I did not like her. When Granny chided me for my attitude, she said "Your Auntie Kate is an angel." Granny was usually fair-minded, but was totally taken in by Kate's fawning sycophancy. I had no skill in hiding my feelings and grieved Granny with my obdurate attitude.

Stella, Mother's twin, was in charge of the family's laundry. The linen cupboard, on the second floor, would have been more aptly called a linen room, for the amount of stuff needed for a household of twelve people was considerable. It was a gloomy place, lit only by a weak light bulb. There was no daylight until, during the Blitz, a bomb caused a crack through which one could see the sky. Several years after the war, Mother glanced up from the drive and saw the whole pediment was leaning forward, about to crash — lethal to anyone passing.

Every week, two men brought a huge wicker hamper of fresh laundry and removed another of soiled linen to be laundered. Trade vehicles parked in the road and everything carried in or out. Ambulances and hearses were the only exceptions. The pleasant smell of fresh laundry was masked by the smell of camphor mothballs protecting woollen blankets from moth, and the mustiness of stored suitcases and cabin trunks.

Racks of slatted shelves in the Linen Cupboard were labelled, with places for everything. Stuff for the maids was stored separately. When something got threadbare, it was demoted to be used by them. Granny would certainly have been rated a good and considerate employer in those days. Nobody would have thought it strange to treat staff so differently from the family. In their bleak bedrooms they had iron bedsteads and bare linoleum on the floor.

I was grown-up before it struck me the annual routine of staff Christmas presents was outrageous. The housemaid and parlourmaid would be summoned to the dining-room, where Granny sat beside the fire. Each would be given a new "best" cap and apron. Each said: "Thank you, Madam", were wished "A Happy Christmas", and departed. Yet Granny was not mean by nature; that is just how it was. I do not know what Nelly, the cook, got.

Most personal washing was done in the bath, by the maids. After rinsing, it was carried downstairs for mangling in a back-yard shed. It took two to work the mangle, a herculean task. Finally, everything was pegged out on lines to dry in the yard. After ironing, it was hoisted on an airing rack, hauled to the kitchen ceiling by rope pulley.

Stella's other task was to arrange the flowers, cut from the garden. Part of the vegetable garden was set aside to grow flowers for the house: sweet williams, asters, chrysanthemums etc. A double row of sweet-peas ensured abundance. I became the self-appointed sweet-pea picker, revelling in their scent, arranging them in a wide cream porcelain bowl in the drawing-room.

Muriel, my eldest aunt, had established she was "not domesticated" and escaped household duties.

There were seven staff to run a house for nine people. Cook ruled in the kitchen. A daily cleaner came in to help with the housework, rooms being given a thorough turn-out in sequence. The housemaid and parlourmaid took five early-morning tea-trays and eight brass hot-water cans to bedrooms on two floors. With only one bathroom, every bedroom had a marble or glass-topped washstand, each with a washbasin and cold water ewer, a soap dish, toothbrush jar and a lidded slop-pail. Under each bed, a po.

Grandaddy monopolised the ground floor lavatory. The maids plus the chauffeur, gardener and garden boy used one in the yard, outside the scullery door. In winter there was anxiety about the pipes freezing, but I

103

never heard of thought being given to those who had to use it in all weathers. The rest of the Family used a lavatory on the first floor. Other smells fought with the powerful aroma of Friars Balsam drifting from inhalers stored in a marble-topped maplewood cupboard, ready for use against the winter crop of colds and coughs. It was often a choice of open the window and freeze, or close it and stifle. I preferred to freeze. There was never enough time between breakfast and the arrival of the school car. The worse the stress, the slower the action. For a time, I was afraid a water rat would come up the drain and bite my bottom.

During the day, the maids laid the fires, made the beds, tidied the rooms, laid the dining room table, waited at table, cleared away and washed up and answered bells. An indicator on the kitchen wall showed which front or back door bell was ringing, or one of the rooms. The girls were never idle. In the mornings they wore cotton dresses, with plain white apron and cap. In the afternoons, they changed into dark dresses with the caps and aprons graciously given at Christmas.

Grandaddy was an early car-owner, but did not drive himself. He engaged Warwick, an ex-coachman, and arranged driving lessons for him. It was soon thought safer to make him the gardener, with a boy to help. He was followed by Wilkins and later by Taylor. As well as looking after the cars, the chauffeur had the annual duty of testing the fire escape. This contraption was rope wound round a drum, screwed to a window-frame in Kathleen's top-floor bedroom. To descend, the victim had to wriggle into a braid loop, hold the rope, and hope to be gently lowered to the ground; another loop came up for the next person.

Choosing a car for Grandaddy was difficult because he was 6ft 2ins tall and liked to sit in the back, wearing his top-hat. Before he retired, one of his daughters had to give his topper a final brush and hand it to him before he set off on his walk to Sundridge Park Station to catch the train for London. By the time I knew him, he'd retired and relinquished the top hat for everyday wear.

There were three cars in the garage — the "Big Car", a Humber and the Yellow Peril. The "Big Car" was stately black, with grey upholstery. A sliding glass partition isolated Wilkins. To communicate, the window could be slid open, but we children greatly preferred the telephone which hung just behind the rear door. Any attempts to use it frivolously were severely frowned on, as we "must not distract Wilkins while he is driving".

Once passengers were ensconced on the back seat, two further seats could be unfolded, affording total seating for six — three across the back, two on the folding seats and one in the front beside Wilkins. After the car left us, it gave many years service as a hire car for a local garage. Ideal for funerals. It was replaced by a more modern dark blue Austin, KP6080. It lacked the glass partition and the telephone, but had the folding seats.

After Grandaddy died, the Austin was replaced by a Standard. This was an orthodox four-door saloon, its blue leather upholstery giving the interior a pleasantly opulent smell. It no longer warranted the name of the "big car", but still inherited the name. In this car, Granny sometimes travelled in the front seat, as it was easier for her to get in and out. As the cars became lower and sleeker, they looked more elegant, but lost the headroom enabling one to step in and out gracefully.

The Humber had style. Grandaddy hand-painted it maroon, the upper part milk-chocolate. It had pale grey whipcord upholstery and a bull-nosed bonnet. The driver's door did not open, the spare wheel being mounted on the running board. Although the gear lever was on the driver's left, the handbrake was on the right. Entry for the driver was made easier by the amount of headroom. Even Wilkins, who was tall, could step in and glide behind the steering wheel. The Humber was easy to find in large car-parks because its roof stood high above surrounding cars — a welcome boon during Wimbledon fortnight.

Pam and I relished the annual joust between Kate and Muriel we named the "Best Route to Wimbledon". Muriel was not much interested in tennis, nevertheless it was a matter of principle for her to state her views. These ran to a well-honed script. Which was the shortest way? Which was the quickest way? Kate got waspish, Muriel mulish. Stella tried to be peacemaker, so both turned on her. Mother, ever practical, did not care which way she went, so long as she was in her seat in time for the first match. If the best route contest flagged, we could instantly revive it by chipping-in with: "But last year you said turn right there."

Mother and her sisters learned to drive, but never drove the "big cars" although Muriel was most experienced, having driven army ambulances in Egypt during WW1. After a while, the chauffeur had to go. There was insufficient for him to do once all the sisters were driving both the Humber and the Standard. In any case, economies were imperative because there were three more mouths to feed and two more school bills to pay. After the war, it became impossible to get spares for the Humber, so she went to Taylor, who was then chief mechanic at Sergeant & Collins garage.

The Yellow Peril was a Baby Austin, belonging to Muriel. The chassis was buttercup yellow, with black mudguards. The celluloid side windows could be lifted out and the hood folded down in fine weather. Muriel had ridden motor-cycles during her time as a VAD in Egypt and, on her return, bought her own. Wearing a long belted brown leather overcoat, with leather helmet and goggles, she roared around, not entirely in control. On it, she once rode to Scotland visiting her friend, Marjory Maclean, sister of her late fiancé, Peter. She fell off so many times her parents bought her the Yellow Peril.

Peter learned to drive in the Humber. On one of his early sorties, he went straight through some roadworks, shouting out of the window: "Can't stop! Can't stop!" Road-menders leapt for their lives. He tried to blame the brakes, but that would not stick, so he turned the episode into an anecdote casting himself as daredevil hero. Unconvincing.

He bought an ancient faded blue Baby Austin, for £15. We called it "Little Miss Bouncer" — (there was a song on the wireless which started "Little Miss Bouncer loved an Announcer, up at the BBC . . .") Like the Yellow Peril, Bouncer was best with the hood down. Then four of us could travel happily. Bouncer was not very fast, but could be turned in a confined space by simply picking up the back and walking it round. One sunny day in the country, we ended in a ditch, but we soon lifted Bouncer out and put her back on the road. She had no garage, so Peter parked in laurel bushes beside the house. When he went overseas in the army, Bouncer was left behind the laurels, covered by a tarpaulin. Although the garden was regularly peppered with shrapnel from local anti-aircraft guns, Bouncer survived unscathed.

After the war, Peter brought home a Sicilian bride, who hated Bouncer on sight. Given that she arrived from her sunny home to face an icy English winter, and promptly became pregnant, it was entirely understandable she preferred the sort of limousine favoured by Il Duce, Mussolini.

The three Aunts did voluntary work, each having her "district". Sweeping slum-clearance programmes had dislodged families from London's East End and decanted them to a new housing estate at Downham. Stella and Kathleen were each allocated an area to visit as amateur social workers. How they were supposed to help was never clear. Tales of coal being kept in the bath were probably exaggerated. What those on the receiving end thought of these well-meaning ladies we will never know. Stella's sweet nature and kindness could scarcely be taken amiss, but Kate's patronising manner might have been harder to stomach.

Muriel's "district" was nearer home. She covered Canon Road, a street of Victorian terraced houses in Widmore. It was also her recruiting ground for the pack of Wolf Cubs of which she was "Akela". She made an imposing figure every St.George's Day, marching at the head of her pack. Her khaki skirt fell just short of stout lace-up shoes. Her pullover was clasped by a leather belt, with Useful Things dangling from it. A grey triangular scarf was worn so the St. George's Cross badge showed at the back, the front points passing through a leather toggle. All was topped by the sort of wide-brimmed felt hat worn by troops who relieved Mafeking, now sported only by Canadian Mounties.

The sisters all had the same blind spot — none knew when to retire. In Muriel's case, the Scouts were her sole interest. As well as the weekly cubs' meeting, she took them to camp in the summer, wrote and produced plays performed by the Scouts, attended international "Jamborees" and finished up as District and County Commissioner. To give it all up would have left a void in her life. She was presented with Scout honours, silver acorns, golden wolves, but never took the hint. She may have been a figure of fun, but her innocent seriousness and total lack of any sense of the ridiculous saved her from mockery. She was well-loved in her "district".

One particular family was a constant pain. The father was often absent, mother had a string of urchins to bring up — and a filthy temper. We came to know their name very well. After I married, we were moving and our house was for sale. An expensively-dressed potential purchaser arrived in an upmarket car to look over the house. I suddenly realised he was one of that problem family, come up in the world, having anglicised the spelling and pronunciation of his name to conceal its Belgian origin. He'd also shed his South London accent. Muriel was still alive and said she'd always thought him different from his siblings. Our house was not sufficiently grand for him; it had no paddock for his children's ponies. They bought another house in the village and settled in very well. I kept schtum.

Biographies of self-made men always leave out the most interesting bits. I want to know when and how they scramble up the ladder. With this man, I knew he'd started married life in a flat over a green-grocer, then moved to a four-bedroomed detached house in the road where my brother lived. After that, the trail went cold. Presumably the foundations need laying around the age of 25-30 and the big leap made by 40. That is the bit that fascinates me, but is always skipped when their stories are told.

Pam and I were able to piece together something of the lives of our mothers and their sisters when they first left school. Kate had been to a different school from the others, so she played lacrosse, not hockey. The other three joined Atlanta Hockey Club, in Bickley.

They all played for Kent. Muriel became goalkeeper for England until replaced by her younger sister, Vera.

Mother was in the team for several years until the First War broke out. She had a white blazer, edged with red braid. On the pocket was the English team badge, three Tudor roses, with little lozenges sewn beneath, one for each year she was in the team. She maintained her interest in the game by sitting on the selection committee choosing the English team.

International matches were often played at the Oval, coachloads of schoolgirls forming the bulk of the onlookers. Consequently when, in a General Knowledge test at school, we were asked "What game is played at the Oval?" I answered "women's hockey". My response was read out to the whole school as an example of imbecility.

In my attic, I have several albums filled with photographs and press cuttings. Early ones show the teams wearing shirts with leg o' mutton sleeves, high starched collars and ties. Skirts were dark heavy serge, cut flared to mid-calf length, with black stockings and lace-up leather shoes. Hair was swept on top, Edwardian style. Their sticks had a short stubby end, then later changed to a type with a longer hook. Now the modern stick has reverted to the original pattern.

A few years later, the starched collars disappeared, replaced by soft collared blouses, ties knotted more casually. The weighty wind-resistant skirt gave way to a knee-length copy of a schoolgirl's tunic, with knotted braid belt. Hairstyles altered too. Most wore their hair taken back in a loose bun, a velvet band keeping stray wisps under control.

Team membership gave them a chance to travel to tournaments where they played either opposing clubs, or regional teams representing North, South, East, West, Scotland, Wales and Ireland. Muriel also visited Holland and the U.S.A.

In the village of St.Mary's Platt, the big house of Great Comp was owned by Mr. and Mrs. Heron-Maxwell. She was a strong character, well-known for her pioneering work in establishing the Women's Institute throughout Kent. At Comp, she had a hockey pitch laid out and a large pavilion built to provide dormitories for visiting teams. Great weekend parties were held. Muriel, Vera and Stella travelled by train from Bromley and on to Comp in a pony and trap.

The name of Comp was well-known to me as I grew up and I saw it for myself after I was married, when Peter and I bought a cottage in the village. By then Great Comp was run-down, the gardens overgrown and the pavilion gone. A couple bought it, worked mightily on it and restored the gardens to some of their former glory.

Fashion changes are clearly reflected in old pictures of tennis teams. The stiff collar and long skirt were abandoned. Madame Lenglen caused a sensation when she first appeared at Wimbledon in a short silk dress. A player of less distinction would probably have been barred.

The team photos which used to hang at Sundridge Park Tennis club showed short hair with velvet ribbons round their foreheads. Short-sleeved silk dresses reached the knee, worn with white stockings and plimsolls. Three sisters made up half the team, leaving out Muriel who did not like tennis. Mother was cheated of her chance to play at Wimbledon by the outbreak of the First World War.

The standard of first class tennis played then bore scant resemblance to the professional circus of today. The gut-strung wooden rackets did not have the power of modern high-tech weapons. There was no professional coaching or training. On the day, players briefly knocked-up with their opponents, then got on with the match. At Wimbledon, old TV footage shows there were no chairs for the players to rest on. Their only respite was a short stroll when they changed ends.

The modern game has become dominated by the power serve. It would be much more entertaining if the second serve was abandoned. Players would then have to decide whether to risk going for a cannonball, or to play more safely on crucial points.

Before the advent of television, we followed Wimbledon avidly on the radio. The commentary was brilliant, clearly conveying the atmosphere. I wish today's TV commentators would talk less.

For several years, a house was rented on the Sussex coast for our summer holidays. The maids came too. It was a major logistical exercise as trunks were packed and sent in advance by Carter Paterson. One year, we took a house in Bexhill at the time of the Eastbourne tennis tournament. I was too young to be eligible, but Mother, Stella, Kate, Peter and Pam finished the week with a good haul of prizes.

Peter, Pam and I did not match the Aunts' standards. Having our own grass court and good training, we were competent. I was handicapped by a dud left hand, so I could not throw the ball up accurately to serve, which led to an embarrassing number of double-faults. We played in the Kent Junior championships and Peter and I entered the mixed-doubles for the week-long tournaments at Tunbridge Wells and Cromer.

I had yearned to ride ever since we left our pony, Brownie, in Padstow. I got my first lesson at Miss Garner's stables in Bexhill. A photo shows me riding, with bare legs, a short skirt and a cotton sunhat. The first time I cantered, I thought my eyeballs would fall from their sockets, but was not deterred. Birthday and Christmas money was saved to pay for lessons. The jodhpurs I got as a birthday present were highly prized. I admired them in my wardrobe every day of the year. I was happier to have the breeches and fewer rides, than more rides in a skirt. No one thought of wearing a hard-hat.

Ours was not a "cultured" family. No one went to concerts. The grand-piano in the drawing room was loaded with framed photographs, but never played. A pianola stood in the morning room but, as it took two men to lumber it into position at the drawing room piano, it was a very rare treat. I could be blissfully happy, sitting on the stool, my legs just long enough the reach the pedals, energetically rendering a selection from "The Chocolate Soldier", or "The Blue Danube".

We had two upright pianos in the nursery. Pam played one, a school-friend played the other, and Peter had a saxophone. The repertoire came from sheet music bought in Woolworths (where nothing cost more than 6d. Marks and Spencers sold nothing over 2/6d). "Red Sails in the Sunset" was top favourite.

I was hopeless. I could bang a drum, but, sadly, any other instrument was beyond me, and I could not sing well enough to merit encouragement. The music I relate to is dance-music. I grew up a Bluebell Girl manquée.

A wall of Globe-Wernicke bookcases stood in the morning room, but the only books read were novels from Boot's Lending Library. Subscribers were each given a little book in which to list titles they fancied, often culled from the critics in The Morning Post, later The Daily Telegraph. Books listed were put aside, making it quick and easy for one person to change books. Muriel read detective stories and hankered to be a writer herself, but nothing came of it, apart from the excellent plays she wrote for the Scouts.

Family knowledge of art was zero. No one painted or made anything creative. Mother did some embroidery, but did not venture beyond chain-stitch, satin-stitch and lazy-daisy-stitch worked on designs from iron-on transfers. Most featured hollyhocks and crinoline ladies, whose bonnets conveniently obscured their faces. Pictures hanging in the house were a mixed lot, heavy portraits of ancestors predominating. A valuable Dutch Old Master flower piece was hardly visible beneath layers of discoloured varnish. Two oil paintings of stiff huntsmen and hounds hung in the morning room, both signed Amy Scott, painted by Granny before her marriage. She used to ride to hounds in those days, side-saddle of course.

When furniture was being moved around after she died, a painting was put aside. It depicted a deeply unappealing baby lying naked face-down on a cross, in shades of muddy grey, jaundiced yellow and sepulchral black. I maintained that it must be valuable, for no other reason could justify its position on the drawing room wall. I rashly volunteered to put it in a Sotheby's sale, certain it would make the family fortune. Wrapping it in a cloth, I could just about manage to take it by train to London and taxi to Bond Street. It duly came up for sale and was unsold. I had to bring it home again. The total cost in fares, Sotheby's charges and wasted effort underlined how flawed my original reasoning had been.

Leisure pursuits included Muriel, Stella and Kate playing bridge. They were peeved with Mother, who refused to learn, thinking a family four would be intolerable. In time, Pam learned to play, which saved them always having to get someone in to make up a four. After I married, I struggled to learn bridge, to please my husband. Another couple, Pamela and Phil, came regularly as both wives wanted to learn. Pamela succeeded but I failed. I was always in tears after they left. Comparing notes many years later, she owned up that she always cried all the way home in the car.

I know that highly intelligent people find bridge fascinating, but it's also true that two of the most apparently stupid people I know are bridge fiends. For me there are two stumbling blocks. Firstly, I have difficulty in remembering things until I have seen them written down. Secondly, no one explained to my satisfaction why the bidding is conducted in a code. If all four use the same code, what's the point?

Other winter evening occupations included jigsaw puzzles, made from plywood, individually cut and much more interesting than the mass produced stamped-out cardboard versions available now. Grandaddy used to cut them on his treadle fret-saw, and taught me how to make them as well. "Monopoly" always broke up in ill-feeling. Granny would "sell" anything to oblige anyone. This irritated Muriel, who took it all in deadly earnest. Kate stifled her sulk lest Granny spotted her being less than angelic. Peter was cross if he did not win. I got bored and just wanted it finished.

I must find out how to play "Newmarket". I know we enjoyed it. We used a bag of cowrie shells as counters. I still have them in my attic. We were aces at Racing Demon, played in pairs. One turned up the cards, the other was the grabber. Any outsider pressed to join in was bemused by the speed and ferocity of our game.

In the summer, we played bicycle-polo in the garden, climbed trees, did gymnastics on the swing and competed for distance by leaping from the seat at the limit of a swing. I did it once, in bare feet, and landed squidge on a frog. It died, I fled, hysterical and no amount of scrubbing could wash the sensation off my foot.

It took a long time to get permission to play tennis on Sundays. Grandaddy did not approve, but Granny won him round; it became church in the morning, tennis in the afternoon.

A big family has much to recommend it. My years at "Hurst" compensated generously for my solitary earlier life in Padstow.

CHAPTER
TWELVE

Grandaddy's girl

When Father dropped out of my life, Grandaddy came in. Everything about Grandaddy was big: his heart, height, girth, kindness and patience, even his bushy white moustache which tickled when he kissed me. (Father never kissed me.) Blue eyes twinkled through small gold-rimmed glasses and he probably saved me from growing up with a warped view of men.

He enjoyed golf and I was sometimes invited to play with him at Sundridge Park. Portly gentlemen who take up golf later in life seldom acquire a great swing, so his shots did not travel far and we got on well together. There must have been smiles from other members as we went to the first tee; I, about eleven, with a skimpy bag of clubs and he, an imposing figure more than seventy. He was never patronising. We played our few holes as two golfing friends. Although Peter and Pam could play, they were never invited to join us. Maybe he'd spotted my bruised ego and determined to give me something of my very own.

His other pleasure was his workshop. A room at the top of the house was divided to form a linen store and a workshop. A telephone from the morning room on the ground floor summoned him for meals. A hefty workbench, with a vice, stood under the workshop window, a lathe at right-angles to it. Tools were tidily racked and small chests of drawers housed nails, screws and other bits of ironmongery. Everything stood in order, to hand when needed. Shelves held glues, varnishes, paints, turpentine and white spirit. The harmonious blend of smells differed from the carpenter's shop at Prideaux Place, where it was the smell of wood that predominated. I savoured both equally.

With endless patience, Grandaddy taught me how to use the tools and work on the lathe. I still have a box I made under his supervision. The dove-tailed joints are satisfyingly flush and the chamfered edges of the lid match at the corners. It is embellished with a classical shell design, done with a painstakingly applied transfer. Surprisingly, it is dead central.

I spent hours french-polishing in the traditional way, applying the polish a little at a time with small circular movements. Although the box is only 6 x 4ins., it took many hours of concentration before it passed muster. Then I spoiled it by putting the hinge on crooked. That wonky hinge must have offered me valuable lessons of the "don't-count-your-chickens-pride-comes-before-a-fall-live-with-your-mistakes-etc." It could serve to illustrate just about every adage.

His huge hands did delicate work. On his lathe he turned tiny round boxes of wood or ivory, with sweetly-fitting lids. He also turned wooden spinning tops, hundreds of them, for children in London hospitals. Finally it became too much for him to manage, so he got the tops mass-produced and the family were enrolled to help with painting them. It was amazing how many different patterns could be worked on a top less than an inch across. I wonder if any of them are still lurking in hospital wards, or have been passed down through families. He always wanted any child who wished to be able to take a top home.

I have his desk, and in a little drawer there are five surviving tops. He had many letters of thanks from hospital matrons, which spurred him on to make more and more. Pam and I did wonder sometimes whether the hospitals really wanted such numbers showered upon them, but we shall never know. I hope they gave as much pleasure to the recipients as they did to Grandaddy's generous heart.

All my memories are happy. My only regret is that his modesty stopped him from telling me about his interesting and distinguished working life. Long after he died in 1938, I got a 20-page account of his career: "LT.COL. CHARLES BUTLER CLAY, V.D." (Volunteer Decoration). A Biographical Sketch. Born in Liverpool on 18th May 1856, he was son of William Clay, an Ironmaster and Managing Director of the Mersey Steel and Iron Company. The grounds of his house at Park Hill, Toxteth, were used as the drill ground of the 8th Lancashire Artillery Volunteers, which he had formed in 1859 and numbered 950 men. William Clay commanded the Corps for 20 years, holding the highest Volunteer rank of Lt. Colonel Commandant.

It was the first Volunteer Corps to have field guns. Clay's Breech-Loader Guns were private property, having been designed and made at the Ironworks. The Company also provided horses for the guns and their limbers. In the early days, all the men were members of the Steel & Ironworks staff.

At the age of eighteen, Charles joined the Volunteer Corps, passing through ranks from Lieutenant until he resigned in 1879, with permission to retain the rank of Lt.Colonel and to wear the uniform of the corps on his retirement. I remember a photograph of him, hanging in his dressing-room. It showed him wearing a pill-box hat, a chinstrap holding it on at a dashing angle. The short tightly-fitted jacket had a stand-up collar and a row of close brass buttons down the front. The trousers had a broad stripe down each side.

Sadly, when I eventually had the melancholy task of clearing the house, the picture was gone, but I have a snap of him in Parade Uniform, with helmet and stick.

Two other treasures from his dressing room were missing. One was a clock, which he liked explaining to us as having "perpetual motion". Its glass-domed case showed the mechanism, with little brass balls running endlessly down a series of chutes.

He also had a weighing machine, standing on a frame, with turned light-oak legs. One side had an upholstered green cut-velvet seat, with low brass arm-rests. The other had the weighing apparatus and a stack of weights.

The appropriate number of weights went in a brass dish hanging from the end of an arm. The final adjustment was made by sliding a small weight along the arm, until perfect balance was achieved. The total of the weights plus the figure showing on the arm, gave the total in stones and pounds. It needed a sturdy machine to weigh Grandaddy. He never told us how much he weighed, but it was several times more than little Granny.

Once, when they were staying with us in Padstow, they were going down the steps to the beach at Chiddley Pumps. The steps were uneven, with no handrail. Ever-gallant, he said: "Take my arm." Next moment, whoops! His leather-soled town shoes slipped and he pulled Granny over and landed on top of her. She was badly winded, but escaped with no bones broken.

In 1988, when staying near Liverpool with our son-in-law's parents, we tried to locate the original site of the Mersey Steel & Iron Works. A little book by Frank Shaw, entitled "Learn Yerself Scouse", says:- " A famous iron foundry stood at the Dingle, on the Northbank of the River Mersey, in the 19th century. Nearby still stands St.Michael's Church (opened 1814) containing much prefabricated cast-iron. The area was known as the "Cast Iron Shore" or, in scouse, "De Cazzy."

In the 1980's, the area was reclaimed as the site for the successful Liverpool Flower Festival. Now it is a pleasant residential area, with a promenade and views south, over the water to the Wirral coast and the Welsh hills beyond. To the north, above a sandstone cliff, parallel streets of terraced houses run steeply up the hill, like a huge "cotoneaster horizontalis". It was the location for filming the popular TV series, "Bread". On top of the hill we found a level Recreation Ground which was probably once my great-grandfather's garden, where he drilled his Volunteers. The house must have been demolished long ago.

In 1864, when Charles was eight, his father left the Mersey Works and established the Birkenhead Forge. It seems the family moved to Birkenhead then, as Charles went to private schools in Liverpool and Wallasey and finished his education at Malvern College.

He was apprenticed at his father's Works for three years. He could not have had a better mentor. William Clay was a first-class inventor, designer and business man. His men "had the most perfect confidence in him. He could take his place, and often did so, at the smithy, the puddling furnace, the shingling hammer etc. and showed that he could execute work with his own hands, as well as design." He was the first to introduce the manufacture of puddled steel on a large scale in this country. The plates of the steamer built for Dr. Livingstone's expedition to Central Africa were manufactured there, the weight being only 4 lbs per square foot.

This combination of imagination, practicality and integrity was amply inherited by his son. After three years apprenticeship at the Birkenhead Forge, he served a further two at Laird Bros. Shipbuilding and Engineering works in Birkenhead.

In 1879, aged 23, his apprenticeship completed, he joined the engineering drawing offices of the Inman

Steamship Co. They were building ever bigger and faster ships, in rivalry with Cunard. For many years they held the speed record between Liverpool and New York. Inman's "City of New York" was advertised as the largest liner in the world. Charles Clay worked on her specifications and went to the Barrow Shipbuilding Co. while she was to being built. Returning to Liverpool, he applied for a job in the offices of various consulting marine engineers, but none of his interviews survived the question "What sea-going experience have you had?" To remedy this, he went back to Inmans and signed on as a junior engineer on the "City of New York" to go to the U.S.A. He got the sea-going experience, but not the coveted job. Re-applying he was told that "they did not set much value on sea experience".

In 1881, Charles Clay joined the United Telephone Company in London. The first telephone exchange in England opened only two years earlier and the public service was still at an experimental stage. The first telephone operators were men, but they were not a success as they could not stand the abuse from subscribers without retorting in similar vein. There were so many complaints that the men were replaced by boys, whose vocabulary was more limited, but it was young women who proved best at the job. As well as good voices, they needed sound lungs and good memories. When a subscriber called for a number, the operator had to know that Coleman Street numbers ran from 1-500; Leadenhall from 501-1000; Chancery Lane 2501-3000; Westminster 3001-3500 and so on.

If it was not on her board, she called across to the another operator to make the connection.

At this time, London had about 1200 lines served by 13 exchanges. There was intense competition between United Telephone Co. and Globe Telephone Co. Once, the Globe Co. maliciously tied together a span of United's wires, at a point near the Wool Exchange, which caused all United's customers' bells to ring. United sued Global. Global were spotted taking photographs on the roof and Charles Clay saw the risk of manipulated "evidence". The camera may not lie, but cunning choice of angles can make it tell whopping fibs.

Together with an architect, he set about making a model of the roofs surrounding the Wool Exchange. After two days, the architect gave up, unable to cope with scrambling over the roofs to take measurements, but the model was made and taken to the Guildhall to be explained to the Court. United won their case.

In 1883, there was a trial in the Court of Appeal to settle important patent rights. Charles Clay was responsible for providing models and apparatus to be demonstrated in Court. The trial lasted nine days and new models were being called for daily. The two mechanics who should have made the models were absent, so Charles Clay and a colleague, Mr Hawes, had to make everything themselves. They had little sleep, but it was worth it; again United won the case. In due course, United took over Globe, and appointed Charles Clay to take over the Globe apparatus.

In 1885, aged 29, he moved to Sunderland to become Manager of the Northern District Company. I have telephone directories of the period. A slim paperback edition for December 1888 — March 1889 measures 3 x 4ins.

The growth of new subscribers was so rapid that directories were up-dated quarterly. The coloured cover has little sketches of Berwick, Alnwick, Newcastle, Durham, Whitby and the Sunderland Head Office. Under the name of each town, the directory listed businesses and private residents separately. It shows that Charles Clay lived at The Elms, Sunderland, Tel.No. 3.

I do not know how or when he met my grandmother, Amy Scott, whom he married in 1888. He could have used his telephone in his courtship, for the directory lists her father, John Scott, of Ford Hall, Sunderland, Tel.No. 345.

To spread and popularise telephone use, Public Telephones were introduced. Usually situated in shops or private houses, they were identified by an enamelled metal notice, with white lettering on a dark blue ground. The public paid a fee to make a call.

A Public Notice announces:

"At the request of several Manufacturers and Merchants, The Northern District Telephone Company, will issue on and after April 6th.1889, ONE PENNY, THREEPENNY, and SIXPENNY TICKETS, which will be accepted at Public Telephones in payment for LOCAL & TRUNK MESSAGES and they can be remitted in payment of their monthly Trunk Toll Account."

Another notice follows up with:- "PUBLIC TELEPHONES. In order to increase the use of the PUBLIC TELEPHONES, it has been decided to Reduce the Charge to ONE PENNY PER LOCAL MESSAGE. Anyone, (whether Subscriber or not), can use the Public Telephone". This was a far-sighted move for, as well as introducing people to the telephone, it led to many becoming subscribers.

The new telephone was particularly valuable for the many coal pits in the area, as this letter shows:

Wearmouth Colliery, Sunderland, 6th October 1887.

Dear Sir,
I have your letter. The Instrument which you placed in our pit is a most efficient one and has given us no trouble. It is in direct communication with my house (1 mile from the pit top), the resident Manager's house, and the Colliery Office, and has been found to be most useful. I know of no application of the Telephone more useful than this which enables one to communicate with works which cannot be visited by the management so frequently as those on the surface.

Yours faithfully,
M.W.Parrington.
To: C.B.Clay Esq., Northern District Telephone Co.Ltd.

As well as the subscriber network, Private Lines were offered. Quoted examples advertised include connecting: "Stables with private houses, theatres with box-offices, barracks with hospitals, private wharves with their central offices etc. The Renter of the Private Wire has the apparatus entirely under his control, and can use it day and night without the intervention of the Company's servants."

In the early days, telephone exchanges were not open at night. Only gradually were the hours increased.

The directory was used by the Company to suggest reasons for installing a telephone, such as: "The Telephone in CASE OF FIRE.

The Company draw special attention to the value of the Telephone as a means of conveying notice instantaneously to the Fire Brigade of an outbreak of Fire. The South Durham Salt Co.'s Works (connected with THIS COMPANY'S SYSTEM) was recently the scene of what might have proved a very expensive Fire, but for the warning which the men were able to Telephone to the Fire Brigade within one minute after the discovery of the outbreak."

Subscribers paid a regular subscription, entitling them to free local calls. Regular scoldings were printed: "CAUTION AGAINST USE OF TELEPHONE BY NON-SUBSCRIBERS.

The attention of the Directors has again been called to the fact that certain Subscribers continue to allow non-subscribers to use the Telephone for the transmission of messages, and the Directors regret that it is still necessary to bring the matter to the notice of Subscribers generally with the view of discontinuance of a practice which is most prejudicial to the interests of the Subscribers themselves as well as to the efficient working of the system."

129

Before the widespread use of the telephone, urgent messages went by Telegram.

At a Post Office, the message was written on a buff form, charged at so-much per word. It was telegraphed to the Post Office nearest the receiver's address.

A uniformed boy on a red bicycle delivered it, and waited for a reply. Composing succinct messages became something of an art form, but efforts to be brief sometimes mystified the receiver, needing another telegram asking for an explanation of the first. Ownership of a telephone gave useful free access to this service.

Incoming telegrams were telephoned through, with written confirmation following.

In both World Wars, a visit from the telegraph boy was dreaded because next-of-kin were customarily notified by telegram when men were missing or killed in action.

In 1889, a subscriber congratulates the Company:-

I frankly own
Your Telephone
Has satisfied us all. Whene'er we ring
The wondrous thing
Instanter comes the call.

For business ends,
Or chats with friends,
Its value none can gauge,
In truth I wot
Who use it not
Are far behind the age.

The interleaved advertisements and notices reflect the lives of the telephone-owning classes. A. S. Holmes, Stockton-on-Tees, taps a vein of fine-tuned social snobbery by making ordinary items a touch more special: "York Ham, Cumberland Bacon, Cotherstone Cheese, Grewelthorpe Cream Cheese, Yorkshire Potatoes, York Brown Bread and Fine Durham Mustard."

There was no refrigeration, but "Finest Norway Block Ice — always on hand, at very low prices," helped to keep larders cool. There was much competition with tea. The Elephant Cash Stores, Stockton-on-Tees, tell us their Ceylon Blend, 2s.lb., "has many admirers"; their Elephant Mixture "is drunk by thousands." A thirsty public is offered Continental Wines by the case. Scotch and Irish Whiskies, Choicest Jamaica Rums, London Gin and Old Town are only quoted by the gallon. If they over-indulged, G. P. Fairman was on hand with a remedy. "For the liver: Essence of PODOPHYLLIN & DANDELION — 1s.& 2/6 per bottle. Prepared by the Proprietor."

J. A. Chapman, Sunderland, had Sewing Machines, Bicycles and Tricycles for sale, with "Riding taught to buyers free." Peter Lockie & Co., Sunderland, enticed with: "New Broughams and Horses for Wedding Parties or Private Use. Brakes, Wagonettes, etc. for Pic-Nics in excellent order and supplied at the lowest, remunerative rates. Funerals efficiently and expeditiously carried out."

The safety and reliability of the railway is vouched for with a two-paged coloured coupon inserted in each directory by "Nestlé Swiss Milk — The richest in cream". The coupon was to be signed and left in the book. Nestlé promised to pay £100 to the legal representative if the signatory was killed in a railway accident during the current quarter. To ensure no cheating, the colour of the coupon was changed four times a year.

The Sunderland and Durham County Institute for the Blind employed over thirty people and taught trades, offering "Baskets, Mattresses (Hair, Wool, Grass and Straw — Old bedding purified and re-made), Feather Bedding, Piano Tuning, Matting, Door Mats, Brushes, Coal Baskets and Sailors' Beds."

A romantic picture of ships sailing from all over the globe is conjured up by the list of stock at Joseph Thompson & Company's Timber Yard, Sunderland. "Norway, Swedish, Memmel, Stettin and Dantzig Firs. Stettin Hewn and Sawn Oak Logs & Crooks. American Oak logs up to 30ins.square, Pitch Pine and Red Pine Spears up to 70ft.long, Black Walnut up to 30ins.square, Rock Elm, Hickroy (sic), Ash, Birch, Yellow Pine, Mahogany, Cedar, Teak, English Elm, Ash, Beech and Plane tree in Logs, also in thoroughly seasoned Planks & Boards. Yellow Pine Pattern Wood of the finest quality always in stock. American & Stettin Oak Wagon Scantlings, Tram Sleepers, Tubbing Deals, Cribbing, Wagon Sprags, Oak Spokes, Ash Cart Felloes, Telegraph Poles, and oak Arms, Spars and Rickers for Ladders, Saugh, Larch, Hornbeam Cogs, Plaster Laths, Slate Laths, Crate wood and Fret wood."

Taken together, the range of advertisements suggest a robust society that worked hard and enjoyed its rewards. To ensure that everyone was in good health to participate to the full, assistance was to hand:-

"HEALTH, STRENGTH AND ENERGY are quickly obtained by simply taking a few doses of EPP'S CURA-CENE (Wine of Ozone). The greatest purifier and enricher of the blood known, its effects are almost immediate and the cure certain. A guaranteed cure for nervous, physical and functional weakness, headaches and singing noises in the head and ears, dimness of sight, and specks floating before the eyes, dizziness, failing appetite, pains and aches, heart disease with palpitations and fluttering, rising of food and acidity of the stomach, vomiting, liver complaints, wind wasting diseases, shortness of breath, kidney diseases, softening of the brain and listlessness, coughs, asthma, and in early stages of chest diseases and decline, impurity of the blood with pimples, blotches and eruptions, flushing, trembling of the hands and limbs, exhaustion, melancholy and loss of memory, indigestion, biliousness, neuralgia, gout and rheumatism, loss of energy, and unfitness for study, society or business, and there is not a disease but what this medicine will reach, and in all human probability cure, as it has thousands of times before, even after everything else has been tried and failed. IT GIVES STRENGTH AT ONCE and gives more strength in ten minutes than any other medicine will in as many weeks and is extremely pleasant to take. This Grand RESUSCITATING ELIXIR has been recommended

133

by the most illustrious Physicians of the age, including Sir Erasmus Wilson, Sir Charles Locock, Physician to the Queen, and Mr Caesar Hawkins, Sergeant-Surgeon to the Queen, who have given their testimonials unsolicited. Sold in bottles at 2/9, 4/6,11/, and 33/- and there is great saving in buying the larger sizes. Sent anywhere carriage free, or through any Chemist. EPPS & CO., 366 ALBANY ROAD, LONDON."

How might readers have responded to this advertisement? It caters for everyone, from pimply adolescent, through a turbulent life towards senile "softening of the brain". And yet, and yet . . . ?

"Health, Strength and Energy" are first promised by simply taking "a few doses", but later contradicted by emphasis on the economy of buying big bottles, but the quantity in each bottle is not stated. The advertisement is targeted at an affluent class, but even so, in 1889, 33/- was a high price. The same sum would buy two gallons of Scottish or Irish whisky. Epps & Co. continued to insert their full-page advertisements, appearing to prosper. We must hope their customers thrived as well.

In 1888, Grandaddy briefly visited America, to study the latest developments in telephony. He also got married that year, but I do not know which came first. The following year, he was very gratified when Mr Lockwood, of the American Bell Telephone Company, in a paper before the American Institute of Electrical Engineers, said: "The best working longlines I found were without doubt those belonging to the Northern

District Telephone Company. This company is in the charge of Mr C. B. Clay, of Sunderland. The lines are all new and are built on the latest model."

The Northern District Telephone Company was taken over by the National Telephone, and in 1893, he was transferred to London as Metropolitan Superintendent. When he left, he was presented with a desk, on which I am now writing. The silver plaque is engraved:

Presented to C.B.CLAY ESQ.

by the staff of the National Telephone Co. Ltd. (Northern District) as a mark of esteem on the occasion of his leaving the district.

MAY 1893.

He bought a commodious house in Albermarle Road, Beckenham, for his growing family. He was to have four daughters, and a son who died in early childhood.

In London, he proposed the same policy of extending the network of public call offices which had been so successful in the North. The General Manager was shocked at the notion of charging subscribers to use public telephones. "Why, there will be a riot!" he said, but he was persuaded to introduce the reform.

An ever-increasing number of call-offices were opened in the London District, where everyone had to pay a call fee, gradually diminishing the number where subscribers had free use, until only that at Head Office still retained the privilege. It was done with scarcely any friction and the foundations of country-wide system was laid. It would not have been a practical or remunerative policy for the Company, if the majority of callers paid nothing.

This "lack of friction" is a thread which runs right through Grandaddy's career. He was obviously greatly respected and warmly liked by all the people he met and worked with. It shows in all accounts of his activities.

The National Telephone Journal of November 1906 gives a comprehensive account of his career and also an article:

"PRESENTATION TO MR CLAY."

"A concert, held at Caxton Hall, Westminster, in aid of the National Telephone Benevolent Society was made the occasion of an interesting ceremony. In October of this year, Mr C.B.Clay completed his twenty-fifth year in the telephone service and it was felt generally that so important an event should not be allowed to pass uncommemorated. Halfway through an excellent concert the presentation of a billiard table and an illuminated address was made to Mr Clay.

Mr Lowe expressed the good wishes of the staff to Mr Clay, and pointed out that as the Company increased in size, so Mr Clay's personal success had increased. Mr Davis alluded to the kindness and consideration with which Mr Clay treated all those who worked under him, and gave statistics of the increase of the Company in London during his period of management.

In replying, Mr Clay, who had a great reception, dwelt with some pride upon the success which had been achieved by the men who worked under him in the old Northern District Company, most of whom were now holding offices of importance in the Company and elsewhere. He was equally proud, he said, of his Metropolitan staff, and had no doubt that they would achieve similar success. There was further enthusiasm at the close of his speech, all present joining in the singing of "For He's a Jolly Good Fellow". The presentation of a billiard table was chiefly subscribed by the Metropolitan staff and by those members in other parts of the country who have been under Mr Clay in the past."

It was installed in Beckenham, and on the move to "Hurst", the Billiard Room went up on the second floor. It must have been a major job to get the table up there.

When space had to be found to give us a home, it was the Billiard Room which became a bedroom for Mother and me. I hope he was not upset at parting with it. I never heard that he was a billiard player, but such was his generosity of heart, he would not have hesitated. Without him, we would have been destitute.

When I was living at "Hurst" again, after the war, I sometimes saw an elderly man standing in the gateway of the drive, looking at the house. He would stay about ten minutes and then walk away. One day, I went out to talk to him. He told me he had worked for Colonel Clay for many years, and it gave him pleasure to come and stand there and remember earlier times.

He would not come in for a cup of tea, but was clearly pleased I had approached him. After a while his visits stopped.

Grandaddy delighted in telling that his staff were "all colours." There was Mr Brown, Mr Black, Mr White, Mr Grey and Mr Green. I did not ask our visitor's name, but afterwards I felt sure he was one of "the colours".

Grandaddy was too old for active service in the First World War, but raised a Volunteer Corps, mainly of men in the Telephone Industry. They gave all their free time and did valuable service in developing army communications systems.

In recognition of his service, he was awarded the Volunteer Decoration and granted the unique honour of keeping the rank of Lt. Colonel, although he had never served in the Regular Army.

CHAPTER
THIRTEEN

Being prepared

Beneath my excitement at the prospect of boarding school lay another reason for wanting to move on. Father could only afford to give Mother an annual pittance when he left, which did not keep us for a week, let alone a year. She needed a job and got a position at K.P. to coach games, drive the school car and handle various other supervisory roles. I was embarrassed by her presence on the staff. Unfortunately, Mother's duties fell within JAL's orbit. Mother was competent, well-liked and respected by staff and pupils, but JAL knew she could never enrol her in her fan club. She got back at her through me, via rice pudding and prunes.

Prunes or dried apricots with ground rice, sago or tapioca were staple diet. Once JAL spotted that I loathed the lot, she started to pick on me and decreed that I could not leave the dining hall until my plate was clean. It was stiff enough to be repellent, not quite hard enough to wrap in a hanky and stuff up a knicker-leg and too bulky to be kept hamster-wise in my cheeks, for later disposal. I had no wish to defy her, but the stress made it daily more difficult to swallow.

The day came when all the other children had left the dining-hall and I was struggling to down the stuff with great gulps of water. JAL had put Mother to supervise the meal and hovered to keep an eye on us. Somehow, Mother got me out and I went home in tears. Providentially, I came out in a rash of German measles the next day.

In 1936, after three years at K.P., I was eager to join Pam, boarding at Ancaster House, Bexhill-on-Sea. Despite Pam crying with home-sickness at the start of every term, she was happy there. Our education there had become possible because the Headmistress, Miss Burrows, had met our mothers when they were all younger on the hockey circuit. Knowing both had been left penniless, each with a daughter to be educated, she generously offered to take us without fees. She operated her own Robin Hood policy, fleecing a few nouveau-riche fathers, whose daughters might not otherwise have been accepted, to subsidise the less fortunate. The secret was well kept. Neither we, nor any other girls, knew anything about it.

I was delighted with my new uniform. The dark green, with touches of red suited my colouring, subconsciously making me comfortable in it. Luckily the school ran a second-hand clothes service, as the clothes list was long. A cabin-trunk was needed to pack everything at the beginning and end of each term.

I came to think my panama had an unfashionably deep crown, so rashly cut the brim off with nail scissors, intending to overlap a little and sew it back together. I had to take out the lining band, but when I did, the whole weave started to disintegrate and I had a fearful job to cobble it together again and make it wearable in time for church. Disaster! It was then too shallow. It sat on top of my head. It would not stay on. I had to hold it all the way on the half hour walk to church, and back.

At the end of a term when girls were leaving, it was the tradition that they should try to throw their hats into the Thames as the school train pulled into Victoria Station. I would have liked to hurl mine away immediately. I had to own up. A new one was bought.

Miss Burrow's mother started Ancaster House, with six pupils. By now it was thriving, with about 120 girls, an economic number to support the necessary staff. Its high reputation owed more to the personality of its headmistress than the academic prowess of the pupils. During my years there, only one girl, the daughter of a doctor, took Higher Certificate for entry to university. She planned to follow her father's career. There was no talk of a career for the rest of us. From this school of excellent repute, some went on to secretarial, others to domestic science colleges, where they learned how to iron a shirt perfectly in not less than half an hour.

Miss B. was a heavily built woman, with mannish haircut and a forceful personality. She knew the force of her own charisma and wielded unfettered power over every soul. We were her power base, rather than her role being to nurture girls consigned to her care. She was a domineering woman and you crossed her at your peril. Her sharp tongue could make girls squirm. Pam was easily swayed by her Irish blarney, happily lacking my sardonic eye, but I was never at ease with her.

My strongest instinctive dislike focused on Miss Smith, known as "Horse". An electric charge of mutual dislike sparked between us. She only taught gardening, but pried and spied everywhere, tittle-tatting back to Miss B. She did not live in the staff cottage, but in Miss B's private quarters in the main house. I was too immature to recognise the common thread linking these women, beginning with my own Aunt Kate.

The nation's war memorials did not list all casualties. For numberless ranks of young women, who might have become wives and mothers, few careers were open. With minimal academic training, they filled teaching posts in the expanding number of boarding schools. Many seemed to have no life outside the protective cocoon of school. Their outlook was restricted, their psychological and sexual development stunted.

The nearest they got to love affairs were fantasies culled from novels. A.H. had its share of these unfortunates, whose existence depended on Miss B. If they incurred her displeasure, they got a term's notice and were out. Possibly a few were lesbian, but most would not have known the word, for this was Bexhill, not Bloomsbury; they were probably neutered by lack of experience.

After the rigorous teaching of grammar at K.P., I found Miss Marshall's English classes futile, teaching us nothing positive. We would be given a choice of three "essay" subjects. I got more and more frustrated, my mind paralysed and unable to even pick a subject.

All were equally uninspiring and anyway I was not prepared to bare my thoughts to Miss Marshall. The only fluent writing I did was on Sunday mornings when we wrote a compulsory letter home. I could cover sheets describing the events of the past week, but when called on to be "creative", I froze.

Our poetry was culled from Palgrave's Golden Treasury. I preferred the hypnotic beat of "Hiawatha" and the dreamy verse of Rupert Brooke. Miss Marshall edited the school magazine and we all had to offer contributions. I did some verses that were a snide pastiche, meriting a severe ticking off for cheek, but she failed to recognise its sarcasm, took it at face value and printed it. My already low opinion of her plummeted.

I felt that many of the lessons we sat through were a waste of time and irrelevant to my idea of real life. Much time was allocated to arithmetic, geometry, algebra and trigonometry. I still do not know the purpose of algebra. What is trigonometry? My future needs would have been met had I left school knowing multiplication tables, being able to add-up, subtract, divide, handle mental arithmetic and tot-up long columns of figures quickly.

A kindly old lady took Art classes, but sketching and then filling in with watercolour offered nothing for the talented. They could have been picked out for proper study and the rest given some knowledge of art history, some smattering of the world of painting, sculpture and architecture.

When we did get good teachers, they did not always last. A dear little Welsh bundle, Miss Jones, favoured allowing us to use reference books during exams, rather than wasting time learning reams by heart for regurgitation. Sadly, such heresy was unacceptable. Two terms and she was gone.

Every hour of our day was mapped out. Lessons in the morning, games in the afternoon, prep after tea. After supper, if not engaged in some activity, we sat with sewing, mending or knitting, for "Reading Aloud." A member of the staff, omitting any remotely "unsuitable" bits, would read some bland novel, often badly. Well-read uncensored Dickens or other classics would have held our attention better. It was an anodyne way of keeping us quiet until bedtime. — 8.15pm for the juniors, up to 9 o'clock for the sixth form.

I'd arrived at A.H., aged thirteen, not knowing how babies were born. Via the navel perhaps? Mother had told me nothing, beyond warning me of pending menstruation. I filled my void of ignorance from the talk of more knowing girls in the dormitory after lights out. There were no pet rabbits to demonstrate obligingly. The only animal was the school pig. It was fattened on kitchen scraps, vanished bacon-wards during the holidays and replaced by a fresh young one each term. Credulous new girls could sometimes be seen before breakfast, going down to the pigsty, with bucket and brush, to undertake "Pig Wash". Pam had warned me, so I was not caught.

The school was divided in three "Houses". Horse was housemistress of Rome, Miss Marshall of Venice and Miss MacPherson of Florence. Thank Heaven I

144

was in Florence. In Miss MacPherson, who had lost her fiancé in the War, we had a honey. She was human, erudite, well travelled, had a fine sense of humour and a soft Scottish voice. She spent her long summer holidays in France or Italy, speaking both languages fluently. She taught history.

Each House had its own Guide Company, which met one evening a week. The first time I changed into uniform after games, I realised that I was being looked at and talked about during tea. Although I had removed my patrol leader's stripes, I still had a sleeve full of proficiency badges. No one else had any. Miss Macpherson was delighted to have me; she could not do knots. Now she had a demonstrator.

Trouble came when I got to the fifth form. Guides were then expected to become Cadets, training to become leaders of Brownie packs. I had no wish to become a Brown Owl. I didn't want to dance round a cardboard toadstool singing pixie songs. I wanted nothing to do with anything run by the androgynous gym mistress.

I did not want to wear a Cadet scarf, a white cotton square, folded and tied in the traditional Guide way, looking like a sanitary towel. In a futile rebellious gesture, I cut a loop off one, and wore it. Wiser friends persuaded me to take it off. Miss Gordon had no sense of humour. I might have been expelled. Sandy Mac worked a brilliant compromise saying she said she needed me to help with her company, so I put up a third stripe as Company Leader and got my "training" that way and her company continued to win knot competitions.

Every few years, a camp was held at Hatfield House, two Guides from each school company being invited. I had a great week. We slept in bell tents, feet to the centre pole, like hands on a clock. As the weather was perfect, our lot voted to sleep outside, under the stars. To construct our sleeping bags, we folded blankets, making envelopes secured with blanket-pins, laid on ground-sheets.

After supper, several hundred sat round a campfire, singing traditional songs. One evening, I sat next to two girls with "1st Buckingham Palace" on their shoulder flash. One of them is now Countess Mountbatten. Lady Baden-Powell, the Chief Guide, spent a day with us and spoke during the evening, uplifting us all. Girls today would think us a pathetic lot, but we were happy, blessed with joyous innocence.

During my second year at A.H., Mother became seriously ill with thrombosis in both legs. There were then no blood-thinning drugs, so she spent months lying motionless in bed, with two nurses in attendance day and night. I never consciously faced the fact she might die, but Mother did. The thought that Peter and I might be shipped off to Father gave her both the incentive and the courage to recover.

After so long in bed, she was very weak but, when Grandaddy died, she was determined to get from her bed into a front room, so she could see the hearse driven away. With Pam and I to help, she did it. We helped her each day as, little by little, she recovered the use of her legs.

Burying of the past when Father left set a pattern for the rest of my life. At times of trauma, I keep going apparently normally and get a nasty reaction later. Nowadays the pendulum has swung too far the other way, as the "Counselling Industry" foments a "victim culture". In this case, my school behaviour and work suffered. Miss B. was very short with me. I was "to pull myself together". One of the times I felt the loss of Father most was when "normal" girls had both parents attending school functions and taking them out for a day. With Mother ill, Pam's mother would come, with Auntie Kate. It was kind of them, but really underlined the void.

Sandy Mac remained constantly supportive. If I'd been in Rome, with Horse as Housemistress, or Venice, with the vapid Miss Marshall, I truly cannot visualise what would have happened. Expulsion probably. I had the comfortable certainty Sandy Mac shared my view of some of the staff. I despised Miss Wilkinson, who taught us geography. Everything came to a head over the fishing industry. From my Padstow experience, I knew she was peddling second-hand rubbish from an out-of-date textbook. My polite interjections were not appreciated and an open row was brewing when the lesson ended. I went straight to Sandy, still fuming, and asked to drop geography, just before the affronted Miss Wilkinson huffed in to complain. Sandy deftly rearranged my timetable, with a grin and the hint of a wink. I could have hugged her.

Mother's reputation as one-time England hockey team goalkeeper put me straight into the 1st XI, with

147

Pam. Hockey was something I could do with her, despite the three-year seniority chasm. The rest of the team were tolerant, not treating me as a bumptious junior. I was careful not to presume friendship off the pitch.

We played against many other schools, with particularly keen rivalry against The Beehive — excellent school, unfortunate name. The niece of the headmistress, Miss de Putron, outclassed us all and went on to become one of England's best-ever players. As goalkeeper, I bore the brunt of her onslaughts. Playing in the first team was great, but because we were so often the stronger team, I got bored. I went through whole matches without touching the ball. With the blessing of Mrs Bryan, who coached hockey, I picked a younger girl, trained my replacement and switched to right-back in the 2nd XI. I soon won my way back into the first team.

We also played netball, but I was too lanky to be any good. The little nippy ones did best, as they did in the gym. They vaulted over the horse, turned cartwheels and climbed ropes with ease, while I struggled to get my long legs under control. In summer, we played tennis and cricket. I liked batting, but my bowling was hopeless. At the time, I saw no point in girls playing cricket. Later I saw its value for:

1. Admiring and/or supporting boyfriends and husbands.

2. Impressing children on the beach.

As the school hall did not have a stage, opportunities for drama were restricted. Girls had to play male roles so, when the seniors did "Pride and Prejudice", Mr Darcy with well-developed breasts rather spoiled the romance with Elizabeth Bennett. The De Le Warr Pavilion had recently opened, causing a national stir with its modern architectural style. Overlooking the sea, terraces, balconies and walls of glass let light flood into the building. In this grand setting, we performed a musical "Robin Hood". Every girl had a role; I had two. I was a starving vagabond, doubling as the village champion archer, needing a swift change of costume, from ragged sacking to a genuine workman's smock and felt hat. My make-up turned from cadaverous tramp to ruddy-faced countryman.

Pam was Little John (with D cups). With the other leading characters, we were equipped with real bows and arrows and had to learn to use them. At first, I found my left wrist was not strong enough to hold the bow steady. A leather support strap helped. It was so good that I shot an arrow right out of the school grounds, over the road and into the playground of the Nazareth House Orphanage next door, mercifully not killing an orphan. We shifted our practice ground to a safer area.

The climax of the show was the great archery contest. It was staged so that we shot at an invisible target off stage. On the first night, Robin Hood's "winning" shot hit a beam and bounced back on the stage. With admirable aplomb, another arrow was plucked from the quiver and shot successfully, to loud applause.

Every Saturday morning, Miss B. took the whole school for current affairs. The rise of Germany was worrying. When Neville Chamberlain returned from his meeting with Hitler, waving his piece of paper promising "Peace in our time", we were given a day's holiday. A picnic was hastily organised and all the girls transported along to Cooden, for a day on the beach. Running at full speed through shallow water, feeling the exhilaration of sand and water on my bare feet, I kicked a submerged rock and broke a toe. The full extent of the damage was not apparent until next morning, when I couldn't get a shoe on.

CHAPTER FOURTEEN

Distant gunfire

World War II was not ushered in with thunder and lightning, but on a sunny September Sunday morning, with a cloudless blue sky. At breakfast, there was none of the usual family chatter. Granny's enquiry: "Who is going to church this morning?" fell into a little pool of silence. The service started at 11 o'clock, the time of the Prime Minister's broadcast to the nation. Mother, the Aunts and Peter opted for church. Pam and I stayed with Granny.

I knew enough of the First World War to swamp me in dread. We sat round the radio in the drawing room, the French windows open to the garden, lawns, tennis court, rose beds and sweeping herbaceous borders. As Mr Chamberlain started speaking, I quailed at what was coming, clinging to a gossamer thread of hope. His measured words rolled inexorably on: ". . . consequently we are at war with Germany."

Hardly had he finished, when air-raid sirens raised their sickening wail. Silver barrage balloons rose gently, silently, into the tranquil sky, to stop swaying slightly on the tension of their mooring wires. They ringed London, defending the city from low-flying planes, looking plump and benign. Air-raid wardens, self-conscious in new tin hats, cycled the streets, blowing whistles to chivvy everyone under cover. The church party arrived home breathless.

What next? An atmosphere of unreality prevailed. Granny struck a positive note: "Kate, go to the kitchen and tell Nelly we will have lunch at 1 o'clock, as usual." It felt wrong to sit idle, but no action felt appropriate. I went through the swing door to the kitchen passage and sat alone on the back stairs. I was sixteen. I was scared. I didn't feel strong enough to face a terrifying future. My tightly shut eyelids formed a cinema screen showing images of death in the trenches, the horrors of poison gas, sailors drowning in blazing oil . . .

The siren wailed the steady all-clear note, bringing me back to the present and the reassuring smells of roast beef wafting from the kitchen. I slipped back to the rest of the family, now all talking to release the tension. That theatrical first air-raid warning had been a false alarm, but gave us all a fright.

Police cars raced to a house at the top of our road, arriving just too late. In the attic they found radio equipment and evidence our neighbours were active German spies. The occupants had flitted. Dramatic stuff. It heightened the atmosphere of unreality; it seemed we were all taking part in a bad movie but nobody knew the script.

Peter, Pam and I helped with the back-wrenching task of filling sandbags to protect doors and windows of the operating theatre at the local hospital. We toiled all day. Aching limbs and blistered hands were of little account, measured against the satisfaction of doing something positive.

Our next job was apple picking. The owner of a small orchard offered his crop free to local hospitals, if someone else would pick them. It sounded a pleasant task, but our bucolic idyll quickly shattered. Our ladder was heavy and hard to manoeuvre on the soft ground. Abandoning ladders, we tried stepladders. With the basket parked on the top step and both hands occupied, balancing was tricky. It was little better than ladders, but not so far to fall. It took hours to fill ten cartons and then load them into a small car.

At the hospitals, our offerings were unwelcome. Anyone who has made an apple-pie knows how long they take to peel and core. They were accepted with bad grace and probably thrown out as pig-swill. We were crestfallen and exhausted. The only person happy was the orchard's owner, smugly feeling his munificent offering had contributed to the War Effort, at no cost or inconvenience to himself.

The Phoney War continued. Nothing much occurred, so at the beginning of the September term, I put on my school uniform and joined my friends on the school train at Victoria.

Having passed my matriculation exams the previous term, I looked forward to an interesting year in the Sixth and being a House Captain. Freed from the stranglehold of the exam syllabus, we might have enjoyed art, music, architecture, history and general knowledge but our formidable Headmistress had different ideas.

Wielding great influence as a Town Councillor, she secured war jobs for us. Four of us issued ration books. We sat in the Town Hall, filling in local citizens' names. Heavy manual workers were entitled to extra rations, but no criteria were laid down for assessing eligibility. We used our own judgment somewhat generously. Was Bexhill the better fed for our efforts?

London schools closed, their pupils evacuated to the country. With luggage labels attached, each carrying a small suitcase and a cardboard box with a gas mask, they left their weeping mothers and were marshalled into trainloads and taken away to alien places. Anyone in a "safe" area with spare rooms was allocated evacuees. The children and their hostesses got some rude shocks as they all learned to shake down together.

Thirty evacuees, aged around eight, had to be entertained for a few hours once a week. I went, with two other Guides. We did not know what to expect and at first it was mayhem. Our best bit of equipment was the whistle. Once we established that the whistle had to be obeyed, order could be maintained and games started. Discipline was foreign to them, but once they realised it was more fun that way, they liked it. We became so popular it was often hard even to move, as they hung to our hands, belts, anything to secure individual attention. "Please Miss, please Miss, please Miss". At the end of a session, they tried every trick to detain us. It meant being very firm indeed with these squirming little leeches, who so badly needed to be cuddled and comforted.

We also sang to the blind — and struggled to learn Braille. To be blind in wartime had its special anxieties. After a shaky start, we got our audience to sing along with us and they loved it. I'd never met a blind person before.

The progress of the war was clearly spelled out in a weekly current-affairs talk. The school assembled to hear Miss Burrow's excellent survey of world affairs. She did not mince her words; we were aware the Germans were over-running Europe at an apparently unstoppable rate. Before long, what she was telling us was confirmed by our own ears. The noise of distant gunfire could be heard from across the Channel. We stood on the window sills at night and listened to the rumbles and crumps. What had started like faraway thunder got a little louder each night, until we not only heard it, but felt the windows rattling in their frames.

I shared a room with another girl. We were above Miss Burrow's rooms. One night, certain that drama was afoot, we crept to the head of the stairs. She was talking urgently on the telephone, discussing arrangements for evacuating the school away from the vulnerable Sussex coast. German plans captured after the war showed one of their invasion points was by the Gas Works, not half a mile down the road.

Next morning the news was broken at Morning Prayers. Great packing-up began. We senior girls were treated as adults and took new responsibilities in our stride. With commendable speed, all 120 pupils were ready to move. At such short notice, a place big enough to take everyone was not available, so the school was glad to shed pupils. As Mother was not paying fees, she thought it right to offer to withdraw me at such a dangerous and uncertain time. A pity, for a year in the Sixth would have been more valuable than the previous years together. I was fetched by car and didn't even have a chance to hurl my hat into the Thames.

CHAPTER
FIFTEEN

Flying free

It took a war to upset the Family routine. The maids left — Nelly, the cook, to drive trucks in the ATS, Winnie to the NAAFI canteens and Irish Madge to the Land Army. Gertrude was too old to go, so stayed as a daily help. The chores were shared. Cleaning the bathroom, upstairs pantry and lavatory became my responsibility. We all shared the washing-up and laundry. Kate did the cooking.

Warwick was also too old to join up. He turned most of the flower garden over to growing vegetables, with the help of George, a garden-boy with a stutter. One day, when a bomb dropped near, poor George could not get a word out. Meeting him down the road, Mother didn't know whether to stay in hope he could tell her what had happened or to hurry home to see for herself. Warwick kept the house supplied with potatoes, carrots, swedes, turnips, cabbages, sprouts, cauliflowers, beans, peas and onions. There were apple and pear trees, raspberry canes, red currant and gooseberry bushes and strawberry beds. Those able to do so grew more than they needed, to give to friends who had no gardens.

Chicken sheds, disused since a neighbour's smouldering bonfire had set them alight and roasted the flock, were re-populated to provide eggs to augment meagre food supplies. Although food became so scarce during the war years, the population enjoyed good health.

With a weekly ration of meat that made only a single meal and 2oz.of butter to last a week, the volume was made up with bread, vegetables and fruit. The ration of cheese would hardly have satisfied a mouse, and egg supplies were pitiful. The imported egg powder that sometimes turned up was a poor substitute for the real thing. Those living in the country managed quite well, but to feed an urban family was a daily challenge, particularly if the man of the house came home at midday. Works canteens had their own allocation of supplies. Before food got scarce, I didn't like cheese, sprouts or tomatoes. Now anything was welcome, bar rabbit.

At first, we went to the cellar whenever the siren went, but soon found that it was usually a waste of time, so did not bother, unless it got noisy. This confused Rover, our bright Springer spaniel. As nobody took him for regular walks, he was in the habit of going out on his own. Somehow he learned to streak for home when the siren sounded. He would arrive, panting, at the front door, bark to be let in and go straight to the cellar door. One day, we were too casual about interrupting a game of tennis on the next-door court to take cover when the siren sounded. We got a fright when machine-gun bullets pattered down.

Ostrich-like, we all dived headlong into some laurel bushes.

When I so unexpectedly left school, at the time of Dunkirk, Peter was already in the army and Pam was about to start training as a physiotherapist at King's College hospital. Her uniform and textbooks were already bought, but she got engaged to Harry Westall, whom she'd met at the tennis club. It was thought pointless for her to embark on a four-year course. Instead, she looked after two small children whose mother was dying.

Pam and Harry married on 21st, December 1940. He arrived back on leave late the previous evening, having just got his commission, but not having had time to get his officer's uniform. After much telephoning, we managed to borrow service dress for him. The jacket was a bit big but, worn over two pullovers, it fitted quite well. He was the warmest one of the wedding party. Pam shivered in her white velvet dress. I shivered as her bridesmaid.

Only one keen-eyed man spotted that the regimental badge on the borrowed cap did not match those on the lapels of the jacket. Peter was expected back to "give the bride away", but had a nightmare journey through air raids and did not arrive until halfway through the reception.

Now I was home for good, I posed a problem. I was a bit young for an adult job, but had to be employed usefully. Each aunt tried to enrol me in her own pet war activity. The previous summer, Muriel sought to use her Cub pack to collect waste paper, which she wanted to sell to raise funds for the Scouts. The small boys were not up to it, so she conscripted the Family instead. At first, Pam and I thought it quite a lark to go round the streets on the back of a lorry, collecting sacks of paper. Sorting it later at the Scout hut was not fun. If the sacks had only contained paper, it might have been tolerable, but the stench of some very nasty things permeated our clothes, skin and hair. I think we all went well beyond the call of duty before we gave in and mutinied.

Muriel was baffled by our unpatriotic attitude, but with her usual single-mindedness, switched to volunteering her VAD nursing experience. In full nursing rig, she spent long hours on duty in a concrete first-aid post in Milk Street, Downham. No regular bombing had yet started and although the Battle of Britain was raging overhead, it did not produce many casualties on the ground.

I knew nothing about nursing beyond the first-aid learnt in the Guides. Nevertheless, I was to be an unwilling volunteer at the first aid-post. Mother improvised a uniform for me, using a white overall, a cook's apron and a large white cotton square folded into a VAD-style cap. With my short hair, an armoury of clips and pins was needed to anchor it, but it remained precarious and certainly would have been dislodged by any vigorous movement. There was not much prospect of that occurring while there were no casualties to treat.

After several days of boredom, we had a "casualty". A mother brought in a child with a bit of dirt in her eye. I had assumed that the nurse on duty with me was competent, so was surprised as she fussed about, uncertain what to do. She tried to flush the mote out, but only managed to get a stream of water running down the girl's neck and soaking her jumper. I couldn't bear it. I took a jug, positioned kidney bowl against the child's cheek, tilted her head, poured gently and the eye was cleaned. All as per the Guide's manual. The remainder of the shift passed rather silently.

Suppose a real casualty had been brought in, covered in blood and rubble, what would she have done? I was not willing to hang around to find out. Mother agreed it was a dangerous farce and told Muriel I was not to go again. Another mutiny.

When the German army overran Belgium, a number of Belgian families escaped to England in small fishing boats. Some came to a large house requisitioned for them in Edward Road. Mother collected furniture and other necessities for them and looked after their welfare. One of them, a grandfather, was ill in Farnborough Hospital. He had problems as he only spoke Flemish, so I went with Mother and his daughter to try to sort things out. He spoke to the daughter in Flemish, she passed it on to me in French, I relayed it to Mother in English. The reply went back along the line, finally being shouted, as the old man was deaf. He was smiling contentedly when we left and the whole ward had been kept entertained.

Sorting through old photographs recently, I was puzzled by one of a baby I did not recognise. Turning it over, I read the inscription: "George Albert

Vandekerckhove, aged 6 months, Belgian, presents his photograph to his dear protectrix, Mrs Ford-Hutchinson. 5 May 1941." The families continued to send her Christmas cards for many years after they returned to their homes at the end of the war.

Next, Kate enrolled me in her causes. She was head of the "Friends of Bromley Hospital". They needed an extra person for the telephone switchboard as a special line was installed to liaise with the emergency services during daytime air-raids, which were becoming frequent. The line could not be left, so I stood-in for the regular operator whenever she left her cubby-hole in the Front Hall. The switchboard had leads with plugs which had to be inserted into appropriate holes to effect a connection. Poor Grandaddy must have spun in his grave at my ineptitude.

The rest of the time I made myself useful running errands, taking delivered flowers to patients, posting their letters and so on. Between jobs, I sat on a chair in the hall, so was the first person seen when anyone came in. A woman brought a screaming baby that had put a live electric plug in its mouth. A navvy arrived, having walked a mile with a foot flattened by dropping a paving stone on it. I had to run after a woman who came to visit her husband, to save her going unwarned into the ward where he had just died. I took the messages through the emergency line when two school-friends were dying under their bombed home.

Compared with today's complex hi-tech hospital and modern drugs, a district hospital then was a simple set-up. Matron was in overall charge, with Sister Pike to oversee the nurses and catering. She was all smarm to Matron and doctors, but a bitch to young nurses. She and Kate thought highly of each other. Finance and general administration were in the hands of the male Hospital Secretary, with a typist. The Lady Almoner looked after patients' welfare problems.

There were four long wards, a surgical and a medical for men and the same for women, plus an X-Ray department and Outpatients. One of two newly-qualified resident doctors was always on duty. The local G.Ps. attended their patients in hospital, calling in specialists as necessary. It all worked satisfactorily with minimal bureaucracy.

Another of Kate's activities was the organisation of the annual Alexandra Rose Day, with house-to-house collections and street vendors selling pink fabric roses to raise money for hospital and nursing charities.

A new flag-day was inaugurated to raise funds for SSAFA (Soldiers, Sailors and Air Force Association), to be held annually on 3rd September, the anniversary of the outbreak of the war. Kate was approached to find a District Organiser. Being under eighteen, I was not permitted by law to collect in the street, but as nothing was stipulated about the age of the Organiser, I was appointed to cover the Bromley area.

I drew up plans and made a list of potential helpers, calling on Kate's list from Alexandra Rose Day, plus family friends. I contacted most by letter or telephone, as I had a credibility problem. Face-to-face, people assumed I was my mother's messenger. Daylight air-raid warnings were frequent, so each collector was told her nearest public shelter, should the siren go. In a shelter during a raid, who could refuse to be generous?

Following the success of the day, I had the ludicrous experience of being taken by Kate to the London headquarters of the Alexandra Rose organisation, to be interviewed for the post of National Organiser. I was astonished at such a silly idea, but they were serious, urging me to take the job. I would have had no idea how to set about it, and said so. They must have been desperate to find someone. Kate was quite crestfallen and cross with me.

I needed a proper job, but had no qualifications. Because of air-raids, travelling to London daily was thought too dangerous. Someone recommended me to the Manager of the local Lloyds Bank, so I went for an interview. He prudently did not take me for his branch, but passed me on to Beckenham, who needed their first girl to replace a man who'd been called-up for the army.

I was not a good bank clerk. The job was not interesting enough to engage my full attention, and not easy enough to be done while thinking of something else. I made careless mistakes. A long desk, with three high stools, ran along behind the cashiers. I perched on the middle stool, making entries with a fountain pen in a huge ledger. If he brought his own quill pen, Charles Dickens' clerk, Bob Cratchit, would have felt at home. The man on my right had been doing the same job for 30 years. He seemed able to glance at a column of figures and know the total. When I got to the foot of a page and had to turn over, it meant adding up l.s.d., and carrying the total forward. I made very heavy weather of it, until he taught me his method.

To "cast", go up each column, pairing numbers making 10: 6+4, 7+3 and so on. To be doubly sure, I run it from the bottom up, then the top down. If they tally, O.K. This trick has been invaluable all my life. It can be faster and less prone to error than using a calculator. It would have been a more useful skill to learn at school than algebra.

The stool on my left was occupied by a retired Manager who had come back, part-time, to Do His Bit and release a man to fight. To be a humble ledger-clerk hurt his pride and I fear my arrival, frivolous and untrained, rubbed the salt in. The worst threat to his dignity was when he tried to get up on the stool. He was short and the stool was tall. His struggles to get up were a subject for pity, not mirth, so I had to be sure to keep my head studiously bent over my ledger while this pantomime went on.

I came to dread Tuesdays. That day, no one could go home until the books balanced, down to the last farthing. If there was an error, the men descended on my ledger, searching for where I had added when I should have subtracted or vice versa. My mistakes caused everyone to be late home. I felt all the worse because they were all so tolerant of my tiresome carelessness.

On the daily bus to work, I made the acquaintance of an elderly gentleman who got on at the next stop. Due to a stiff leg, he walked with two sticks and had difficulty getting up the high step into the bus, but people were patient, the conductor helped him and the driver waited till he was seated before driving on. A problem arose when he started to pause on the top step while he scanned the passengers. If he spotted me, he transferred a stick to the other hand, so that he had one free to raise his hat to me. The hat was replaced, the stick moved again, and eventually he moved towards a seat, while I squirmed with embarrassment.

Over the weeks, I learned that he grieved the loss of a daughter who had become a nun in an enclosed order. His other daughter was a BBC producer, and later became the wife of the British Ambassador to Washington. From his manner, I thought he was an academic; perhaps a university lecturer, or maybe an antiquarian bookseller, but there was nothing of that nature in Penge, the bus terminus. My curiosity overcame my good manners and I asked him point blank. His business was sanitary ware. He had a factory making lavatory pans.

A WRNS officer often joined the bus. Getting off at Beckenham, she made for the station, doubtless heading for the Admiralty. She was a walking recruiting poster. I was hooked. I devoured every perfect detail of her immaculate uniform. I swooned over the tilt of the tricorne hat. I could only daydream. My eighteenth birthday was still many months away, an eternity. At the bank, I was training as a cashier. There was much to learn, the task made more difficult by having to chat to customers at the same time. As a topic, the previous night's raid pushed the weather into second place.

The Blitz had started and air-raids were a nightly menace. Now we have a fuller picture but, at the time, news was scarce because secrecy and security prevailed. We had a narrow focus, according to our role. I was later astonished at the open way the Falklands War was reported — as though it were a football match.

Throughout the Blitz, people living 50 miles west of London could be naïvely ignorant of the severity and extent of the damage caused by air raids. They might think damage was limited to the docks, whereas great swathes were laid waste throughout London, its suburbs and in the other major cities as well.

During the nights, those lucky enough to have cellars, slept there. Others went into Anderson shelters dug in their gardens, huddling together, sleeping as best they could, to emerge in the morning, never knowing what they would find. Some went to public shelters and Henry Moore's sketches of the London Underground show jumbled masses spread sleeping over every platform.

From the East End, women came by special "caves trains" to sleep in the safety of the Chislehurst Caves. From Sundridge Park Station they straggled along, with laden prams and pallid children. At first they had to return to London every morning, but later many lived in the caves, their own homes being flattened. Muriel started a cub pack there to occupy some of the boys. Local residents gave unstinting help, but there were many problems, food and sanitation being two. The caves proved far more extensive than had been realised and the throngs of evacuees extended ever further into the labyrinth. The men stayed in London, working every night as air raid wardens, firemen or rescue teams, toiling to put out fires and seeking victims buried in the rubble, carrying on with their jobs during the day. Women drove the ambulances.

Our house, solidly built in 1888, had good cellars. Down there, we slept on narrow wooden bunks, wearing trousers and sweaters, just in case. Snoring was a problem. I could sleep through the racket of anti-aircraft fire and the crump of bombs, but the combined snoring of Mother and three aunts was hard to ignore. No one would believe herself the culprit but by common consent we evicted Muriel. She was indignant, but got the best deal as a full-sized sprung mattress fitted neatly under the main staircase and she slept most comfortably there. The others snored on.

Granny could not manage the cellar, so her bed was brought down to the morning-room. The ceiling was shored up with sturdy posts round the bed, supporting sheets of corrugated iron. Net glued to the windows, plus heavy curtains, kept her safe from flying glass. Lying in my bunk, I felt more anger than fear, furious I was likely to be killed at seventeen, inwardly railing at God and the adults who had let this happen. Had they learned nothing from the First War?

As we did night-shifts as fire-watchers, we were allocated two helmets made of compressed cardboard. Shrapnel rained down from the anti-aircraft guns stationed on the nearby golf-course. Each morning we collected jagged chunks of metal from the garden, to be returned to factories for melting down and re-use.

There was a parade of A.R.P.(Air Raid Precautions) workers in a local recreation ground and an inspection by the Duke of Kent. Why? I went with John Alexander, from next door, who was waiting to be called-up for the Navy. We found the Fire-Watchers lined up, men and women in separate ranks. John suggested we stayed together, so I tucked my hair up a bit, under my cardboard helmet. Being tall and wearing navy trousers and sweater, I was not conspicuous. We stood for two hours before the official party turned up. The Duke dutifully walked along the ranks, stopping now and again "for a word". As he came along our row, he suddenly spotted me, with lipstick. He paused, he hovered, he panicked, he moved quickly on.

For fire-fighting, we had a stirrup pump. It was meant to be used by one person. Held steady on the ground by a foot on the metal stirrup, one end of the pipe went in a bucket of water, one hand worked the pump, the other directed the hose. The snag was refilling the buckets. The designer forgot that "Jack AND Jill went up the hill to fetch a pail of water." In practice, we needed a pair to keep the buckets replenished, usually Pam and I as we ran fastest. Water would not extinguish an incendiary bomb; that needed sand, which we hadn't got and anyway would have been too heavy to shift. We tried to stop the surrounding area from igniting. The feeble little squirt of water was useless once a fire got hold.

On the long winter nights, evening meals were early. The sirens sent us to shelter when the first German bombers crossed the Kent coast soon after dark. We were acutely aware of the night sky. With total blackout, no chink of light must peep through carelessly drawn blackout-curtains and vehicles had screens over the headlamps, reducing the beam to a pinpoint. This let the stars shine diamond-bright. When we could see them, we expected a raid. Thick cloud was our comfort blanket. Above all, our fate moved with the moon's phases. When it was full, a Bombers' Moon, it boded ill.

One bad night, as usual the first wave of bombers dropped flares and incendiary bombs to light up the target area for those that followed. Instead of the London Docks, a wood-yard near Bromley North Station was set ablaze. Wave after wave followed, showering down bombs and incendiaries until the town was on fire from end to end. We did not escape. The house seemed clear, but an incendiary pierced the garage roof, bounced and skidded under the car. Mother and Stella tackled that one, one working the stirrup pump, spraying the tank to keep it cool, while the other inched the bomb clear with a garden rake. They worked with urgency prompted by having that morning got the paltry petrol ration allowed for cars on essential work.

Running down the drive to alert our neighbour that the top of his porch was alight, I met John coming to tell us we had one on the roof and our chicken sheds were burning. A sprint to the top landing showed a bomb burning in the lead-covered gully between two gables. By climbing on top of a cupboard and wriggling out of a small window, I pushed it clear of the melting lead with a broom, yelling to warn anyone below to stand clear. Pam and I ran up the garden, ignoring an empty kennel that was alight, to find an incendiary had pitched in the centre of a coiled garden hose, belching thick black smoke from the burning rubber. Singed chickens were demented. We hadn't a stirrup pump, so grabbed watering cans from a smouldering shed and ran back and forth to the garden tap, some thirty yards away.

Granny spotted Muriel about to go out bareheaded and insisted she took protection. On the hall table stood a potted plant in a cache-pot made from an elephant's foot, complete with toenails. The base was only paper. A friend, who often slept under our dining-room table, relished recounting how he saw this apparition approaching, with a bucket and stirrup-pump in one hand and the other struggling to support the upturned elephant's foot helmet. At the seat of the fire, she took it off, stood it on the ground, and started pumping.

So it went on all night until the all-clear sounded an hour before dawn. I had been too busy to feel frightened. Adrenalin drove out fear. I was invincible. We had seen the blaze in the heart of the town, so Pam and I cycled in for a quick look. The Parish Church looked bad, but the tower was still standing. Not a shop seemed unscathed. The whole length of the High Street was awash, fire hoses snaking everywhere.

Shopkeepers struggled to salvage their stocks. Down the centre of the street great heaps of sodden clothing, boxes and anything that could be carried, were piled together in a continuous wall as far as we could see. Roofs were gone, windows had showered glass everywhere. Churches and halls were hit and not so much as a Scout hut remained. It was well after the war before there was a place big enough for a meeting or concert.

But I could not dally, I had to get to the bank. No buses were running, so I cycled. Between Bromley and Beckenham is a steep valley. I skirted part of it with a detour, but still had to push my bike up the long hill from Shortlands. It was after eleven o'clock when I got there, full of apologies. I received an emotional welcome, hugged by everyone. They had all seen Bromley burning and feared for my safety. Mr Crang, the Manager, plied me with hot coffee (ground acorns), saw I was unfit to work and kindly sent me home. I would rather have curled up under a counter and slept, but I had to muster energy to get home. I slept all the afternoon, to be ready for another night.

By the time I got home, we had a new addition to the household. Kate had found Beryl wandering in the town in a dazed state. During the night, her home had been destroyed and she had lost everything. In earlier years our families were neighbours, until her father was plunged into bankruptcy by the failure of his once-prosperous business importing ostrich feathers. A change in ladies' fashions ruined him. Poor Beryl felt an imagined social stigma ever after. Ill-equipped to earn her living, she had the same lowly clerical job for forty years and lived as a "paying guest" in other peoples' homes. Now even that was gone.

She became part of our family for the rest of the war. Her non-stop gratitude was a trifle tiresome. She would spend her lunch-hours scouring the shops for scarce items, always hoping to find some rare thing, such as a valve for a bicycle tyre, a torch battery or light bulb. She could not pass a queue without joining it, in the hope of bringing back some morsel to show her gratitude. That in turn made the recipient obliged to be grateful, with the cycle of gratitude going round and round until overload caused Gratitude-Fatigue.

Our other arrival caused problems. She had been many years with the family, as nanny to Mother and her sisters. After she retired, Grandaddy bought her a little flat. Her mind started to deteriorate. Every evening, she came round before dark, was given a cup of tea, then departed with the same words every time: "Well, I'll say 'Goodnight' Mrs Clay and I hope it will be a GOOD night!" One night it wasn't. Firemen pulled her from the wreckage of her flat, and we took her in. By the end of the war, her dementia was serious. She could not tell night from day, she roamed the house, often taking things and hiding them under her mattress. Scissors had to be hidden, since she had found a pair and cut all the buttons off a coat, leaving a big hole in the cloth round each. It was a great nuisance, but everyone got used to locking doors and putting the key on the ledge above.

Mother had to give-up getting out in the night to put her back to bed as she only got out again a few minutes later. Bedroom doors had to be locked and her knocking on the panels, with "anybody there?" had to be ignored. Her room was next to Mother's, who would hear her switch on the brass light-switch outside her door and then go down the backstairs to the kitchen. It was a miracle she did not gas herself or blow the house up in her efforts to boil a kettle.

One day, she could not be found in the house or the garden. Local streets were scoured, but no sign. Finally, the police were told. They asked what she had been wearing, but all her dresses were still in the cupboard. She might have been wearing a white cotton Victorian nightdress, a pink lace-up corset over it, or any other random assortment of garments.

The police eventually returned her, no worse for wear, after riding to and fro on the 227 bus, until a conductor took her into Beckenham police station. She came back with a shilling and an umbrella. She was wearing a long skirt and a cardigan pinned across with a huge safety pin.

After she died, Mother was surprised to hear the familiar click of the light switch outside her bedroom door. She asked Kate if she was unwell, thinking she had been visiting the lavatory during the night, but she had not left her room. Shoulders were shrugged and it was facetiously blamed on Nurse's ghost. Mother continued to hear the unmistakable click of the switch at night. After a few weeks of this, she woke to find Nurse standing by her bed, her white hair awry, her blue eyes staring, looking worried. Mother managed to stammer something soothing and reassuring. The apparition turned and walked through the wall into her old bedroom. Mother never heard the light switch click again.

But that episode lay in the future. I was still at the bank, still yearning to join-up, still waiting to be eighteen. In the spring, came brilliant news. The WAAF had dropped their age requirement to 17. I was overjoyed, until my excitement was dashed by finding that working in the bank was a "reserved occupation" and I could not leave without permission from Head Office. I was distraught but the Manager was very understanding, doubtless mindful of the late Tuesday evenings, and obtained the necessary permit, just in time, as no more were allowed to leave. Clutching it, I went to London to enlist. A further snag arose. The WAAF said they would take me, but only as an Accounts Clerk. In vain did I protest that I was a bad bank clerk, and could get a letter from the Manager to prove it.

Returning home on the bus, deeply despondent, I met a family friend and tearfully told her my problem. "Write to your M.P." she said. I did. It worked. After an agonising wait, my papers came through. On June 21st, 1941, I was reborn as Aircraftwoman 2nd Class Ford-Hutchinson No.449652.

CHAPTER
SIXTEEN

Mapping the future

After all the waiting, longing for this day, I got it wrong. I went to the right place, on the right day, at the right time; Adastra House, Kingsway, London, June 12, 1941, 9a.m.

I had my identity card, ration book, and parental letter of consent. It was not enough. Being under age, I needed my birth certificate. I had already been among the throng several hours, waiting for my turn. Now I was turned away, shattered. Through a mist of tears, I saw a phone box, scrabbled in my purse for change, dialled and was speaking to Mother. She would find the certificate. She would bring it. Weak with relief, I stumbled to a chair and sat for as long as it took for her to walk to the bus, catch a train to London, catch a bus, find Adastra House.

When she arrived, she could not find me. We wasted another hour standing within yards of each other. At last, we connected, hugged and she melted away as I got back on the end of the queue again. I was feeling that the war would be over before I even got into uniform.

As soon as girls were recorded, given a cursory medical check and sorted into batches, they were put on a bus and departed. After hanging round all day, I was on my way. The bus was ancient, camouflage-painted, with no glass in the windows.

Once aboard, the atmosphere changed from uncertainty to a holiday outing. As we went along Oxford Street, we found ourselves being cheered and waved to by passers-by, all becoming a hilarious royal progress. We waved, we laughed, we sang. Heroic stuff. All too soon we were at Paddington Station and our hilarity evaporated. We were packed into a train and set off slowly, grittily, to our unknown destination. The girl on one side of me was dirty and smelled disgusting. The one on the other side was homesick and snivelling tearfully.

By dusk, we were at Innsworth Depot, near Gloucester, in a camp of wooden huts in rows round a huge tarmac parade ground. Each hut had 30 beds, with sheets like sandpaper and stiff grey blankets. Having been at an expensive boarding school, this was acceptable to me. I went to bed hungry but happy. The muffled sobs all around suggested that the other twenty-nine volunteers were having second thoughts. Conscription for girls started several months later.

Every morning, the bed had to be "stacked". The mattress was in three sections, called "biscuits". These were piled on top of each other. One blanket was folded in four lengthwise. The rest, with the sheets, were folded and stacked, with each fold precisely showing along the front edge. The stack was enclosed by wrapping the long blanket around it. This went neatly on the biscuits, topped off with the hard sausage bolster, which served as a pillow.

For the next few weeks, this was home. We were formed-up and marched to meals, lectures, medical inspections, showers, anti-gas drill, films and eventually to the stores for our new uniforms.

For nearly everyone, bitter disappointment. They had run out of average-sized uniforms, so the unfortunate girls were given a cap and an institutional grey overall and, the ultimate humiliation, had to keep their civilian gas-masks in cardboard boxes with a little carrying string, instead of a service respirator in a khaki canvas haversack with brass fittings.

Dressed like that, the poor souls were sent away to face ridicule with the RAF.

Me? Being tall, I was in luck. There was a uniform, bearing a 1939 label, of excellent cut and superior cloth, and even my cap was a good one, uncrushed whilst in the store. I was the envy of all in my hut. The only snag was that since we arrived a heatwave had developed. Even the tarmac parade ground melted, tar sticking to our shoes. While still in our own clothes, we had abandoned stockings and wore our pyjama tops as cool blouses. Once in uniform, we were muffled in thick grey lisle stockings, shirt and tie, skirt and jacket and a cap to be worn at all times when out of doors. It was a couple of years before regulations were relaxed to allow us to shed jackets in summer and roll up our shirt sleeves.

The depot lay midway between Gloucester and Cheltenham. Those of us with proper uniforms were allowed passes to leave camp. Four of us decided to try our luck hitch-hiking into Cheltenham, little thinking there would be lots of other airwomen with the same ambition. We were about to give up and go back into camp, dashed and disappointed, when the perfect vehicle drew up for us and there was a rush to clamber aboard. It was a "Queen Mary", a low loader used for carrying aircraft fuselages. It was unsafe, as we were all standing up, holding on to each other. Only those round the edges had anything to hold on to, and that less than waist high. But we were delighted, got safely to Cheltenham, had a meal in a Services canteen, saw a Carmen Miranda film, and returned to camp less dangerously, by bus. Our poor overalled hutmates were wildly jealous.

Emboldened by this successful spree, at the next chance we headed for Gloucester, and four of us were quickly picked up by an open-topped lorry. Only after it had set off did we realise that its last trip had left it thickly coated with white dust. In no time, our airforce-blue uniforms were grey, and with the powder in our hair, we looked a good deal older than when we set out.

Thinking it was probably cement dust, we anxiously scanned the summer sky, fearing to solidify if it rained. When the lorry stopped for us to get off in the middle of Gloucester, we found what the rushing wind in the open lorry had disguised. The stuff was not cement, it was fertiliser, and we smelled appalling. To go to a canteen was out of the question. We could only find a secluded spot, shake off as much as we could and make our way back to camp, vowing to be more choosy in the future.

Hitching was best done in pairs, standing where the driver could see us well in advance. We always began with "Where are you going please?" so we could refuse if the driver looked leery, on the grounds that his destination was unsuitable. It was rare to meet anything but helpfulness. Lorry drivers were kind, often taking us into roadside cafés and buying us food and cups of tea. The lorries were slow, hot and noisy, but far more reliable than private cars. We hitched a hearse once, sitting on the little seats beside the empty coffin, all the way from Didcot to Hammersmith Broadway, getting surprised looks from passers-by.

After two weeks at the Innsworth Depot, everyone was supposed to be posted away to the real war. However, one of the functions of the Depot was to sift and allot each girl to a trade . . . cooks, batwomen, clerks, accounts, parachute packers, telephonists, technicians, radio operators, drivers and so on.

At that time they were looking for the first dozen to be trained as Map Clerks. The qualifications seemed to be education plus height. It took another two weeks to get the group together and meanwhile we were to "volunteer" for jobs around the camp. Seeing some of the awful tasks on offer, I promptly opted for "Officer's runner", and a good choice it turned out to be. I was detailed to a WAAF Officer (Admin) and sat on a chair in the corner of her office. (Routine: enter office, salute, remove cap, sit down. Be called, stand up, put on cap, salute, take message, salute, leave office, complete errand, return, enter office, salute . . .) Some errands could take a pleasantly long time, strolling round the camp, having a chat here and there, before returning for the next job.

Duties included acting as escort to girls up on a charge for disobeying some regulation. What a litany of lame and/or ingenious excuses for being late, losing equipment, being AWOL (absent without leave) the miscreants gave. My real education was starting. After my sheltered upbringing and having had no contact with girls outside the narrow social class to which I belonged, it was a wondrous eye-opener. For the first time I saw that not everyone would automatically conform to rules and regulations. Those deemed incorrigible were sent home, where they would probably be directed to munitions factories instead of wreaking havoc in what was supposed to be a disciplined, albeit female, force.

Finally, the twelve Map Clerks were selected. Being tall, we all had proper uniforms. The heat wave persisted and we had inoculations and vaccinations. My arm was a mess and I was feverish when our order to move came through. We were to go to GSGS (Geographical Section, General Staff.) at Harrow for training. To the Army? The shepherding abruptly ceased and we had to organise ourselves. An RAF lorry got us to the station, with the shaming civilian gas masks hidden in our kitbags. Then a train to London and by Underground to Harrow, where we asked the way.

No taxis, of course. With the heat, my festering arm throbbed. We straggled along. I was reduced to trailing my kitbag along the ground by its rope, until a boy aged about twelve took pity on me. He swung my kitbag up on his shoulder in smart military fashion. He wobbled a bit, got his balance and gallantly escorted me the rest of the way.

Hot, tired and dishevelled, we entered the smart foyer of this army/civil service establishment, dumped our kitbags and flopped. Slips of paper with our billet addresses were handed out and we were shooed off the premises. Thankfully, my place was not far and a dear kind woman took me in and looked after me as though I was her own daughter.

After supper, I went out and walked around until I saw a doctor's plate on a garden gate, went in and rang the bell. A woman doctor dressed my arm daily until it was healed and refused to take payment. This sort of kindness by strangers was part of wartime life. Money was unimportant, which was just as well — eleven shillings a week did not go far.

After our inauspicious arrival, we smartened up and presented ourselves as a neat clean class and were rewarded with an excellent education into the world of maps. The blunt fact was that the maps available to the army were totally inadequate and, for the RAF to fly by, virtually useless. Even we raw recruits could see how little value they would have to aircrew, but nothing so tactless was even breathed. The head of the unit was brother to the celebrated cartoonist "Fougasse", and the map catalogue, which was to be our bible, was adorned with his cheeky little drawings, a constant pleasure. At the end of the course, having mastered the principles of Mercator's projection, conical orthographic projection etc., we were given a little exam and then posted to stations in Bomber or Coastal Command.

Twelve Map Clerks for twelve aerodromes. We were to choose our own postings in order of the exam results, but there was no time to weigh pros and cons. I had first choice, saw a bomber station near Cambridge, and picked that.

CHAPTER
SEVENTEEN

Virgin territory

Waterbeach railway station was the stop after Cambridge, no more than a halt with a hut on it, surrounded by flat fenland country. The only other passenger alighting was an RAF Squadron Leader who took my kitbag and ushered me into a waiting staff car.

I had been in the service long enough to know that Squadron Leaders do not normally give lifts to mere airwomen. "You are our first WAAF at Waterbeach," he said. A signal had preceded my arrival. I was expected. There were about 1200 airmen at Waterbeach, and every single one seemed agog to look me over. I was swept up to the front door of Station Headquarters escorted to the Adjutant's office, and presented as booty.

Three WAAF Cypher Officers had an office doing a job of stultifying tedium, endlessly coding and decoding messages. They lived at "The Laurels", a biggish house a couple of miles away, looked after by a cook and an orderly. I was to live there and cycle to and fro.

I had my own little bedroom and became firm friends with Muriel, the orderly. She was glad of company and an ally, as the cook was a tartar who did not give us enough to eat. We had to creep down at night, raid the larder and blame the cat.

Waterbeach aerodrome was built on the standard pre-war pattern. A straight road led into the camp, past the guardroom, and up to the main door of Station Headquarters. A brick two-storey building, it housed the Station Commander, the Adjutant, the Station Warrant Officer, the Operations Room and Intelligence, which included the Map Store. I had a fine big room upstairs, overlooking the front door, which was strictly for officers only. Other ranks went round the back, even when they were all members of the same aircrew.

Crews for a night's operation gathered in the adjoining Briefing Room. In advance, I pinned up relevant maps and had a satchel ready for each navigator, containing the maps and charts I thought he would need. The available maps were woefully inadequate. They covered Europe, but their small scale and general layout gave scant help to a navigator. To do his calculations and plot his course, he also had a disposable paper chart, on a Mercators projection.

When everyone settled down, Briefing began. The Intelligence Officer described the details and importance of the target, using an epidiascope to put up illustrations. With night bombing, pin-pointing an individual building was unrealistic; it had to be "dock area", or "factory area". If the target could not be found, standing instructions were to bomb SEMO or MOPA, standing for Self Evident Military Objective or Military Objective Previously Attacked.

185

The Met. Officer had his charts, and lovingly described the technicalities of fronts, isobars and the like. But all anyone really wanted to know was anticipated windspeed and direction and, most importantly, the pattern of cloud cover. The Signals Officer addressed the wireless operators, giving them frequencies, D/F stations available, identification procedures and signals of the day. Details were typed on a rice-paper "flimsy", which could be swallowed in an emergency. I never met anyone who ate one, but it emphasised the need for security.

The Navigation Officer discussed the route, and the C.O. wound-up with a general survey of the whole operation in relation to other squadrons on the same target. Take-off times were allocated, and crews went off to make their final preparations. The chat was amiable, but I would never say "Good Luck" or any variation of "Goodbye".

In summer, the nights were short, so trips were necessarily limited in range. The slow heavy Wellingtons could not risk being caught loitering over enemy territory in daylight. In winter, they ventured further afield, even as far as Berlin. Dusk take-offs and dawn returns, left a deadly interval between. When the last plane was safely away, I cycled back to The Laurels, set my alarm, and tried to get some sleep — but with an ear alert, in case of an early return by a damaged plane. The old Wellingtons were wonderfully reliable. Flak or tracer bullets could go right through the doped fabric that covered the fuselage, leaving the geodesic metal framework intact, but always with the risk of hitting one of the crew as it passed through. Even with one engine gone, the plane could be nursed home on the other.

Returning to the camp from The Laurels in the middle of the night posed choices. There were two driveways leading from it, both lined with dense shrubberies. The quickest way was via the drive that led straight to the main road, but with a longer gauntlet to run in pitch blackness with the boojums after me. If I'd overslept and/or felt brave, it was that way. If in good time/timid, the shorter drive and the longer way round. In summer on a moonlit night, the ride was routine, but on a black wet night it was hard pedalling against the bitter winds that swept straight off the North Sea. Although I knew that the guard would call a challenge, it always made me jump and instead of giving the password of the day, I could only squeak "It's me." It was adequate. I was the only squeaker they had.

As my map stock increased, I rearranged storage. By edging some of the stacked map chests forward, I made myself a secret burrow, equipped with mattress, bolster and blanket. I slept there unobserved on nights when it was not worth pedalling to and from the Laurels.

In the Briefing Room, a blackboard listed the crews. As they returned, I entered their landing times. One would come, then another, then several together, then the anxious wait for stragglers, and I'd pop down to the Operations Room for up-to-date news. I brewed a great urn of tea and dished it out in a pint mugs as crews came in, red-eyed, weary and quiet. I had a small ration of rum in my charge and used my discretion to slip a dash in the tea where I felt it was most needed. God knows they could all have used it.

As the planes came in, cameras were unloaded and photographs, taken automatically as bombs were released, were processed. I inspected them, in the hope of plotting them on the target map, before giving them to a dispatch rider to take, by motorcycle, to Group Headquarters. Sadly, they often showed little but open fields, and we would not starve the Germans into surrender by killing a few cows. Nothing seemed to resemble the target, so minutely described at Briefing. It would have been heartbreaking for the crews to know how little some of them were actually hitting. I quietly sealed the pictures in a big envelope and sent them on their way without remark.

This lack of accuracy prompted great research activity into the development of navigational aids, leading to the introduction of "Gee". It worked by sending synchronised pulses from three British stations. Operating from Marham, three aircraft of 115 Squadron were equipped with "Gee" and used as an early form of "pathfinding" for the rest to follow. Results were excellent, but unfortunately one of the three was shot down in a raid on Hanover, in August 1941. This caused consternation, lest the enemy picked up the new equipment, despite the fact that detonators had been fitted in case of such an accident. To put them off the scent, hoaxes were employed to lead them towards a totally different scheme employing beams, code-named "Jay". The ruse worked. Bomber

Command had a clear run with "Gee" for five months before the Germans cottoned-on and produced viable jamming.

I had never been up in a plane, but one of the crews offered to take me. There was no point in asking for official permission, as it would certainly not have been granted. When I agreed to go, I did not really think it would happen, but one afternoon I found myself walking, with long manly strides, among a crew heading for a Wellington parked at dispersal. Over my usual battle dress, I wore a leather flying jacket, boots and a leather flying helmet hiding my hair. A parachute was slung nonchalantly over my shoulder.

Once the engines started up, the noise made communication difficult; I went where I was put. After take-off, I stood in the cockpit, by the pilot. The sensation of the plane remaining level, while the earth tilted always seems odd. I have never been able to get the feel of a plane banking over level ground. The crackling inter-com was hard to follow, but I nodded and grinned. I nodded once too often. The pilot slipped out of his seat and bundled me in.

No panic, I knew he was just teasing and the autopilot "George" was switched on. So it was, for a while. Then it wasn't. I gripped the steering wheel, frozen rigid as reality penetrated the film of make-believe. After eternity, nothing dire happened and I relaxed a little. As my grip slackened, the nose of the plane dipped. In shock, I pulled back to get level again. That manoeuvre completed without disaster bred heady over-confidence. I forgot that I couldn't drive a car, let alone a plane, and essayed a gentle banking turn, but without even knowing which foot to press to deal with the tail. There is so much fresh air under a plane, and it gave me an utterly false sense of security. I flew over Cambridge, then north to Ely. But enough was enough, it was over to "George" again and out of the seat I hopped.

Having, apparently, failed to scare me with that, I was tested for airsickness, with a good deal of steep banking, but the rear-gunner called for mercy first. We landed back at Waterbeach, where I was dropped off, while they took off again. All I had to do was to make my way back, with masculine mien, until I was out of Flying Control's view, get out of flying gear as fast as possible, and be a WAAF again. The plan was simple, but on regaining firm ground, my legs were so wobbly, my tummy so fluttery, my head so dizzy, that it was difficult to carry off. All the station knew I had been up, but no one said a word. I think I'd passed some sort of boyish initiation test.

When all planes were fitted with "Gee", a new type of chart came with it, initially rated so secret every one I issued had to be accounted for and destroyed after use. Tired navigators did not always remember to bring them back on their return and going out to dispersal to search each plane for missing charts was tiresome when I was dying to sleep. The new navigation system improved accuracy enormously, and the bomb-aimers' photographs began to show more built-up areas and docks instead of open country.

At this time too, I was being given bundles of propaganda leaflets, printed in Dutch, Flemish and French, to be dropped over the occupied countries en route to the target. We all grumbled about handling them, but I heard after the war that they were greatly appreciated by the recipients, despite the harsh penalties suffered if the Germans caught anyone with one.

We had one American pilot on the squadron and, whilst grateful to him for coming to help us win our war, he wasn't very competent. One night, he managed to turn his plane upside-down just as the leaflets were being off-loaded. They all blew back and whirled about wildly. He righted the plane and returned with his very shaken crew. I went out in the morning to retrieve the leaflets and found paper from one end of the fuselage to the other, lodged in every nook and cranny and tucked into the geodesic framework, like crazy wallpaper. Our American ally left the squadron.

When there was no flying, I was free to join the camp entertainments, with films and dances. A big ENSA variety show was billed in the airmen's mess, so Muriel, the cook and I went together. We intended to get there early and be inconspicuous, but when we arrived, the hall was already packed. The door was at the front, so when we three walked in, we were greeted with cheers and wolf-whistles. Scarlet-faced, we bumbled into the first empty seats we could see, which turned out to have been reserved for RAF officers, but it didn't matter.

Our fundamental blunder was not realising the show had been tailored for an all-male audience. As the jokes got bluer, we got redder. Everyone was craning to see how we were taking it. When a merciful interval came, we bolted, grabbed our bikes and pedalled away as fast as we could to the sanctuary of The Laurels.

Muriel and I sometimes braved the dances in the village hall, enduring baleful looks from the village girls. I loved dancing and quickly improved. The standard of dancing was very high, with first class bands playing waltzes, slow and quick fox-trots, tangos, rhumbas, jive and the conga. Uniform is not ideal for dancing, with brass buttons jangling together. I had a pair of illicit civilian supple shoes, which I had dyed black. As WAAF officers did not come slumming at Other Ranks' dances, I wore them with impunity, unhampered by standard issue clod-hoppers.

During winter, if night raids were to closer targets, operations could be over by 02.00 or 03.00. I then faced bicycling back to The Laurels, and the choice of the longer route or the shorter scary one. The Chaplain was usually around when the squadron was operating. One night he asked me how I got back. He was shocked to find that I made the trip alone, at all hours, by bicycle. I had never contemplated any alternative as only officers used cars. Other ranks cycled.

The WAAF officers at The Laurels had certainly never given a thought to my welfare and were probably not pleased to have me there, in case I carried news of their doings to higher ears. When they entertained, the racket was alarming.

My small bedroom lay off a little half-landing. One night a drunken Squadron Leader barged in, and wouldn't go. I was hugging the cat, for mutual protection, and finally flung it in his face. He went, with a scratched face, in a furious temper. The cat was none the worse for it. After that episode, when things started getting rowdy, I went up and joined Muriel in her attic, and we reassured each other.

As a result of the Chaplain's concern, I was moved to a billet just outside the camp gates. My new home was owned by elderly Miss Scott, who fostered girls from Dr. Barnado's. I had a small sitting room, where she brought me my breakfast and evening meal. At midday, I ate in the airmen's mess. It was rather a dark room, because there were so many layers of curtains, beyond those needed for the black-out. If I inched the lace curtains back a bit, they were always tweaked back again while I was out. I struggled to get a bit of daylight, without upsetting my landlady, and ended up with half-gloom and her half-upset, so I gave up.

The ground floor was lit by electricity, but the wiring had never been taken upstairs, so I had a candle for my bedroom. It's not easy to get ready to go to a dance by the wavering light of a single candle. The huge brass bedstead rattled, as all the parts were loose. It was covered by a suffocating feather mattress, but in those days I could sleep on anything. There was no running water or indoor lavatory. The privy was some 20 yards down a muddy garden path; just a hole in a plank seat over a bucket. No Andrex then, only the Farmers' Weekly torn up, strung on string, hanging from a nail. All water was carried in buckets from a pump along the road.

Before I realised the labour involved for her, I was invited by Miss Scott to have a bath and I accepted gratefully. What a performance. A tin bath was set in front of the kitchen range and the good soul carried all the water, bucket by bucket, from the village pump and heated it on the range. When all was ready, she shooed the children out and called that my bath was ready for me.

I was most appreciative of all that she had done for me, but in the future made arrangements to have baths with friends in Cambridge, or nip into The Laurels when the coast was clear. The back door key was ceremoniously presented to me, so that I could get in during the night. It was about 7ins. long and heavy, so I hid it in the hedge when I went out. The children called Miss Scott "Auntie", and I soon followed suit. They were fascinated by my arrival and until they got used to me, I could feel pairs of eyes following my every movement. Kathleen, aged seven, was a lovely child, with big grey eyes. The next was an anonymous little scrap. Alicia was black, with a vicious temper when roused. Then came a new arrival, scowling, tiny, fierce and with a flow of foul language learned, no doubt, at her mother's knee. Aged about six, she could have outsworn any average RAF erk. (To be fair, I heard very little bad language from airmen. If I chanced, say, to be passing through a hanger when a fitter dropped a spanner on his foot, the subsequent apology would be fulsome.)

One night, one of the Wellingtons was in trouble at take-off and had to try to land again, with its bomb-bay fully loaded. In the Operations Room, I realised it might come down near Auntie's house, where the children were all in bed asleep. I ran for my bike, dashed back, whispered hurriedly to Auntie and then bundled the children out of bed, wrapped them in blankets and huddled them all in a little cupboard under the stairs. I grabbed a candle and a book and read to them, on and on, and on, while listening to the plane limping round and round as it jettisoned its petrol and prepared for an emergency landing. After what seemed hours, finally all was quiet, the children put back to bed and I got back to the Ops Room again. The plane had crash-landed successfully, the only casualty the rear-gunner with a broken jaw.

My hours of duty were erratic, governed by the squadron's operational pattern. If there were enough planes and crews, and the weather was right, there could be sorties night after night. A few nights of 10/10 cloud were bliss. As well as being up most of the night, by day map stocks had to be checked and re-ordered. No positive preparation could be made until the signal came from Group HQ giving the target. The Wellingtons were slow and of limited range, so my decisions of what maps to stock were simpler than later on, when the crews flew in four-engined long-range Halifaxes and Lancasters.

I wanted no individual "boy friend" among the crews. I knew them all, but did not want to get too close. When a pilot, Deryck, asked me to go out with him, I relaxed my safety-in-numbers routine. He was good-looking, blue-eyed and glib. After rather a short acquaintance, it chanced that we were both going on leave and I was invited to stay at his home in Wimbledon. I went home first, and there was rather a silence when I casually mentioned my planned visit, but to Wimbledon I went. His parents were both pleasant. They both went out to work, so we would be alone in the house all day. His mother was unhappy on my behalf, seeing my obvious naïveté. Sure enough, as soon as she was out of the house next morning, Deryck swaggered into my bedroom, clad in a handsome dressing gown of red silk, embellished with green dragons. He blithely assumed his right to hop into bed with me. He got quite peeved when asked to go. As he turned round, I saw that the dressing gown, so dashing from the front, was split right across the seat. It summed him up so well; from then on I could handle the situation. I did not want to offend his parents or lose face by re-appearing at home again too soon, so I stayed one more day, left a polite note of thanks to his mother, and departed.

Soon after, he was posted to Egypt and sent me a photo of himself halfway up a Pyramid. Some months later, he wrote from a place unknown to me and I asked one of the officers where it was. He was a bit cagey about answering, as it was where they sent LMF (Lacking Moral Fibre) aircrew. Deryck had already crashed two aircraft through incompetence. It was time to take down the photograph of the glamorous pilot in tropical kit, with which I had sought to impress hutmates and myself.

I had settled down happily at Waterbeach. It was a sunny summer. Then came news that more WAAF were coming. In many ways I would welcome the company, but it was bound to upset the cosy and cosseted little life that I'd built around me. Memories of the depot at Innsworth had not entirely faded. I neither had, nor needed, "discipline". My life revolved round the demands of the job and I'd become used to being treated as a responsible adult. Conforming to all the rules and regulations of a WAAF contingent would be irksome.

I had to move from Auntie's house to the new Waafery, not far from the Laurels. It was a tearful departure. Auntie mopped her eyes with her apron. The children were crying and trying to hang on to me. There did not seem to be any sergeants coming, and as I was now a corporal, I reckoned I should take the NCO's bunk room, and moved in, before twenty girls arrived to fill up the rest of the hut. I needed the privacy as I worked and slept such odd hours.

Occupying that room turned me into an agony aunt (by now all of 18 years old), as those in love, out of love, homesick etc. liked to come and confide. It certainly helped to broaden my education. There was Lil, with a baritone voice and short cropped hair, who terrified pretty Pat by pressing her to go out for bicycle rides with her on summer evenings. Lil would come into my room to tell hair-raising tales of the dimensions of her husband's penis. She had fled to the sheltering arms of the WAAF to escape from this alarming phenomenon. "You wouldn't like it" was her recurrent theme. I did not concur. I did not intend to have sex before marriage and did not intend to marry in wartime, so it was all irrelevant anyway.

Late one night, a sobbing hysterical little airwoman hurtled into my room and collapsed on my bed. After much soothing and comforting, she gulped she had been raped. I called Lil in to help and she was marvellous. Under her blunt questioning, it was soon apparent no real harm had been done, beyond scaring the girl, who had innocently led a large black GI to think he was in luck.

I had never been in a pub until a crew took me with them for a day in Cambridge. We had a great time on the river and ended up in a riverside pub, where I ventured my first exploratory shandy. It was necessary to learn to drink beer, as that was what everyone usually drank, but I never really liked it. Smoking was not known to be a health hazard then, and to be a non-smoker seemed a bit eccentric. We had a weekly ration of cigarettes from the NAAFI. I never smoked at work or for pleasure, but in the smoke-laden atmosphere of a full pub, it seemed less oppressive if I smoked as well.

Gradually, as more girls arrived, more huts came into use, and when some genuine senior NCOs arrived, I was happy to move out and join a group of friends including Muriel, in a Nissen hut.

Muriel had escaped from The Laurels, by re-mustering as a telephonist. From her, I learned invaluable tips about working the telephone system. I was able to keep in touch with friends all over the country free, until the system was changed. Then I had to queue up with everyone else at the telephone box and pay for the calls.

The huts of the Waafery were set in one of Tiptree's Victoria plum orchards. We had to put up with wasps, but had an abundant supply of free fruit. We climbed the trees wearing our standard issue pyjamas of blue/white/fawn striped thick cotton fabric, giving excellent protection against scratches.

This amused airmen going along the main road, whose whistles of encouragement were rewarded by fruit thrown over the hedge to them.

Keeping clean was difficult. One ablution block served the whole site. Doors at each end were always open, so the wind blew straight through, summer and winter. Eight lavatory cubicles were at one end. Lidded pails were provided for disposal of sanitary towels, but for some inexplicable reason, there was a recurrent problem with them being put down the pan and blocking the drains. It happened in all Waaferies and was a constant puzzle. We were lectured about it, but still it happened. Finally came the threat that the next time it happened, all WAAF would be confined to camp. It did happen again. Girls had to explain to their boyfriends why they could not come out for the evening.

In the centre of the block, two rows of basins stood back-to-back, on a concrete floor, with no shelf to put anything down, nowhere to hang a towel, no plug and bring your own soap. To get a hot bath needed guile and good luck. If off duty during the day and the water seemed hot, it was a race to gather up towel, sponge bag, bath plug, Vim, and get in fast. First clean the bath, then while it is filling, try to undress and hang clothes on a nail without dropping anything on the floor, as it would be awash with dirty water, and the sodden duckboard little drier. During that winter, I suffered several bouts of sickness and diarrhoea, and had to get out of bed, put on greatcoat and lace-up leather shoes and go 100yds through rain or snow to filthy lavatories with their wartime hard shiny toilet paper.

Service life, with its minimal options was a fairly straight-forward affair. Once you had joined, there were few choices to make or to fret over. Where you lived, what you wore, what you ate were all outside your own control. Camp life was our little world and we spoke little of our lives outside, what our home was like, who our families were, or what we had done.

Going on leave, one stepped back over an invisible threshold, appreciating home life with relative warmth, comfortable beds and hot baths. We were strangers to our families and perhaps a disappointment to them, for we had travelled too far to be able to be really back for just a week. People returning to camp from leave brought a small aura of foreignness with them, but it would be gone by morning. "Had a good leave?" "Yes, thanks." "Good."

Six Russian officers paid a goodwill visit. After drinking most of the Officers' Mess under the table, they turned up at a village dance. They wore Cossack-type belted tunics over breeches tucked into high leather boots. With much clicking of heels and bowing,

I was swept off to dance with one of them. Most of the other dancers stopped to witness this. Russian style is to be held in an iron grasp, well apart, whirled round giddily, then suddenly WHAM! Rib to rib, thigh to thigh and little chance of breathing.

We had an Inspection by the King. Much spit and polish. I had my back to the door when the official party came in. Turning, I was shocked by the royal face. King George VI was normally a pale man, but he seemed to be plastered with Max Factor pancake make-up. He glowed like a Hollywood sunset.

During the long lovely summer, we usually spent our days-off happily in Cambridge, often on the river, rowing or punting up towards Granchester. Rowing is unsatisfactory on such a narrow waterway, so I learned to punt. I also acquired the knack of wriggling out of uniform and into a swimsuit before taking up a punt pole.

The strict rules about always wearing uniform, unless on leave, were eventually relaxed to cover sports. We reckoned punting was a sport, also cycling. It was a cat-and-mouse game played with WAAF officers, who greatly disapproved of us cycling out of camp on a summer evening, wearing cotton dresses.

The outside world impinged on my life from two directions in Cambridge. During my bathless sojourn with Auntie, I was invited to tea by an immensely kind elderly couple and their middle-aged spinster daughter. He was a distinguished retired general, much decorated, knighted, the epitome of the finest regimental traditions. His lady wife was silver-haired, elegant and charming. Their only child, Ruth, was tall, angular, dowdy, gawky, plain, with hair raked back into a straggly bun. She was an endlessly kind, well-meaning, guileless intellectual, riding about Cambridge on a high old-fashioned bicycle, doing errands for anyone in need.

I was a little bit of their war effort. They offered me afternoon tea, with all the delicate porcelain and silver tea-service routine, so starkly in contrast with the airmen's mess and tea out of thick pint mugs. Tea was scarce, like all imported things, so I scrounged some from the mess to take to them. They thanked me graciously, as though it were the finest Darjeeling, but it was really rubbishy stuff. I hoped that in future they would keep the good stuff for themselves, using my contribution on others like myself, who had grown used to nothing better. Above and beyond that treat, I could have a lovely hot bath with fluffy towels.

Ruth invited me to go with her to a matinée performance at the Arts Theatre. The play was "Desire Under the Elms". The set divided the stage, so that simultaneous action could be seen in a room in a house and in the garden outside, under the elm tree. The plot concerned an old man with a young wife and his pride in the baby son which he believed he had fathered. But the audience knew better, for there, before our eyes, we had seen the young wife with the handsome young man under the elm tree. Poor Ruth was in an agony of embarrassment at having brought me to witness sex on stage. It was indeed a bit daring for those days, despite discreet lighting and a flurry of petticoats.

My other civilian contact was with the University. Charles was an undergraduate there and we had known each other since we were children, living next door to each other at home. With him, I went to parties and met his friends, but I didn't really fit in. They had their enclosed world, just as I had mine, and they seemed to me a touch immature. After all, I was nearly nineteen.

Their May Ball sounded glamorous, but proved disappointing. I had smuggled in a real dress to change in the cloakroom, feeling safe from WAAF officers. The dance was held in a dreary civic hall and was a very dull affair. I had become used to an excellent standard of dancing and first class bands. The civilian dance band was made up of elderly musicians without much swing left in them and the undergraduates' efforts at dancing were embarrassingly bad. But Charles was an old friend, and I was happy to have an extra dimension to service routine. I saw a glimpse of university life that would otherwise have been closed to me.

A news bombshell exploded. No. 99 Squadron was posted to India. What a shock. I was upset at the idea of them all going. Several made kind and flattering suggestions about trying to get me posted out with them, but it was out of the question for a WAAF to go. Much as I loved them all, I wasn't keen on India, as I knew there were snakes. In the event I had a recurrence of tummy trouble which led me to report sick and within half an hour I was in an ambulance en route for Ely RAF Hospital, with an appendicitis.

The Ely hospital was a proper pre-war brick building, with one ward for WAAF. I was seen by a S/LdrMO, and felt lucky to have been sent where I could be operated on by an experienced surgeon. On coming round from the anaesthetic, I was shocked to find the long-lashed young newly-commissioned doctor, whom we'd dubbed "Viola", bending over me. The anxious expression in his lovely eyes told me I was the first patient he had been allowed to operate on. I trust he improved with practice. I had twinges for years.

When I was able to get up, I went into the gardens. There were several long wicker-topped trolleys with one patient waving to me. At first I didn't know who he was. His hair was shaved, he was apparently unable to speak and had a twist of silver wire sticking out of his jaw. That was the clue. He was the rear-gunner from the plane that had crash-landed the night I huddled under the stairs with Auntie and the children.

After sick leave, I returned to Waterbeach, to find the squadron had already left for India. There was now a Conversion Unit, re-training pilots to fly the new four-engined Stirlings. On the ground, they were like ungainly stick insects, long legs pushing their noses high. Their tall undercarriages were insufficiently robust, and dotted around the airfield were several lying at grotesque angles, their undercarriages buckled.

Clearly Waterbeach was now no place for me. With a discreet telephone call to the Army Captain who was Map Officer at HQ Bomber Command, a move was arranged. Still unfit for an operational squadron, I had to settle for a spell at an Operational Training Unit at Harwell. He duly sent a posting signal. I duly expressed surprise, packed my kit and moved.

CHAPTER
EIGHTEEN

Oh! Knickers!

At Harwell, the WAAF lived like sardines in the former Airmen's Married Quarters, an estate of brick-built semi-dets. The beds were packed in, twelve to a two-bedroomed house but it was great to live in a house with the bathroom and lavatory under the same roof. Hot water came from a back-to-back boiler, which only functioned when there was a fire in the open grate of what had originally been the sitting room, but now had three beds in it; one of them mine. Fuel being scarce, hot water was never taken for granted and often heated in a paint tin on an illicit electric ring.

Instead of being in Station Headquarters, the Map Store was in the Navigation Dept. After being on an operational station, just doling out maps to crews on training courses was dull. At Waterbeach, I had established a role which excused me from routine chores, such as duty NCO, which my corporal's stripes now entailed. Here I had to take my turn.

The Waafery was separated from the main camp by a wooden fence, known as "Pay Accounts Fence", being by the Accounts office. Girls without late passes had to be in by curfew. It was the job of the duty NCO to take a big torch and go along Pay Accounts Fence prising airmen off WAAFs and WAAFs off the fence and shooing them back to their own quarters. My education was proceeding apace. After booking-in the late-pass girls, it was a short night before setting off again with the list of early calls to rouse the cooks and orderlies on early turn.

Having got to know Cambridge quite well and been so happy there, I was looking forward to Oxford. A bus ran from the camp, so on my first day off, I went, arriving in the city by about 10a.m. I had given no thought to how I would spend the day. The return bus was at 10p.m.

Twelve hours on my own in a strange city suddenly seemed a long time. A cup of "coffee" filled half an hour, then what? Wartime shops were not places to browse and the colleges did not seem as accessible as those in Cambridge, so I mooched around.

I remembered the name of a restaurant where we had been when taking my brother out from Radley before the war, but I couldn't find it and asked a policeman. It had closed years ago, so I asked the way to the river. He gave me a sharp look, as I appeared despondent enough to be contemplating jumping in. Reassured, he directed me and I found a seat where I thought I'd sit until I could go and have lunch and while away the time until the cinemas opened. My respite was soon disturbed by a scruffy old man who came and sat by me and started chatting. I expect he was just as lonely as I was, but I moved away and was back to meandering round the city.

I counted my money and promised myself a really good meal. I innocently went to the Randolph Hotel but an implacable doorman would not let me in. No unaccompanied women admitted. I was amazed, indignant and humiliated. I tried another hotel and again my corporal's stripes debarred me from getting past a hatstand in the front hall, filled with gold-laced Naval Officers' caps, scarlet-banded khaki Army Staff caps and RAF caps with peaks loaded with scrambled egg. I ended up in the Salvation Army Canteen, with sausages, baked beans, egg and chips. At least I could sit there in peace until the cinemas opened at 2p.m.

I saw a film round three times before it was time for the bus. I couldn't even relax in the cinema, because, being on my own, I attracted men looking for a pick-up.

I got to the bus station rather early. It was crowded with snogging couples and tipsy airmen, but once safely on board, the singing got under way. The soulful rendering of "Nellie Dean" was cheering, and there were more verses to "She'll Be Coming Round the Mountain" than I had ever heard before. If I'd had someone, anyone, with me, the whole day would have been a giggle. Alone it was miserable. I'd never ever spent a day alone before.

In another room in our house was Bobbie, whose adored husband, Hardie, an ex-Battle of Britain pilot, was stationed about 100 miles away. She had joined-up after suffering a miscarriage, thinking that she would see just as much of him, by co-ordinating their leaves, as she would if she were called up for a munitions factory.

Coming in after work one evening, I found her elated and bursting with the good news that she'd just had a telegram from Hardie, asking her to telephone him. Sure it must be to fix a long leave, she ran off to queue at the call box. She returned distraught, sobbing and hysterical. He had met someone else and wanted a divorce. He had written, but she hadn't received the letter. Her instinct was to rush out of the house, but I begged her to wait, while I hurriedly changed out of battle-dress and retrieved the missing letter from the Guard Room, where it had slipped down the back of the letter-board.

There was a pub a fair way from the camp, where I'd recently been with one of the Navigation Instructors, and I thought we would make for that, if I could find it. The effort of cycling on a dark night, with only feeble battery lamps, demanded Bobbie's full attention and seemed to soothe her a little. By fluke, I found the place, and there were no RAF there. Installing tear-stained Bobbie in a dark corner, I asked the startled landlord for two whiskies. The good man poured them, and two more later, sensing perhaps that his minute stock of spirits was being used to meet a crisis.

From Hardie's letter, it was clear he had been two-timing her for ages, even when she was in hospital losing the baby she had so dearly wanted.

Fortified by the whisky, we wobbled our way back to camp, just in time to avoid being put on a charge for being out late without a pass. It was amazing how effortlessly our bicycles sped us along. I'd never before drunk anything stronger than beer. Once over the initial shock, Bobbie came to realise the man she'd idolised was really a rat. She pulled herself together bravely and entered into the social life of the camp. She became friendly with a professional double-bass player in the station band and sometimes went with them when they played at other stations.

One evening, I went too. We travelled in the band-wagon, passing as singers. The dance was in a large hall with a good floor, but of course we did not know anyone and our chums were fully occupied onstage. I was asked to dance by a tall West Indian air-gunner. We started off a bit stiffly, then the band started to swing. His face lit up and he was off. It was electric. He was all lithe grace and rhythm and relaxed me so that, all inhibitions shed, I simply fell in with him and it was easy. The band spotted us, the floor emptied and we jived until I could go no further and we left the floor to loud applause. Fantastic! I had no idea I could dance like that. I was on a high for days.

My job in Navigation seemed a footling waste of time. I was used to using my own judgement over possible targets, weather considerations, possible diversions and so on, when providing operational navigators with their maps and charts, which they always took without checking.

I also took a lot of care in briefing crews on action to take if shot down, providing a kit with foreign money, a map of Europe printed on a silk scarf, and a compass. If they could get into France, they were to make their way to Marseilles and ask discreetly for Pat.

Here at Harwell, the sense of purpose was missing. The Chief Navigation Officer was pompous and tried to make me act as his personal secretary, accompanying him to meetings to take notes, thereby boosting his image. He was crestfallen at my insistence that I could neither take shorthand nor type.

HQBC sent me half a dozen girls to train. I was not popular when I reported back that they did not have enough education or common sense to be let loose on an operational station, however long I trained them. By this time, conscription had been introduced and the fall in the quality of most of the new recruits was noticeable.

Instead of putting the job first, fitting in leave, boyfriends and social life around it, my job now meant so little that I hitch-hiked to London and home as often as I could.

Being used to long irregular hours on duty, it was strange to be free every evening. We only had our beds to sit on unless we went to the Sally Ann (Salvation Army) canteen. Our nearest town was Didcot and that offered nothing, except a railway station. All other diversion had to be on camp. We had a cinema and regular dances in the Airmen's Mess, but little else. I got together a group of amateur "instructors" and advertised a weekly dancing class for beginners. We were swamped with pupils.

Among them a tall apparently-fit immature young man, Henry. He was seriously keen but seemed too inhibited and shy to relax and dance; a large young puppy desperately wanting to please, but falling over his own feet. We worked on him, wanting to boost his self confidence and loosen him up a bit. We overdid it and I was landed with an adoring millstone. He was the only child of elderly parents. His widowed mother worried about him, loading him with lovingly-knitted mufflers. He worked in the Education Office, the safest place in England. We should not have meddled.

Somehow the situation crystallised into a choice. Should he stay safely where he was and live to comfort his mother in her old age, perhaps ashamed of himself? Or should he go for death or glory by volunteering as aircrew and earn his own self-respect? Knowing we had gone too far, we tried to soft-pedal and distance ourselves a bit. The situation seemed to settle but, some weeks later, I received an emotional letter from him. He had already gone for aircrew training. He died in a crash before even getting to the end of the course. He is on my conscience still.

As part of a campaign to promote the sale of War Bonds, twenty-four of us were detailed for drill training, forming a contingent to march through towns and inspire the local populace to lay down their money for King and Country. Being part of a professionally trained squad was surprisingly satisfying, once we became proficient. It had the rhythm and precision of the Bluebell Girls, if not the grace, sequins and feathers.

Marching with the men needed a longer pace than was natural for us and our skirts were cut a bit tight. Other difficulties came with a band. If they were far in front, the time the sound took to travel could distort.

Even a sudden blast of wind from a side street could cause a tremor. Worse still was being caught between two bands, the one in front with one beat, the one behind with another. Luckily I was gone before we had to perform in public.

One quiet evening was disrupted by a summons to the WAAF Officers' Mess. I always maintained the maximum distance between myself and WAAF Admin Officers. Their petty rules and regulations did not restrain the naughty and were a tiresome irritant to the majority, who were quite able to behave responsibly without their supervision. Anyway, it seemed that a bus-load of WAAFs had been invited to a dance at a USAAF base and there was to be an NCO in charge. Me. Rank: Corporal. Age: 19.

Reluctantly I changed into my best uniform, press-ganged the most stolid airwoman I could find, and joined the bus. I should have turned tail there and then. The bus was loaded with potential trouble. The regulars from "Pay Accounts Fence" were aboard, and one we called "the Station Bicycle". All were in giggly high spirits and sporting some very adventurous hair styles and an over-abundance of make-up.

At the base, we found a big dance hall, a dance band playing and lots and lots of American GIs. Their uniforms were of sumptuous quality compared with the hairy scratchy cloth of standard RAF issue. All started off well, but the hall soon started to empty, as couples vanished into the night.

I was trying to shake off one weedy chap, claiming to be a Texan cowboy, whose only conversational gambit was to keep telling me I had "bedroom eyes". It was not worth the band's time to keep playing in an emptying hall, so they packed up and left. I saw what I had let myself in for. The airwoman I had brought with me proved a good choice. The poor kid was bewildered until I took her off to the cloakroom and explained that we would probably have to spend the rest of the evening there, and she was not to leave me.

Finally I reckoned it was time to go, but then the problem was rounding up my errant flock. I asked our driver to sound the horn, in the hope that they would hear it and come. Some drifted back, but we clearly had many missing. I had not thought to count them at the beginning of the evening.

To my relief, an American Duty Officer turned up and I explained my difficulty. My relief fizzled out fast. He was drunk. He swept me and my faithful helper along, an arm round each reluctant waist, to search for the rest of the girls. His initial good humour turned sour and he became nasty. We had no option when he insisted on taking us right through the men's sleeping quarters, switching on lights to reveal rows of bunks, many with two heads on a pillow. I could not tell a WAAF from a local village girl, and was left foolishly re-iterating that the Harwell bus was about to leave.

After a good deal of this, I knew I could no longer even find my own way back to where we had left the bus. The nightmare of it going off without us rose in my mind and I tried to will the driver to sound the horn again, so that I could get a bearing.

Then, when I was beyond the point of seeing the funny side of anything, and a bit scared, I felt something strange round my knees. My knickers were slipping down. The service issue "blackouts" being unwearable, I was wearing "french knickers" made from off-cuts of parachute silk. One button at the waist had sufficed up to this moment. There was no way I could step out of them and stuff them in my pocket without being seen by the surly officer, who would certainly think I had been won over by his manly charm and was giving him the come-hither. I could only wriggle a hand in through the placket of my skirt, clutch the slipping pants and hang on.

We eventually regained the bus, shook him off, and got aboard. I had passed through dismay, embarrassment, humiliation, fear and now anger rose to the top. Most of the girls seemed to have returned and a number of Americans with them. They were loaded with gifts of perfume, nylons, lipsticks and sweets.

I told the driver to shut the door and drive back to Harwell. Unfortunately, he did not know the way. With the black-out, plus all the signposts and village name boards being removed to confuse any German parachutists, it was several hours before we arrived at Harwell.

I had the bus driven not to the Waafery, but to the Main Gate, where there would be RAF police on duty. I got off first, pulling my poor helper behind me, found the duty sergeant, waved a helpless hand towards the bus, burst into tears and walked away from it all.

I had intended to go straight to bed, but on passing the WAAF Officers' Mess, I stopped, marched up to their front door and knocked and rang, and knocked and rang, until the door was opened. I announced that I had come to report to the Duty Officer. She finally emerged, very grumpily, and got a terse and fierce account of what she had let me in for, before I bolted, as I felt tears welling up again. I got no apology, but I think that any future invitations of that nature were politely refused. I didn't even get any nylons or sweets.

There was one quite atypical airman, Marcus, in the Navigation Section, who did not fit in at all. He was the other side of the coin from lesbian Lil. Her chromosomes had slipped a bit one way; his had slipped the other. I found him good company, with public school background and a quick wit. We got along well. This shocked the other men, who couldn't see why I was friendly with him.

This same kindly spirit of joint responsibility for my welfare which had enveloped me at Waterbeach seemed to be shared by all the Navigation Section, where again I was their only WAAF. My brother's protests to my Mother for allowing me to join up were ill-founded. My obvious green naïveté made all these good men chaperone me with the greatest solicitude.

Marcus and I went to Oxford on a day off and went to lunch at the hotel with the rack of high-ranking hats. The head waiter, seeing we were not officers, was so sorry that they were full up and, where I would have slunk away abashed, man-of-the-world Marcus knew better and we sailed into the near-empty dining room. Those impressive caps had no matching heads.

The delicate art of tipping is beyond me. When? How much? Who? Too soon is a bribe, too late is too late. Perhaps, like tight-rope walking, if you don't have the knack, you cannot be taught. Marcus was off to London on leave and asked me to go with him to the Chelsea Arts Ball. It sounded fun, so after duty, we cycled down to Didcot and caught the London train.

First, we went to see his Aunt Violet, a raffish old lady with a house in Chelsea. She wasn't expecting us. Some of her friends were coming later in the evening for a party. The sideboard was loaded with extravagant food, obviously black market, and bottles of normally unobtainable drinks stood on a side table.

As her guests started arriving, Aunt Violet's eyes sparkled, matching her diamonds. Whisky tumbler in hand, she waxed expansive. Having forgotten my name, she introduced me to everyone as "the best girl Marcus has brought for a long time." This was all new to me, this ritzy, glitzy world, where everyone was "darling", and the harsh realities of wartime London austerity seemed blurred and distant.

The Chelsea Arts Ball turned out to be a very poor affair at the Chelsea Town Hall, so we gave it a miss and went on to the Coconut Grove. I had never been to a night-club before, never seen fat bald old men with young peroxide blondes. We drank awful champagne, but I knew no better. We danced, we watched a cabaret. Finally we made our way to the all-night Lyons Corner House for a 4a.m. breakfast. Refusal at the front door, a quick flash of money and a welcome at the side door. Bacon and eggs, coffee and rolls, then time for me to get to the station and the train back.

It was a long hard climb with a bicycle from Didcot up to Harwell. I was just in time for a quick wash and change and get back into the office again. Marcus did not return with me, as he had leave, and that was fine by me. He really was rather awful, but I had greatly enjoyed my glimpse of his world.

Shortly after, I saw a headline in the Daily Mirror: "Chelsea Gambling Party Raided". It was Aunt Violet. She got a whopping fine for gambling and black market food. All those present were named.

The most riled by my slight friendship with Marcus was the big Australian Chief Instructor, who expected all women to fall for his beefy Aussie macho charm. To me, he was an awkward cuss to handle. It came to a head when he accused me of skiving off without leave and had me stopped at the Main Gate. My passes were perfectly in order, so I went.

On my return, the Chief Navigation Officer appealed to me to stop feuding, but I assured him it was all one-sided. I just was not impressed by those big blue eyes. Next day, to my astonishment, Australia came to my office, put a huge bag of chocolate bars on my desk (6 months rations) and apologised for his behaviour. After that, we got along fine.

One of the gadgets used for training aircrew was the Link Trainer, a hooded replica cockpit with all controls. While safely bolted to the floor, the whole thing simulated the movement of a plane, with the pilot flying blind by instruments. I had a go one day and was useless at trying to follow the instructions that were coming through the headphones. There seemed no way of communicating outwards, so I was imprisoned inside until my tormentors had laughed themselves to a standstill outside. I never did find out if they were feeding me rubbish instructions for fun, or if I was really as daft as I seemed. What a mercy I had not been in the Link before being pushed into the pilot's seat of the Wellington over Cambridge.

All this was just playing about, to pass the time. Now I was fit again and it was high time to recall that there was a war on, and to get back to it. A covert call to the Map Officer at HQBC, and a signal came, posting me to Linton-on-Ouse, in Yorkshire.

CHAPTER
NINETEEN

Mission impossible?

Arriving at Linton-on-Ouse, I was puzzled at the atmosphere of gloom. Overheard snatches of conversation seemed to include "Wing-Co" and "Chesh". The reason? Wing Commander Cheshire, 76 Squadron Commander, was leaving. There had been a big farewell party for him in the Airmen's Mess the previous night. N.B. Not in the Officers' Mess.

Fighter Command had its individual heroes in the Battle of Britain, but hero-worship of this kind was not the ethos of Bomber Command. This man clearly possessed a charisma which had made its mark on every person on the station.

That Leonard Cheshire probably survived more operational sorties than anyone else was not just luck. His skill was based on thorough preparation. He went through his plane blindfold, simulating night conditions, until he was so familiar with it that he could deal with emergencies in action. He was awarded the VC, DSO, DFC and was the RAF's observer when the atom bomb that stopped the war was dropped on Nagasaki.

The Cheshire Homes which he founded after the war will stand as a memorial to this remarkable man.

All those who met him in wartime revered him. I had missed that privilege by one day.

Much had changed in Bomber Command since 99 Squadron went off to India. Linton-on-Ouse was a pre-war station, the base for 76 and 78 Squadrons, equipped with four-engined Halifaxes. Navigational methods had advanced with the introduction of radar and pathfinder techniques. The RAF had made progress, but so too had the German defences and losses were becoming insupportably heavy. In 1941, an operational tour of about 30 sorties was a fair target. Two years later, such a total seemed fantasy; anyone getting into double figures was a veteran. Operations were now limited by the supply of replacement planes and crews, as well as by weather.

Bill Dixon, ex-76 Squadron tells me they received the first "R" type in April 1943. "It was delivered — to our complete astonishment — by a "mere slip of a girl" ATA (Air Transport Auxiliary) pilot — alone — no engineer — no navigator. We could not believe our eyes when she tripped down the steps." (I think perhaps Bill was so dazzled by the pilot that he did not notice a flight engineer behind her. No one could handle so big a brute single-handed.)

The appearance of ATA pilots, in their dark blue uniforms and dashing fore-and-aft caps, became a regular sight. We were in awe of these girls, with pilot's wings on their jackets. Their skill and courage in delivering these great planes never seemed adequately recognised.

The Waafery was a collection of damp Nissen huts, situated too near the River Ouse. A welcome new arrival came to fill a vacant bunk in my hut. Mollie had not joined up as early as possible, as I had done. She had first taken a degree at Manchester University and this was her first posting.

On arrival, she took a look at the list of personnel in each hut offering an empty bed, saw my double-barrelled name, and moved in! Having no trade but Orderly, she was what I needed. I got her on to the Intelligence Staff and trained her as a relief Map Clerk. Until I had someone responsible, there wasn't much prospect of being able to go on leave with an easy mind.

It all worked out fine, off duty as well as on. Mollie had an army officer fiancé, Kim, so she was not looking for boyfriends. I reverted to my arm's length strategy, not wanting to get too close to anyone whose life expectancy at that time looked so horribly short. We stuck together, looked after one another, worked hard and enjoyed life.

At a camp dance one evening, I noticed a new aircrew come in and stand near the door. One of them was a West Indian. Blacks were very rare and there were no others on the squadrons. As the floor emptied between dances, he walked straight across to me, a huge white smile splitting his dark face, greeting me warmly. I felt every pair of eyes in the hall riveted on me. I was slow to realise it was the fantastic dancer I had met at Harwell.

To my undying shame, I panicked, made some feeble excuse, slipped away and left the dance, cursing myself for being so craven. I did not want to hurt his feelings, but was afraid of what "other people" would think of me dancing so flamboyantly with him. I was bitterly ashamed of myself and anxious to make amends, but I never got the chance. He went missing on his first operational trip the next night. I wept for him.

A favourite evening outing was cycling along the towpath for several miles. Leaving our bikes in the hedge, we hollered for Nick-the-Boatman, a surly old boy, to punt over and take us across. Walking up the path from the river, we suddenly stepped into a picture-book village, complete with village green and duckpond, surrounded by pretty cottages and a pub, "The Alice Hawthorn". The way round by road was too far for anyone from the camp to go there and very few knew our route. We loved the peace and tranquillity there, after the hurly-burly of station life. My working hours were very erratic, and when I had time off during the day I needed sleep. It was tiresome to have to get into uniform and cycle up to the Airmen's Mess to get a meal. The WAAF Admin Officers did nothing to help, so I made my own arrangements. Mollie was very good at smuggling food back to me.

A run of bad weather now and then gave everyone a welcome breather. Being too far from home to take short passes, I let time accrue, to make longer leave from time to time.

One night, our Station Commander, a Group Captain, elected to fly with one of the crews. It was a brave gesture, as he was too old for operational flying

223

and had no obligation to go. His plane did not return and we were all distressed that his gallant effort at boosting morale should have misfired so badly. No replacement was forthcoming.

A while later, a taxi pulled up at the front door of SHQ, right under my window. Out got a tall man dressed in rough clothes and a black beret, like a stage French peasant. Our CO was back. His plane had been shot down, but he was picked up and put into one of the escape lines which returned aircrew via France, Spain and Gibraltar.

Having enjoyed Cambridge, then failed to crack Oxford, there was the chance to explore York. Mollie and I went there for a day off; no more solo sorties for me, after the misery of my first day alone in Oxford. Mollie knew the city a bit, and our priority was to get a civilised meal at the Station Hotel.

We were determined not to be put off by any haughty head-waiter. We were not out to pick up men; we had plenty of those around us every day. We wanted to sit in comfortable chairs, with carpets underfoot, to have a meal at a table with a cloth on it, with silver cutlery rather than the knife, fork and spoon we carried everywhere in our respirator cases.

With persistence and Mollie's poise, we were grudgingly admitted to the three-quarter empty dining-room. When the waiter showed us to a rotten table near the kitchen door, Mollie would have none of it. She demanded a table by the window, the waiter quailed and, with what we hoped was the aplomb of a brace of dowagers, we took our seats. The meal was far worse than we might have got in a Services Canteen, but the ambience was the thing. We counted our day a success.

York, for me, was a huge improvement on Oxford, but lacked the charm of Cambridge. No idyllic punting on the river. York Minster, with all its stained glass removed for safety and replaced with plain glass, was an austere and chilling place. The little shops in the Shambles had nothing much to sell and most were closed and shuttered. Shops in general had little to offer and all clothes needed "points" from ration cards, which we did not have. Cosmetics were hard to come by. We kept lipstick cases and a powder compact and got refills when we could find them. As a result, we wore some weird colours.

The range of the big Halifaxes extended over a great swathe of Europe and my map stocks reflected this. For a change from bombing Germany, attacks were launched on Northern Italy, particularly Turin, where the Fiat vehicle factories were. It was a long haul for a heavy Halifax, having to get over the Alps, which were uncomfortably near the target and then to make the long return to the Channel, where enemy fighters had plenty of time to be lying in wait.

After the first of these raids, a captain and his navigator came to me to discuss, confidentially, the possibility of going on to North Africa, if returning over the Alps seemed impossible. Clearly it would never get official blessing. What if everyone tried it and Bomber Command found itself embarrassed with all its planes vanished to the sunshine?

I got together the best set of maps available and quietly slipped them into the appropriate satchel at Briefing on the next Italian night. Amongst several planes missing was the one with the extra maps. We heard nothing, I said nothing, but I wondered anxiously.

About a week later, the father of one of the missing crew came to the station to collect his son's belongings. He was still there when his son's plane arrived unannounced, having returned from Africa via Gibraltar, laden with pineapples, lemons and oranges we had not seen in England for years. I got a generous share. They never let on that I had given them maps. It was put down to inspiration and luck that enabled them to limp to safety.

Shock and consternation hit everybody when news came that we were all to move; SHQ and both Squadrons. After shock, came indignation. We were to make way for a Canadian squadron. It seemed hard that we should have to leave a good pre-war station to go to a war-time hutted camp in the middle of nowhere. My office was inundated with people wanting to see where Holme-upon-Spalding Moor was. They were not encouraged when they saw it was isolated, that there was nowhere near to go for a day off and it was miles from a railway station.

To rub it in, an advance inspection of the Waafery by a Canadian Officer had shown it quite inadequate for the Canadian ladies. Great improvements were planned for them.

The logistics of the move were complicated by the fact that we were to remain operational throughout.

We had to plan for both squadrons taking off from Linton, then while they were away over Germany, we were to belt across Yorkshire in the dark, and be ready to welcome them landing back at Holme-upon-Spalding Moor. At first, we thought it was a hoax, but it wasn't. I was allocated a large lorry and kept Mollie. On the day, a skeleton staff remained to get the planes away; the rest set off in advance. Their kit went by lorry. The total personnel were formed up and marched to the railway station. Mollie and I thought it was the funniest sight and hung out of the window, waving to our friends, until shooed in by an irate WAAF Officer.

I sent the bulk of the map store on ahead, keeping back what I fervently hoped would meet the needs for the coming operation. I was still appalled such a crazy scheme was going ahead. Mercifully the matter was settled by the Met.Office, who predicted 10/10 cloud all the way. No flying. Operation cancelled. It felt very strange when the station became almost deserted. Mollie and I spent our last night alone in the empty Waafery.

Next morning, we loaded a truck with the rest of the maps, chucked in our kitbags, plus a bedside rug I was not leaving for the Canadians, hoisted up our bicycles, clambered in ourselves and set off for our new camp.

CHAPTER
TWENTY

Middle of nowhere

Holme-upon-Spalding Moor proved to be as bleak as we feared, and it was only summer. The Waafery lay at the end of a long lane, signposted to the Land of Nod. Mollie and I planned to get off to a good start, so we dumped our kit in our Nissen hut and went across the fields to make the acquaintance of the nearest farmer's wife. We wanted to be first at the back door for a source of butter, eggs and fresh milk. We introduced ourselves and were treated most generously. Adjoining farms had some disease among their livestock, and there were dead piglets and lambs strewn around, but we tried to ignore them.

The Map Room was horrible. No window, only a desk, floor-to-ceiling racking, a step-ladder and a naked light bulb. All the maps were in heavy rolls. When opened up, they stayed obstinately curly. Getting the store operational was a challenge.

The shelving was not sufficiently shallow for only one type of map per shelf. To insert new stock single-handed at the bottom of a top shelf was a formidable task. Stuff already there had to be got down, the new put up and the balance put back on top. My technique for extracting a single map was to grasp the wad above the map I wanted with one hand. A vigorous flick of the wrist then lifted them for a brief moment, while I whipped out the required sheet with the other hand. It looked easy, but needed practice, particularly from the top of a wobbly step-ladder. If the stack was several inches thick, it couldn't be done; wads had to be lifted aside and then replaced. At the Innsworth Depot I noticed they were only taking girls over 5ft 9ins for Map Clerk training.

With two squadrons of long-range aircraft to supply, judging stock levels became tricky. I must never be short, but over-stocking presented severe storage and handling problems.

Admiralty charts were a headache. I held some to cover coastlines and ports. Not only were they useless for night-flying, but their large scale meant a lot of sheets to cover a small area. Added to which, I got frequent signals from the Admiralty giving up-dates on the position of buoys, beacons, wrecks etc. I was expected to make all the changes on each chart with a fine pen and Indian ink. Fat chance. It would have kept a couple of full-time cartographers busy. I tried to pick out anything important, and left the rest. They were seldom used, except occasionally at Briefing.

The only real mistake was made by GSGS, when they produced maps with the airfield at Detling, Kent, in the wrong place. This certainly had to be amended, as it was an emergency landing place for damaged planes unable to get back to base.

The rate of operational losses continued to be dreadful and the atmosphere was brittle. Replacement crews and planes could scarcely keep the squadrons up to strength. Although the better methods of navigation had greatly improved accuracy and effectiveness, the price in crews and aircraft was not sustainable. Anti-aircraft fire accounted for many casualties, but night-fighters, directed by ground-based radar, took the greatest toll. Radar picked up the position of approaching aircraft by the radio echoes to which they gave rise. One possible counter-measure was jamming, but that could jeopardise any aircraft carrying a jammer; fighters carrying suitable receivers could home in on it.

Another way was to use reflectors, with the purpose of hoaxing the enemy into believing either that a) you are where you are not, or b) not where you are. The reflectors, code-named "Window", were thin aluminium strips, whose length was equal to half the wavelength being used by the enemy radar. As they tumbled slowly through the air, the resonances from a few hundred strips, each 25 x 2cms., could imitate the energy given out by a Halifax. The material was produced and made up into packets, each weighing about 1lb. The idea was that the leading aircraft in a bomber stream would drop these, at the rate of a bundle a minute, to produce a "smokescreen" through which the following aircraft could fly. Although Window was ready for operational use by April 1942, arguments within the Air Ministry raged. Prof. R. V. Jones had put up the idea in 1937, but he had to battle against dinosaurs. The main argument against its use was fear of reciprocation. These arguments were ill-founded, because by 1942, what remained of the German bomber force was tied up on the Russian front. Prof. Jones had a meeting with Churchill and the deadlock was finally broken. Churchill gave the go-ahead and authorised the use of Window from 23rd July, 1943.

John Crampton, skipper of Halifax "Q for Queenie", gives a crew's eye view of Window. "The bundles of Window, dumped beside each aircraft before take-off, were frequently wrapped in old newspapers or brown paper, all tied up with rough wartime string. Having ejected Window, many aircraft returned with an untidy mess of paper and string littering the fuselage. But not the Queen Of All The Skies! Q for Queenie always returned spick and span because Flash Gordon, our wireless operator whose duty it was to chuck Window out, reckoned that it wasn't Window that foxed the Hun, but the brown paper and string which was ceremonially shovelled down the chute next to Flash's seat. "Best rubbish dump in the world down there, Skipper!"

Mollie and I wanted to get some riding during the summer evenings, so we approached our friendly farmer. To our surprise, he was glad to get his horses exercised. It was arranged that Mollie, who was competent, would ride a pony which, though broken, was scarcely schooled. I was to ride the farmer's hunter, a great brute with a mouth of iron. Before lending me his horse, he naturally wanted to see me ride. I mounted and circled the field. I was not really capable at all, but I looked better than I was and he was satisfied. He usually brought both horses in from the field and saddled them for us. Mounted on this ill-assorted pair, we rode for miles round the Yorkshire countryside. One evening, my horse had been brought into the loose box, but it was up to me to get its bridle and saddle on. It played me up. It stuck its nose high in the air, so that I could not reach to get the bit in its mouth and the bridle on. It blew out its stomach, so that I could not get the girth done up. The farmer turned up, cursed the horse, dug it hard in the ribs with his elbow, and mocked my feebleness.

Nothing went right that evening. My hunter bolted and Mollie's pony followed. On the grass verge it was safe enough, but I could see that we were heading for tarmac. As long as I thundered along, Mollie had no hope of stopping. Unable to stop by orthodox means, I gave an almighty tug on one rein as we came to a bush. It was scratchy, but we stopped.

After that episode, we walked sedately for a while, until we came to a fork in the road, with a grass triangle at the junction. I wanted to go to the right, but the horse fancied left. We slogged it out. If I did not win then, I knew I would never control it again. It bucked, it reared. I needed a third hand, two to hold its head straight, and another to whack its rump with the stick I had been given, and told to use if necessary.

In the end it was a draw. I slid off, led it the way I wanted to go, and remounted. I was exhausted and my hands were bleeding. To finish off a very unsuccessful evening, a violent thunderstorm broke over us. We finally got back to camp, utterly drenched, utterly limp.

The nearest village was some miles away, but we sometimes cycled there on a day off and patronised a services canteen run mainly for the army in the area. One day, there were some tanks parked outside and I was offered a ride in the clattering, vibrating, shattering, deafening monster.

I stood with my head sticking out of the turret, as we rumbled along the road and then across the moors. It was exhilarating, but the noise was overwhelming and every bone and organ was rattled and shaken. On the return trip, I was invited to drive. That added a yawing movement to everything else, as I found it difficult to steer by co-ordinating the two tracks. Steering a plane, a tank and a horse had all proved hard. My trusty bicycle was best.

It was high time I went away for some leave. Looking after two squadrons was tough, particularly during the summer when there were fewer cancellations due to weather. I was very pleased to leave Mollie in charge in my absence.

Having a university degree was rare in girls of our age then, and Mollie understandably felt that she should be an officer. Her parents thought she should be an officer, so did her fiancé. Our views on the matter of being commissioned differed. She wanted to be an officer first and foremost, but was not all that particular about trade. I would have been very happy to be commissioned in Intelligence/Operations, but that had been closed to WAAF for years; there were ex-aircrew needing that kind of job. I preferred to remain a Corporal doing interesting work.

At that time, there was to be one intake of WAAF Signal Officers, and the OCOps insisted that my name should go forward. In vain, I explained that I would be untrainable. Despite my distinguished grandfather, a pioneer of the telephone, I had never mastered the principles of that, let alone wireless and radar. My protests were swept aside. I earned a bogus aura of modesty, and he recommended me in glowing terms. This spurred Mollie on and, heedless of my warnings that she might be sent somewhere awful, she applied for the only trade then available: Equipment.

Unfortunately, my doom-laden prophecies were fulfilled. She was duly commissioned and sent to a rat-infested warehouse beside the Manchester Ship Canal, in charge of a rough crew of civilian dockers. The crowning indignity was having to live at home with her parents, as there was no RAF mess in the area.

I went on leave, with my free rail pass made out for Cornwall. Mother and I were invited to stay with friends from our Padstow days, Sir Cecil and Lady Carr. This was Mother's first return to the area, since her bitter divorce, some ten years earlier. She had many friends to see round Padstow and Rock. I was fascinated to see it again through adult eyes, having left so sadly as a ten-year-old.

The Carr's house was a beauty. The wide bay-windows of the sitting-room faced south-west, with cushioned window seats for enjoying a panoramic view of the Estuary. Norman Wilkinson, a distinguished war artist in both World Wars, was a friend of theirs and they had several of his fine marine paintings. It was my first introduction to first-class contemporary painting.

The week was marred for me by a virulent tummy bug, which left me prostrate until it was time to return. I had no chance to go to Padstow. Efforts to contact an RAF MO in the area, to get sick leave, came to nothing. Still unfit, I made my way back to Bromley and on to Yorkshire. Mother saw how groggy I was and gave me a flask of brandy to take with me. Wartime travel was slow and the trip comprised a walk to the bus, a train to London, Tube across London, train to Yorkshire, bus to the village and a long trudge to the Land of Nod and the Waafery. The last mile was too much.

My legs were wobbly and I felt faint. Luckily I had not scoffed all the brandy on the way, so I proceeded by walking a bit, then sitting on the grass verge and having a swig of brandy, then tottering on again. I came to the end of my strength and the brandy, so just sat. A passing truck stopped, and the driver drove me straight to the sick bay on the main camp. I was a fool to have come back. After being ill for a while, the MO discovered the very long and erratic hours I had been working over a long period, without adequate rest. It was time to get away from an operational station for another spell. And I had missed my opportunity to, maybe, become a Signals Officer.

Another quiet call to the HQBC Map Officer explained the need to send a competent replacement, as Mollie was leaving too. Margot arrived and I was happy to hand over to her. She had been properly trained at Harrow on the next course after mine in 1941. Mollie went off to her OCTU. I took some sick leave and then reported to RAF Pershore, thankful to be off the Yorkshire Moors before winter set in, and away from the depressing rate of aircrew losses. I was resigned to a boring job in the Navigation Section again. I had been upset when I left Waterbeach, but leaving Holme-upon-Spalding Moor was different. I had not had the same personal involvement with the two squadrons. The sheer numbers involved, coupled with the sadly short time some of them were with us, meant I did not get to know the crews so well. The work was heavy, the hours were long, sleep was inadequate.

Also, as a southerner amongst WAAFs mainly from the Midlands, friendships, apart from Mollie, were not automatic. All in all, Pershore had plenty to offer to offset the lack of value in the job.

CHAPTER
TWENTY-ONE

I can, Can-Can

Little by little, my attitude and outlook changed. From schoolgirl to bank clerk, through air-raids, nights in the cellar, then gladly, if warily, into the new world of the RAF. I'd become dedicated to my personal war-winning, with an overdone sense of self-importance. I'd felt No. 99 Squadron could not manage without me, been disappointed when taken out by appendicitis, then fretted at being non-operational at Harwell. Back with the real action at Linton and Spalding Moor, things were far grimmer, gone the cheerful insouciant air and relaxed atmosphere of Waterbeach 1941.

Four years of war had left its mark on all of us and we were more aware of the global spread of the conflict. All war news seemed bad, and going home on leave brought us up against the drab and difficult life of civilians, struggling to feed families on meagre rations, to clothe them by mending and patching. Curtains were closed at night to show no chink of light, streets unlit, petrol was only for essential work.

The WAAF took care of our housing, albeit damp and cold, and our clothing, which was of reasonable quality. Our food was plentiful, if sloppily cooked and served. I knew now how to be so hungry that even food I did not like was welcome. Anything, bar rabbit and coconut, was acceptable, and there was no coconut.

By the time I left Yorkshire, I was ready for the lighter atmosphere of the Operational Training Unit at Pershore, Worcestershire. I was prepared to modify my personal responsibility for winning the war. All those bombs dropped, all those crews lost, and still we did not feel we were winning. Thanks to Churchill, losing was never an option, never envisaged.

I was ready to allow closer friendships, but implacably opposed to relationships with married men and no sex yet. This view was shared by my WAAF friends. The ground rules were well understood. Keep clear of the point of no return. Lots of optimists tried, but appreciated that my "No" meant "No". I had no real problems. I was ready to enjoy camp life, with dances, concerts, films, and sports, to sleep through every night and work routine days. There were no private parties, all entertainment was there for everyone. For dances, a group went together. If you could dance and/or were reasonably attractive, partners were plentiful.

Vital manoeuvring came at the end, to ensure the right partner for the last waltz — "Who's taking you home tonight, after the dance is through . . . ." If you misjudged it and did not fancy being escorted to the Waafery by the partner you had landed with, it was quickly into the Ladies, whisper, giggle and slip out with some others, bless the black-out and scamper away.

The Waafery was the usual cluster of Nissen huts on a very wet site, the bedding on our double-deck bunks and our clothes were often damp. It was great to be in a hut with such congenial company, with girls who worked in Signals, Flying Control and Operations. We had much in common and the atmosphere was good. It was easy-going and life seemed southern comfort after the rigours of Yorkshire. We got along fine, a bit sorry for one girl engaged to her wonderful Julian. She lived for letters from him. We thought Julian a ball and chain.

I shared with Gay, she had the bottom bunk, I the top. She was interested in acting and a concert party was formed by the Entertainments Officer, who had assumed the role of producer. He was an awkward character and, as he was the Assistant Navigation Officer, I saw him daily. He was often sarcastic and offensive and I found myself being drawn in to smooth down feathers he had ruffled.

It was not easy to organise that type of undertaking, with the practical difficulties of shift workers, leave and postings. With Gay's help, I wrote a sketch in doggerel, an irreverent skit on our camp life. It was facetious, but funny, and it went down very well. The cast was about a dozen, with Gay in the leading role. The other half of the show had singers, a chorus line and a Can-Can. What started off just for local amusement became far more ambitious. The Station Commander's wife had been "on the stage" and coached the dancers.

I was sent to London to hire costumes. My list was:- one set of cowboy/cowgirl outfits for "Deep in the

Heart of Texas"; a set of pretty dresses for the girls and flannels, blazers and boaters for the men, for "Me and My Girl"; one set of Can-Can frou-frous. Black fishnet tights were unobtainable, so we formed a circle and each drew on the legs of the girl in front, using eyebrow pencil. It was quite effective, but hell to get off afterwards. For the finale, national costumes of the Allied countries. All these were packed into two wicker hampers and brought back to the Station.

Finally the First Night. Although it was pretty bad, it was a smash hit.

Requests came to take it to other stations. After a short break the company was re-formed to fulfil a busy "touring" programme. Inevitably postings had depleted the cast and I got drawn further in, first in the back row of the chorus. I couldn't sing very well and had no dance training, but was amazed to find it was fun dressing-up and making-up. Given strong enough footlights to render the audience virtually invisible, I didn't feel self-conscious and could fool around and improvise. With concentrated practice in the hut during the evenings, I mastered the Can-Can and lined up with the others, for once my long legs being an advantage.

The costume felt wonderful. Over frilly knickers went layers of frou-frou petticoats, topped with a low-cut dress and a black velvet choker round the throat. A large-brimmed black velvet hat swept up, topped with red curled ostrich feathers.

In a whirl of petticoats, lights and music, we burst onto the stage, exhilarated and transformed from our everyday selves. The curtain had to fall smartly as we crashed into our final "splits". It looked fine from the front, but in fact a spare leg was folded under. There was no graceful way to rise and a quick check needed to see we could all still walk before the curtain rose again and we made our exit in a line, waving as we went. It was bliss and always a hit with our audiences. One night a small barking terrier got on stage, just as we were finishing our Can-Can, nipping at us as we made our exit. He was the highlight of the show that night, but not readily repeatable.

My boss remarked : "I never realised you had legs." The battle-dress I normally wore was more suitable for a role as the back end of a pantomime elephant.

We took the show to a Station which had an awkward stage, with wings only on one side, so we re-organised entrances and exits. It all seemed to work well enough. We were therefore puzzled by the frosty atmosphere when we were entertained in the Officers' Mess afterwards. It finally dawned the sketch was the trouble. There was a scene where a plane came in unexpectedly to make an emergency landing. The duty RAF and WAAF had to dash hurriedly into Flying Control to cope. Because entrances and exits were confined to one side of the stage, the RAF and WAAF both came on from the same side, dressing as they came, with obvious implications. Vainly we tried to explain, but the damage was done. Our name was mud and we were very upset.

At one performance, Gay was away on leave, so I took her part, but my stage-fright was numbing.

Although I'd written the thing and knew every word perfectly, once on stage, panic gripped me and I could not remember my lines so the rest of the cast had to nurse me through. I was quite happy on stage so long as I did not have to say anything; a speaking part was beyond me. I never risked it again.

A notice went up for volunteers to train as Air Transport Auxiliary pilots. Gay and I rashly put our names down, thinking of their glamorous uniforms, with fore-and-aft caps and pilots' wings. I could never have gone through with it. I was not brave enough. Called for Medicals, we failed on eyesight. Whew! What a let-off.

A new Station Commander arrived. The poor man got off to a bad start, as he had some skin trouble. His chin was unshaven and painted with gentian violet. In addition, a nasty nick-name followed him, the only malevolent one I ever came across. An earlier operational tour had apparently included too many sorties when an assortment of mechanical faults had caused him to turn back before reaching his target. So the Group Captain "Blank" became known as Dutch Coast "Blank".

He thought our discipline was slack and we needed Smartening Up. The band, which until then had only produced dance music, was instructed to practice martial music, in readiness for the introduction of a new weekly Station Parade. We were not good at that sort of thing.

The Station Warrant Officer, with many years of regular service behind him, came into his finest hour.

The football pitch sported new white lines in most unsporting places. On the command, "Markers" had to march out first and take up position. The rest had to fall in and form up, in three ranks, on the markers. Being tall, I was the WAAF marker.

On the "fall-in" command, everyone ran about in an unmilitary muddle and the band's martial music kept veering off into little syncopated swingy bits. The CO fumed, the SWO sweated. Finally all was reasonably straight, and the Chaplain stepped forward to take Prayers. The SWO barked : "Fall-out the Roman Catholics and Jews." With no indication of where they were supposed to go, they hung around in embarrassment on the touch-line. The Chaplain intoned the prayers, which were inaudible. Then it was "Fall-in the Roman Catholics and Jews". By this time everyone had entered into the spirit of the farcical occasion and the gaps where the R.Cs and Jews had been standing had gently closed up. They scurried up and down the ranks seeking sanctuary. The joke was not meant to be on them, of course, and they were soon kindly absorbed, with the exception of one scarlet-faced airman. Now livid, the CO intervened. "Airman, what is your name?" "Brown, sir."

"Who was standing next to Brown?" Up went a forest of hands. "Here, sir; here, sir . . . " The CO's pep-talk was carried away on the wind, even the front rank could not catch a word of it. Another Station Parade was never ordered, but we got the message and set to with vigour to Smarten Up.

The path to the Navigation Section was lined with big stones, to stop trucks going on the grass. Nearby was a heap of coal. A bucket of whitewash and a brush were procured from the Sports Shed. Such a transformation! Spanking white coal, immaculate white stones. We were supposed to be camouflaged. A week of juvenile joking was greatly enjoyed, and then we all relaxed into our happy old ways. We were not really sloppy and we all worked hard. After years of war, a touch of levity was in order.

We came to the end of our concert party tours, and the costumes went back to London. It had been a heavy schedule, going off to do shows at night, often getting back very late.

A few weeks later, I went home on leave. Sleeping in the cellar as usual, we heard an unusual-sounding plane, the engine note different from the usual drone. A sudden silence and we thought the ack-ack had got it. Then an almighty crump and we all flinched. Had the plane crashed in our garden? Apprehensive, we went upstairs and peeped out through the curtains, but it was a dark night and we could see nothing. Armed with pokers and torch, we ventured timidly into the garden, but found nothing; mystified, we went back to our bunks.

With chilling certainty, the truth dawned on me. Flying bombs! I knew about these terrifying weapons from intelligence reports. I was frightened, but could not even tell the family until the BBC made the news public. I felt vulnerable and angry and was concerned to be going back to the relative safety of camp and leaving my family behind.

A week away from a wet hut meant damp blankets, so we always took care to air the bedding for anyone returning from leave. Somehow there was a muddle over when I was expected and I came back to a cold wet bed and shivered all night. A severe sore throat developed and I was quickly really ill and lay miserably in my bunk. The girls brought me food from the NAAFI, but I could scarcely swallow it. Someone went to the WAAF Admin Officer on my behalf, and was sent back to tell me to report sick in the ordinary way at the main camp. I got up, dressed, got my bike and set off.

About half way, a truck passed me and I wobbled right off the road, on to the grass verge and just lay there, past caring. The driver, very perturbed, came back, saw my plight with croaky voice and trickling tears. He tenderly helped me into the truck, put the bike in the back and drove me to the door of Sick Quarters. The MO, whom I knew well and who would have helped me, was not there. I was given throat lozenges and one day off sick.

I do not remember how I got back to my hut. Gay returned from leave, was shocked at my state and stormed straight off to get help. Mercifully, my friendly MO was back. He arrived with an ambulance. I was put on a stretcher, my tin hat and respirator balanced on top, and I was on my way to the RAF Hospital in Evesham.

CHAPTER
TWENTY-TWO

Red ties, scarlet women

At Evesham RAF Hospital, the MO asked me to open my mouth. Impossible. That's why I was there. His instant diagnosis: tonsils to be removed. I had none, they were taken out years before. Confidence in MO zero. M & B drugs were new, the panacea for all things, so they were prescribed and I was tucked up in the WAAF General Ward. Gay telephoned Mother, who faced a difficult journey to be with me. She arrived next day, but had not been warned that a side effect of the drug was to turn the patient an alarming shade of mauve. She saw her daughter with the left side of her face so swollen that only the tips of the eyelashes were visible and the jaw-line vanished under swelling that ran from nose to ear and straight down the neck.

Mother found lodgings and stayed several weeks, until it seemed safe to leave me in the capable care of the Ward Sister. When I recovered a bit, I found that the hospital comprised five hutted wards, each with twenty beds. No 1: RAF Surgical. No.2: RAF Medical. No.3: WAAF General. Nos.4 & 5: WAAF Venereal Disease.

For a month, I had hot "Kaolin" poultices slapped on my face and heavily bandaged. I had to remain propped up on pillows, day and night, with a "donkey"

246

bolster under my knees. I craved above all to be able to snuggle down to sleep like everyone else.

The pain was severe if I moved or was touched. One Sister was a gem of skill, understanding and humour. The other was not. She should have been "at the Front", with buckets of blood, amputating limbs. She was heavy-handed and I dreaded her changing my poultice. One day, she decided to scrub the walls of the ward and advanced with bucket and brush. Without warning, she yanked my bed away from the wall so roughly that I yelled. My scream summoned the angel sister. Bucket, brush and sister vanished and she was not seen again on our ward.

Little by little, my swelling subsided until I could get a spoon in; bliss, after feeding for weeks with a straw which went through a handy gap in my teeth on the unaffected side.

Visiting doctors were brought to have a look at me. Zoo time. "Very interesting. Never seen anything like it." One had a better idea though and, God forgive him, he carried it out. He reckoned that under the swelling, which was hard as an apple, there must be fluid he could draw off. He brought a syringe, borrowed from the local vet by the look of it. I was laid on my side, without any anaesthetic, while he drove the needle in, pressing me forcibly into the pillow. Up plunger, empty. Withdraw needle, lifting me off the pillow by my neck. No luck, try again. I fainted.

In time, I progressed until I could join the other walking-wounded from the ward and wander out into the town. As hospital inmates, we had to wear red ties in place of our usual black. In the eyes of the local people, red ties signalled V.D. There were seldom more than half a dozen of us, but maybe 30 or more from the V.D. wards, including a familiar face, "The Station Bicycle". We were spat on, nudged into the gutter, moved away from in the cinema, banned from entering local service canteens, with the shining exception of the Toc H, who took pity on us. We put in a request to Matron to be allowed to wear our black ties, but were turned down flat on the premise that it would make the V.D. girls feel conspicuous.

On sunny days, we hired a rowing boat to go on the river. I usually rowed as the rest had wounds or broken limbs. My next-bed neighbour, Pat, had come a purler off her bike, broken her arm and ground grit into her face. Kate had tangled with a tank, getting her hand trapped between the track and its wheel. Others had had appendicitis, and so on. So I rowed.

We were to be inspected by the Princess Royal, who held some high honorary rank in the WAAF. Everything was polished and polished again. Laid out on a table were some awful bits of embroidery we had done to please the occupational therapist, mine outstandingly hideous.

The lucky ones in bed could just lie there and not wrinkle their bedclothes. The rest of us had to stand by the end of our beds. The girl opposite me was a funny East-Ender. She had lost all her hair from shock when she was buried under the rubble of her house when a bomb hit it. She even made that sound hilarious. Her new hair was coming through as pale golden fuzz.

We waited and waited and waited. By the time the retinue arrived, I should have been back in bed, for I tired very quickly. The Princess picked up my vile tray cloth and "admired" it. My cockney chum winked at me and I started to giggle and could not stop. I shook, tears streamed down my face. I was ashamed, but couldn't stop. I apologised to Sister as soon as I could. She understood and generously blamed herself for not putting me back to bed earlier. Matron was a touch frosty, but accepted my apology gracefully enough. HRH must have thought we were a mental ward.

May 20th was my twenty-first birthday. I woke to find several over-bed tables had been put together across my bed and smothered with flowers. In addition, a crowd from Pershore had organised a celebratory dinner for 20 at the local hotel. Pat and I got special permission to go, had black ties brought in for us, and set about getting ready. Pat's face was still pitted and scarred and mine had strange marks and bruises round one eye. My hair also looked weird, due to inexpert cutting with nail scissors and a bare area where the careless aim of Kaolin poultices had scorched away a 2ins. swathe down the left side. We set about each other with liberal application of Max Factor pancake make-up till our scars were hidden, though we looked like circus clowns. We went to the party, both unfit and groggy, but it was a great occasion and much appreciated. We tottered back to bed and lay there all the next day, too exhausted to stir, tactfully ignored by Sister.

When Pat was due for discharge, a problem arose over her dog. Against Regulations, she had a dachshund. We were used to seeing it patter down the ward to her bed, well ahead of the visitor bringing it. To be ready to go on sick leave with her, it had to be brought in two days in advance and hidden from Matron's sharp eyes. At night, the nurse kept it in her office. During the day, patients took it in turns to keep it in the garden. During Matron's morning inspection round, the only safe place was in my bed, where it lay quietly under my raised knees until the danger had passed.

Peter, my brother, was in England having returned from a long spell in North Africa, Sicily and Italy with 50 Div. Now they were all back, preparing for the invasion of Europe. He came to see me, an impressive sun-tanned Royal Engineers Captain, with one of the first Africa Star ribbons on his tunic. He was shocked that I had been in hospital so long, with no satisfactory diagnosis or treatment. He went to see the Medical C.O., spoke forcefully and extracted a promise that a specialist would be called in. Not long after Peter's visit I woke to hear the steady drone of planes overhead and rushed outside to see fleets of gliders being towed south. The Invasion was on and I was missing it. I fretted and fumed, deeply upset to be stuck in hospital when the day we had all been looking forward to had finally arrived. Peter might be in one of those gliders.

His remonstrations with our C.O. brought results. An Air Vice-Marshal Medical Officer was coming to see me. Matron fussed nearly as hard as she did for the

Princess Royal. When the great man examined me, he clearly had no more idea than anyone else and suggested I should be "boarded out", in other words, discharged as medically unfit. This was too much. I was already smarting from missing the Invasion and in no mood to be chucked out into dreary civilian life at this stage of the war. My indignation overcame any fleeting respect for his rank. He relented. I could go on a month's sick leave, once my blood-count was normal. If I then passed a medical, I could stay.

After three months, I went home to convalesce. Mother was worried about Peter in France, but relieved to have me home. I had not seen myself in the mirror during the bad times. I learned what a shocking sight I had been. Full marks to my mother, brother and all the friends who came to see me, never flinching or betraying their feelings at such a nasty sight. Over a long period, my face and neck recovered and I could turn my head again, but it was years before it all went away. When fit again and passed by a Medical Board, I returned to Pershore. Everything had changed. The Station had switched from Bomber to Transport Command. Most of my friends had left. I could not find any photographs of our Concert Party, no proof that I could do the Can-Can.

Forty years later, living in London, I met a neighbour who often wore an RAF tie; his face seemed familiar. The penny dropped. It was Dutch Coast "Blank". I cringed to think of all the rotten jokes at his expense, the nasty nick-name and the sketch I had

251

written which had sent him up so hilariously. He seemed delighted to reminisce, placed me as soon as I told him my maiden name. From his attic, he unearthed photos of the concert party, including the Can-Can. Now my family had to believe my unlikely tale of being a once-upon-a-time Can-Can dancer.

Pershore held no job for me now, so I rang the HQBC Map Officer. Still not strong enough for an Operational Station, I settled for Chipping Warden, an Operational Training Unit, near Banbury. The signal came a few days later, I expressed my customary surprise, collected my stuff together and made my way there.

CHAPTER
TWENTY-THREE

Trivial pursuits

Chipping Warden Waafery was a group of wooden huts in a woodland setting; crisp autumn leaves crackled underfoot. In a hut on the edge of the wood, I got a corner bed at the far end, away from the constant comings and goings by its main door. I unrolled my mat, a souvenir from Linton-on-Ouse. Quite snug, with a bedside locker, an ammunition box for clothes storage and a shelf from which to dangle anything liable to be eaten by field mice, who nosed into everything. I also treasured a radio made for me by a friend out of bits and pieces. It worked for him, but for me it crackled and stuttered.

When the cold weather came, the advantages of a corner bed faded a bit and perhaps those nearer to the central stove had an advantage, although shortage of fuel restricted its use. We scoured the wood for fallen branches we could burn and I am afraid one or two five-bar gates became four-bar gates. With only sodden green wood and a handful of coke, it was hard to get the stove alight, despite liberal sprinklings of Silvo and Brasso.

At night, we wore our issue pyjamas, plus sweater, socks, mittens, balaclava helmet and a scarf and still were not warm. By day, I often wore my pyjama trousers under my battle dress to prevent chapped legs from chafing by the harsh cloth. Chilblains on fingers and toes burned and itched, rheumatism needled into shoulders.

Regular kit inspections were held, when our official kit had to be meticulously laid out on the bed, while the WAAF Admin Officer did her round, checking nothing was missing and appraising the polished state of the brown linoleum of each bed space. Every day, polish, polish, polish; cap badge, buttons, shoes and lino. Someone always had something missing. The trick was to pass along the wanted item from a bed that had already been checked, getting it to its destination unobserved before the omission was noticed. It brightened up a dull procedure.

Expecting kit inspection one day, I opened my bomb box to get out the never-worn "blackouts" to lay out with the rest, but they were moving about. A field mouse had chosen them for a nest for her young and, bless her, had nibbled them extensively. With glee, I bore them off to the stores, at last able show them "worn out" and exchange them for the more wearable "Knickers grey rayon locknit directoire WAAF for the use of." Known as "twilights".

Because I was the N.C.O. in charge of the hut, I had one valuable privilege. Instead of daily stacking my three "biscuits" and folding the bedding in the exact manner laid down in King's Regulations, I could leave my bed made up all day. When life was rough, such trivial pleasures were sweet.

It was a long cycle ride from the Waafery to the main camp, where we went for work and meals. The trip could be much quicker by a short cut round the perimeter track and across the end of the main runway. Rightly, this unsafe route was forbidden. If caught, I was ready to say that I was visiting one of the planes at dispersal. I got careless, failing to notice an incoming bomber till it whooshed over my head, caught me in its slipstream and sent me and my bike sailing though the air to land gently in long grass some distance away.

In Navigation, the instructors were all aircrew with operational tours safely behind them. Among them, Hugh. A bit older than the rest, from North Wales where his parents ran a pub. He had been a Borstal Officer. His charges were fortunate to have such a compassionate and understanding man, but he had scars that showed some of his lads were slow to appreciate him. I saw his goodness to trainee aircrew. He brought one terrified young airgunner to the privacy of my office, so that he could talk to him in his native Welsh.

Few of us were old enough to have done much before the war and the difference in maturity was marked. In many ways, the war had made us wise beyond our years, but within limited parameters. Hugh had always refused promotion to commissioned rank, preferring to remain a Warrant Officer, a rare NCO aircrew rank, most being Sergeants or Flight-Sergeants, but his seniority and character merited something higher. He was as keen on dancing as I was, so we were instant friends.

255

Just before my arrival he had become engaged to marry the WAAF Admin Sergeant. She was highly regarded by everyone, a few years older than most, accentuated by grey hair. She had been posted away to OCTU, to become an Admin Officer. Hugh was such a nice man and we went off to every dance in the neighbourhood, cycling up to ten miles each way. Sometimes we cycled all the way to a tiny pub opposite Sulgrave Manor, George Washington's birthplace. It was worth the long ride to have bacon and eggs and sit comfortably round a fire, away for once from the constant bustle of a big Station.

Another Instructor was a giant man called, inevitably, "Tiny". He had been a professional wrestler, was a gentle lamb and very shy. Hugh and I undertook to teach him to dance. Although so huge, his wrestler's training had made him well-balanced and light on his feet. He progressed well. One evening, we fixed to meet him at a village dance a long way from camp. Hugh and I cycled and Tiny came on his motorbike. While Tiny and I danced, Hugh found more partners for him, as he was still too shy to ask them himself.

At the end of a successful evening, it was late and I risked being on a charge if not back in time. Hugh gallantly offered to ride his own bike and wheel mine, so that I could return on the pillion of Tiny's motorbike. We set off, but the lights soon failed. Our only light was a feeble beam from my pencil torch which I shone over his shoulder, which was too high for me to see over. Thus we got along, sometimes on the road, sometimes on the verge, sometimes nearly in the ditch. Finally arriving safely back, I congratulated him on his masterly steering. He modestly replied that he had steered where I pointed the torch. Poor Tiny had a problem. He'd married a petite bride, without considering if they were physically matched. Their honeymoon was sad.

As Hugh's wedding date drew inexorably nearer, he became despondent. He felt that perhaps his fiancée had rail-roaded him into the engagement and he had been weak to go along with it. If I would have married him, he would have broken it off, but much as I liked him, marriage, no.

He went on leave to face a slap-up smart wedding, as befitted the daughter of a Brigadier. The bride, now an Officer, expected him to accept the often-offered commission, so that they could be posted to the same Station.

While he was away, came the scarcely believable news. The war in Europe was over. VE Day. With the relief, the almost disbelief that it was finished at last, came the dawning realisation that we could all stop what we were doing. No more bombing. We were redundant.

A friend came back after flying over Rugby, seeing it no longer blacked out. We resolved to go and see this marvel on the ground. We worked out a complex timetable of bicycle/bus/train to get there and back. Perhaps it did not look all that spectacular when we got there, but we felt the trip was worthwhile and a suitable way to celebrate.

He asked me out again a few days later and I suggested bacon and eggs at Sulgrave. We walked into the pub parlour and there, sitting disconsolately alone by the fire, was Hugh.

He had returned early from a disastrous honeymoon, rendered impotent by the realisation of the mistake he'd made. My arrival at the Station had been unfortunate for him, but if his engagement was so frail that I unwittingly shattered it, he was foolish to have gone ahead. His kind heart had over-ruled his head. To the surprise of all but me, he still declined the offer of a commission. As a Warrant Officer, he could not serve on the same Station as his Officer wife. I never knew how the story ended. I hope he untangled his life and found happiness.

After many years, a batch of WAAFs were to be commissioned as Intelligence Officers. Although the European war was over, the Japanese war was still raging, seemingly doomed to run for ever. I was posted to OCTU at Bowness-on-Windermere. I gave away my wonky radio, my gramophone and records which had been played over and over so many times, but never got stale. Bing Crosby, Frank Sinatra, The Inkspots, Hutch and the Andrews Sisters. My prized little carpet was abandoned and I was stripped down to my official kit list, my "twilights" still as good as new.

So, with many mixed feelings, I left. Sad to leave the easy companionship and freedom of being part of something big. The atrocious living conditions were irrelevant weighed against the riches of friendship and solidarity which we took for granted and which I have never found again in such abundance.

After four years, the art of living surrounded by a mesh of rules and regulations was finely tuned. I had never been up on a charge, not because I never broke the rules. I tried not to transgress in front of the Admin staff. If I was going to be late back to camp, I made sure I was really late, so that the duty NCO would be in bed and asleep. Now that my job as Map Clerk had lost its relevance, it was the right moment to be moving on. I went off to OCTU with a feeling of rising excitement.

CHAPTER
TWENTY-FOUR

Eight in the Bridal Suite

Daffodils trumpeted spring, sunlight sparkled on the lake, riffled by the breeze. Home for the next two months at OCTU was the Belsfield Hotel, Bowness-on-Windermere, with lecture rooms in the Old England Hotel, by the water's edge. It was hard to concentrate on lectures when the eye wandered to the window framing a perfect picture-postcard view of the lake up to Ambleside.

On arrival, beds were allocated and I shared the Bridal Suite with seven other Cadets. Only eight to one bathroom, with constant hot water, was sumptuous luxury. We had fitted carpets and no lino to polish.

Our first task was to fit white Officer Cadets' bands round our caps and to write our names on white tape to be sewn above the top left hand pocket. Having a name 14 letters+hyphen long and using rather large letters, my tape stretched right across the width of the pocket. When I lined up next day beside a Cadet with a short name written in small letters, the Officer gave us long hard look. Were we being cheeky? Our innocent expressions, followed by apologetic regret and keenness to make amends were perhaps a shade overdone. I shortened my tape; she lengthened hers. On the basis that no-one-would-do-anything-so-silly, we escaped censure, just. This was clearly no place to lark about.

I was pleased to find Margot on the course and hear how she had got on at Holme-upon-Spalding Moor after she took over the Map Store from me. Crew losses had continued to be dreadful. I was glad to have left when I did.

Our days were filled with button-polishing, shoe-polishing, uniform-pressing, lectures, note-taking, drill and P.T. There was a lot to do and it had to be done properly. After a while, I realised I had given up smoking. It was not a conscious choice, I had every minute of the day filled, leaving no time or wish for a cigarette. I have never smoked since.

An RAF Drill Sergeant marched us up and down on the car park by the edge of the lake. As we got better, we began to enjoy it, except for one unfortunate girl with no sense of co-ordination. The harder she tried, the more her left arm would go forward with her left foot, her right with her right. Off duty we tried and tried to help her, singing marching songs, tying her wrists to the girl in front, but it was no good. We had not only to learn to march properly, but to take big parades, acting different roles from Parade Adjutant to Inspecting Officer. It was straightforward enough to be on the receiving end of orders, but to be put out in front was terrifying. Our course had only fifteen girls on it, but other courses there at the same time made up a large body of girls. We each had to be able to get everyone onto the Parade Ground, formed up, dressed and presented for Inspection. On my first effort, I was doing all right up to the moment when I gave an order to move, without first bringing them from "At Ease" to "Attention". The reaction was for everybody to try to step forward, but unable to do so with feet still apart. The effect was of wind rippling through a cornfield, as they swayed forward in unison.

Margot and I were prepared to work hard, we had to, but we also wanted to make the most of our surroundings. We found rowing boats for hire and often went on the lake in the evenings. A flying boat base was at the head of the lake. We held our breath each time one of the heavy Sunderlands took off. They did not use the length of the lake as a runway, but took-off across the narrow head of water, getting just enough lift to get away through a cleft in the surrounding hills.

At week-ends we explored further afield. Our course-mates thought we were naughty to go off enjoying ourselves, instead of studying our notes. The lure of the Lake District overcame any twinges of conscience and we had a wonderful time. We hired bicycles, hitch-hiked, took buses and, above all, walked. After the austerity we were used to, we were in a different world, right away from the wartime atmosphere of food shortages, rationing and air-raids. Bacon, eggs, meat, butter, cream all seemed plentiful

262

and we had splendid high teas, all home-made and generously served.

The owners of a small hotel in Grasmere warmly welcomed us and invited us to stay for a weekend. Greatly daring, we asked for an overnight pass and got it without demur. We had a lovely break there. We were both pressed to consider coming back to the hotel after we were demobbed, to join the staff and be trained in hotel management.

The OCTU course progressed and as the end came in sight, life became serious. Perhaps not everyone would pass. Failure meant returning ignominiously to the ranks, the new uniform for which we already had been measured, never worn.

The function of the OCTU was not only to teach us King's Regulations and drill, but was also for turning us into Officers and Ladies, au fait with the etiquette of an Officers' Mess.

The habit of carrying our "irons" in the respirator case had gone. Now it was separate cutlery for separate courses, cruets, glasses and being waited on by orderlies. In the evenings before dinner, we toyed with dinky glasses of sherry, not paid for with vulgar cash, but put on our Mess bill for monthly settlement (i.e. deducted from our pay). We stood round making polite small-talk to each other under the ever-watchful eyes of the Officer Instructors, who held our fate in their hands. I found this pantomime a bit silly, but we needed it. Most of us had no idea how to behave in this formal setting and would have floundered if pitched into a serious Mess, making humiliating social blunders.

We were put through a series of tests and exams, but above all our future hung on the general impression we had made on the Officers who had watched us so closely. Would I be marked down for flippancy? Should Margot and I have stayed in, swotting with the others and foregoing the joys of the Lake District? It was too late now. The morning of the results fell on the day I was Duty Cadet, a normally mundane task. When the list of passes was read out, one name was missing. Poor girl, not only could she not march, but her gaucherie and shyness were a handicap. Now, poor soul, she had to go. As Duty Cadet, I went with her to her room, helped her pack, walked with her to the bus and saw her off.

She was out and away within an hour for the miserable trip home to tell her family she had been rejected. I waved her good-bye, both of us in tears.

Not one of the Officer Instructors came near. It was disgraceful. Anyone could see she would not have made an Admin Officer, but she had been selected as a potential Intelligence Officer, where she could have been brilliant. These factors should have been fully considered before even sending her on the course and the Instructors briefed accordingly.

To our amazement, Margot and I found ourselves top of the course, with only a few marks between us. At the final Passing-Out Parade, I had to march forward, halt, salute and be shaken by the hand, there being no actual sword of honour to present. I misjudged it, halting a pace too soon and had to lean forward over an invisible chasm to reach the outstretched hand of the C.O. To have got nearer and still had the proper foot to halt with, would have risked ending nose-to-nose with her. I saluted again, turned about and marched to take up a position at the head of the parade.

This we had not practised. Marching alone out in front was most disconcerting. I daren't listen to the footsteps behind and found it difficult to keep an even pace. A band would have helped. We got off the parade ground successfully, dismissed and hugged each other with relief and glee.

We packed and returned to London to collect our new made-to-measure smooth barathea uniforms. I was lucky, getting a greatcoat of Crombie cloth, which was no longer available. Most new officers had to make do with inferior Melton. A gabardine raincoat with a red/blue shot lining was extra welcome. Other ranks only had vile rubberised ground sheets, with a head hole, worn poncho-style. Shoes were still black lace-ups, but of supple leather in place of rigid pimply leather which took months to break-in, working on it with a bone to make it smooth. Topping all, a new cap with a handsome gold thread badge. Gorgeous.

I never returned to Grasmere, but Margot did. She was a darling, but unfortunately her size, plus the thick glasses she had to wear, hampered her social life. Plain girls are the vulnerable ones. Pretty ones have plenty of choice, they can discard the undesirables, safe in the knowledge that there are plenty more better men around. The plain girl does not have that self-confidence and can fall victim to the first rat that flatters. When a Polish pilot made advances, Margot fell heavily in love. She was demobbed and took up the Grasmere offer. All went along nicely, until the Pole turned up, scrounging for a job. He hung around for a while, working as a porter, but was so unsatisfactory he was sacked. Margot found herself pregnant. The Pole had vanished, she was distraught, refused to tell her family and made an unsuccessful attempt to drown herself in the lake.

I knew nothing of this tragedy while it was going on and was puzzled when my letters went unanswered. After a while, I got in touch with the hotel and heard the pitiful story. She had left them, had the baby, but left no address. Knowing she had a brother in London, I rang up all possible numbers, but without success. Several years later, travelling along Piccadilly in a bus, I saw Margot on the pavement, but by the time I could get off, she had vanished. I never heard from her again.

CHAPTER
TWENTY-FIVE

Enemy secrets

After a short leave, eight of us met at the Intelligence School, Highgate, joining a course with about 20 RAF. Most of the subjects were familiar, but it was interesting and a chance to shake off the girls' boarding school atmosphere of OCTU and get used to being an officer. I practised what I hoped was a suitable salute, quite different from the "longest way up, shortest way down" that had become second nature. My new salute conveyed gracious thanks to the person who'd so courteously saluted me, with a hint of blasé boredom to show I'd been an officer for absolutely ages. Acknowledging salutes took a bit of practice; it did not always dawn on me I was being saluted.

The first time I walked across the front of Buckingham Palace I passed two sentries before I realised they were jumping out of their sentry boxes to present arms and I was supposed to return their salutes. I kept to the other side of the road after that, except once for fun, with an already-demobbed boyfriend in civilian clothes. He'd never been saluted there, and did not quite believe me. He was a touch put-out when I got the full treatment. The guards did it to amuse themselves on a dull day.

Towards the end of the course, four WAAFs were interviewed, with no hint of the purpose. The arrangements seemed very ham cloak-and-dagger. We were driven to an unidentified spot and called, one at a time, into a caravan. I went in first and was addressed in English-schoolboy-German by a Group Captain. I could make out his question, but only reply in English, although I had taken German at school. Some general questions, in English, followed. I emerged, sure that whatever the mystery job might be, it would not be for me. We were all left in the dark, finding no common denominator.

Carol and I were picked and told to go to Latimer Station, where we would be met, but under instructions to tell no one of our destination. Still mystified and very glad of each other's company, we went. A driver with a staff car met us. After a while, we arrived at a barbed wire gate, with sentries. Passwords were exchanged, but it seemed we had come to the wrong entrance.

As the car was backed and turned, Carol and I clutched hands in shock. We had seen real Germans, in Luftwaffe uniforms. What had we come to? We drew up at the front door of a mansion and went in, still gawping. Our kit followed, off-loaded by the driver. Officers do not carry their own luggage. We were shown to a twin-bedded room in a modern annexe and left to unpack.

We whispered, trying to make sense of all we'd seen. Obviously it was some sort of Prisoner-Of-War camp. We did not dare ask where we were or what was going on. We were thankful to be sharing a room, so we could each pick up clues and compare notes. We reported to the Admin Office and were given a coded address to which all our mail should be sent. We wrote postcards home, giving our new address. There was nothing for us to do until next day, so we walked down the drive to explore. Finding no guard on the gate, we strolled into the village. Seeing a letterbox, we popped our postcards in. As they dropped, we realised the enormity of what we had just done, but it was too late to retrieve them. All the secrecy of the coded address would be nullified by a Latimer postmark. We were shattered at our folly. For days we expected a heavy hand on the shoulder, but as time passed it seemed our awful secret had not been discovered, so we relaxed.

We gradually worked out we were at the interrogation centre for German POWs. The unit was called ADI(K) to confuse the enemy (Assistant Directorate of Intelligence "K"), staffed by Air Force officers plus a few Navy and Army types, with WAAF Sergeants as typists and telephonists. The mysterious Group Captain who'd interviewed us was our C.O., known behind his back as "Daddy" or the "Old Man".

He was highly-strung and charming, worked at tension-pitch and got dreadfully wrought-up, often talking into several telephones to several people at the same time. He never relaxed, was never mentally off-duty. His desk, with four telephones on it, was flanked by desks for four assistants. He liked to have his team close by and thrived on bedlam.

269

He used his "bad" German with great skill. His atrocious accent was misleading; he was perfectly fluent. If one of the interrogating officers was having difficulty getting information, the Old Man was called in. He would make conversation with the prisoner, often stumbling over a word. Having got round to the vital point, he would stutter, as though stuck for the right word. The prisoner often obligingly filled it in for him.

Most of my time was spent maintaining a card index of all the prisoners interviewed since the start of the war, when the unit had been located in the Tower of London. I was in a fog, but too shy to ask questions. All the others had been there for years. For security, once posted in, there was no way out except via coronaries and ulcers, which took a fair toll.

I was nervous when the Old Man called me in, not understanding enough to feel more than a twit. Answering his summons, I was likely to find that before he could ask me his question, telephones would ring and one would be thrust into my hand. Most of the lines were "scrambled", making it hard to hear clearly. A call might be from Germany about an unknown subject with technical and German words thrown in. I was not a secretary, knew no shorthand, and struggled to respond half-intelligently. I often had to handle highly technical stuff to and fro with Professor R. V. Jones, at War Station X. His post-war book *Most Secret War* giving the story of the technical development of Radar became a best seller.

270

I do not like floundering in unfamiliar territory, but the habitual atmosphere of secrecy precluded asking many questions, making progress towards self-confidence grindingly slow. Carol and I were grateful to be together and helped each other along until little-by-little we got the hang of things, became less shy and could start feeling useful. The other officers were all older, cosmopolitan and multi-lingual, having lived and worked on the Continent before the war. "Daddy", unlikely as it seemed, had been the head company representative in Paris for Ideal Boilers. I had never been abroad and as a typical product of an English boarding school, had poor French and worse German.

Michael Dennison, the actor, was an army major there. He took Carol and me into the control room to watch the work of staff monitoring the bugged cells of the prisoners, round the clock, often picking up useful information. Although the war with Germany was now over, the work continued. Now we had access not only to captured personnel, but to senior German staff officers specially brought over to us.

On the plus side, my living standards had zoomed. I was living in comfort and style after years of cold damp huts, draughty primitive ablution blocks and rough food. The crippling chilblains and rheumatism faded away but the loss of the companionship and atmosphere I had taken for granted on big bomber stations was a deprivation I had not envisaged. After some weeks, a few ex-aircrew joined us. I was overjoyed to have the company of people from my own past, for I was still feeling out of place in this totally different culture.

In an Airmen's Mess, our evening meal had been a high tea between five and six o'clock, leaving time to change, smarten up and have a long evening ahead. Meals in the Officers' Mess did not finish until about nine o'clock, so if we wanted to go out for the evening, we missed our meal. Consequently, we did not go out much, but the grounds were extensive, with a lake and two bad-tempered swans.

Carol was a lovely girl, but a lousy judge of men. She worked her way through a series of misunderstood husbands. Her expensive but sheltered upbringing, with Mother vetting all young men and disapproving of nearly all, was followed by a WAAF career in a small unit, far from the educating hurly-burly of a big mixed station. It had left her sweet, kind, trusting and vulnerable, a soft touch for any sob story.

Another mansion, not far away, housed more prisoners. Carol and I were sent over one day, ostensibly to catalogue a captured collection of books. We found heaps of books piled on the floor, but they were all in Russian. We scarcely knew which way was "up", never mind translate them. We tried vaguely to sort them into piles of "Very Technical", "Rather Technical", "Might Be Technical" and "Sundry", according to illustrations, figures or any other clue we could glean.

During the lunch break, we walked across the gardens to the main building in search of food. We passed, at some distance, a hard tennis court with high stop-netting forming an enclosure in which Luftwaffe officers strolled, including one swaggering in a cloak. This was only our second glimpse of real Germans since the day of our arrival. Normally we did not see them as their quarters and the interrogation rooms were distanced from the main building by a tunnel.

On our return to Latimer House, we were greeted by grinning faces telling us Daddy was howling for our blood. All sorts of facetious remarks were flying round our baffled heads. We went quaking to face the Old Man, with no inkling of our transgression. He was incoherent with indignation. We struggled to discern what solecism had caused this storm. It emerged the cloaked figure was the famous Luftwaffe hero General Galland. (We'd never even heard of him.) He had spotted us, judged correctly from our uniforms that we were Air Force Officers and had returned to his bugged quarters bragging some tale of how Carol and I had talked to him in the gardens in terms of hero-worship.

Finally, the Old Man accepted we had been nowhere near Galland and the whole rigmarole was his fantasy. We were ragged rotten in the Mess, despite our protestations of innocence. We were left feeling humiliated, embarrassed and furious at being made to look so foolish.

The dropping of atomic bombs on Hiroshima and Nagasaki stopped the Japanese in their tracks and ten days later the whole war was over. The Mess cat started the celebrations by giving birth to a litter of kittens, named Winston, Dwight, Monty etc. She chose to have them in my bed, but in the nick of time

I went into my room and saw the bedclothes moving rhythmically up and down. There was just time to turn back the bedcovers, lift her gently and offer her an alternative nest in a warm cupboard.

I went to London with two RAF Officers to cheer with the throngs outside Buckingham Palace. It was difficult to keep together as we swayed this way and that in the flowing tide of happy, singing, laughing people. For a while we could not get through the wrought-iron gates from Green Park. In one surge forward, I got pushed sideways, missing the gate opening and feeling the pattern of the iron tracery being impressed on my flesh forever, like branding. After a few more surges, we were though. We sang, we cheered, we called for the King and Queen, who came out on the balcony time after time, with Princess Elizabeth in ATS uniform and Princess Margaret. Strong emotions bonded the crowd, expressed through laughter, tears, and above all singing, running through the repertoire of the National Anthem, Land of Hope and Glory, Rule Britannia, Nellie Dean and Auld Lang Syne.

Our next big news was that Latimer House was to close, most of the prisoners having been repatriated and our own staff starting to get their demobilisation papers. The rest of us were to move to London and occupy a floor of the Gas Light and Coke Company's office block in Monk Street, SW1. First there was to be a celebratory party in the Mess, the only one ever held. Elaborate plans were laid for a buffet supper followed by dancing. I borrowed a poppy-red velvet evening dress from my cousin, Pam. The colour suited me far better than her, the rich red swamped her delicate complexion. When all was arranged with great enthusiasm, we heard that although the war was well and truly over, permission could still not be given for outsiders to come in for the evening. Consternation and dismay among the prohibited wives, but Carol and I had a splendid time.

The party started with a white-haired Staff Officer from the War Office making a rambling pompous speech. Beneath the very convincing make-up was Michael Dennison, giving a brilliant virtuoso performance which was very clever and extremely funny. He got us all off to a good start. By the time Carol and I got to bed, it was getting light and the birds were halfway through their dawn chorus.

One by one, staff were starting to leave. Conversations went round and round plans for the future. War had become my normal way of life; I knew no other. I had no idea what I would, or could, do. The men airily dismissed my concerns with: "You needn't plan. You'll get married." No help.

I had progressed from perpetually up-dating the Great Card Index to working with an Anglo/Turkish ex-pilot. He owned a factory making ladies' handbags in Lancashire. He wanted me to become his Factory Manager. I knew nothing about managing, nothing about manufacturing and my home was in Kent. He nagged on and on, amazed that I was turning him down. At the same time, another was pressing me to work for him. His firm, near the Oval, was a main importer of marble and other stones. The backbone of their trade seemed to be gravestones. That did not appeal either.

Meanwhile, the move to London had to be organised. The Old Man sent me to London to reconnoitre the new offices, but I found none. We had been allocated an open floor space with neither walls nor partitions. "Offices" were to be chalked out on the floors and enclaves constructed by carefully positioning bookshelves and filing cabinets. We went "open-plan" before it had been invented. Great cunning was employed as we all staked out our territory.

The Old Man was calling on me more and more for an assortment of errands. On the move to London, I had hoped to get further out of his range, but no. A tall rack of shelves stood behind his desk. I was the other side, with a shelf left clear between us, so he could call me. I tried to close it by surreptitiously adding another book each day, until he rumbled me. I tried just adding a few sheets of paper, but it was no good.

He was used to having four assistants flanking him, now he had only two. When he wanted something done, it had to be immediately and someone must always be on hand for instant action. He was not a natural tyrant, he drove no one harder than himself. He was utterly single-minded, caring passionately about the job. He was distressed if anyone seemed to fall below his own lofty standard of dedication. It was impossible to be cross with him for long. He had long since worn down most of his staff, but I was new and flattered to be thought useful.

My real job now was dealing with B.I.O.S. and C.I.O.S. reports, the product of investigations in Germany to obtain details of their industrial processes and designs. These were not protected by patents so could be used by British industry. I dealt with all this as best I might, with nothing but my native wit to guide me. I was gratified to learn, many years later, that these reports had proved valuable and my untutored efforts had not been in vain.

Across the road was an Express Dairy café where four of us had long happy sessions over coffee or lunch. The other three were splendid raconteurs. Eddie, alert, foxy, with darting brown eyes and crinkly auburn hair, was a Glasgow newspaper reporter/part-time lion tamer. He owned a pair of lions, performing with them in a circus. I have a photo of him in a cage with them. They had never hurt him, but he had a nasty scar where a monkey bit him. During the war, they were lodged with a farmer, who gave them vermin to augment their diet.

Dickie was a six-footer with the easy self-assurance of an old-Etonian. He was the product of Lord Trenchard's scheme to recruit from the public schools direct to Hendon Police College. He had been in charge of Hampstead Police Station. The third was Philip, who ran his family firm of internationally-known Bond Street jewellers. His sardonic manner concealed a mordant wit. His glamorous wife was a famous actress. With this trio, the conversation was spellbinding, ranging over circuses, crime, jewel robberies and truth far beyond the realms of fiction. I sat saucer-eyed.

The Old Man was upset if he found us all missing at the same time. Once he encountered Dickie making for the stairs and challenged him. His instant response was that he had absent-mindedly come to work in a red Paisley tie (true) and was going out to buy a black one (false). But it did not do. He was hustled into the official car and the driver instructed to take him to a Jermyn Street haberdasher where he had perforce to buy an outrageously expensive black tie. He was demobbed a few weeks later, but the tie probably graced funerals for the rest of his life. As there was no Officers' Mess in London, I lived at home. Mother had been working at a little munitions factory in an old Organ Works. The ladies there assembled fiddly electrical components. One of her fellow-workers offered us the use of a flat in her garden, overlooking Chislehurst Common. It was her chauffeur's flat, but he was still in the army. Approached by an outside staircase, the flat had a sitting-room, two bedrooms, kitchen and bathroom. If left empty, it might have been requisitioned. We were delighted to move in and live above the laid-up Rolls Royce.

CHAPTER
TWENTY-SIX

Abroad at last

Arrangements were being made to repatriate the German High Command, who had been brought over en bloc for interrogation. As there were twenty-seven female clerks and secretaries, it was thought seemly to have two WAAF escorts in addition to three RAF Officers. I was dying to go, but really I was the most junior. Putting scruples aside, I flannelled and crawled shamelessly. I got the job, to go with Betty Masterman. She had been in charge of admin there throughout the war and was a staunch and faithful officer who richly deserved a bit of excitement.

Our escort party was joined by a Polish RAF Sergeant. He seemed to speak all languages fluently, knew his way around anywhere and could produce whatever was needed with the facility of a conjuror pulling a rabbit from his top hat. He could cajole or threaten as the occasion demanded and would have used the revolver he carried had he thought it necessary. His whole family had been destroyed by the Germans. He had been in, and escaped from, two PoW camps.

When it was finally fixed that I would go, I just had time to dash down to Chislehurst, pack a bag and leave a note on the kitchen table that I had gone to Germany and would be back in a few days. Our instructions were to return to Latimer Station, where a special train would be waiting to take us to Dover.

Our train was at the platform, so we put our kit aboard. Nothing much seemed to be happening that needed our attention, so we went to the station buffet for coffee. After a while, we strolled back and found the platform empty and our train gone. How were we to get to Dover to catch up before we were missed? Frantic calculations about trains/taxis/hitch-hiking were flung about desperately. Nothing seemed remotely feasible. Court-martial loomed. I spotted our sergeant. All was well, the train hadn't gone; it had been moved into a siding. We acted unconcerned, pretending we had been there all along, but were badly shaken at having so nearly fallen at the first hurdle.

British trains are designed for high platforms. Getting in from ground level in a tight straight-cut uniform skirt presented a challenge. Years of hitch-hiking in lorries had taught me to hitch up my skirt to free my long legs and jump. We needed two to pull and one to push to get Betty more modestly aboard.

Thus far, we had no role to play, having armed RAF Police in each coach. When we paused for a few minutes at Clapham Junction, they got out and patrolled the platform, to the stupefaction of commuters waiting for their trains home. On we crawled again and finally pulled into Dover Marine Station. Our job now began. Betty and I were responsible for the twenty-seven women, a number forever graven on my heart.

A Cross-Channel ferry was waiting, soldiers of all nationalities thronging the quay. The Embarkation Officer and both his sergeants were drunk. With difficulty, we got some deck cabins cleared of their protesting occupants, piled our female charges in and told them to bolt their doors and not to come out. Betty and I commandeered the Sick Bay, with two bunks. Scarcely settled, loud knocking made us open the door to an ashen-faced Belgian soldier with a gashed and bleeding hand. We found first-aid equipment, bound him up, and put his arm in a sling. He went away well satisfied, but we wondered whether the red cross on the door was going to bring anything more challenging, but we had no more visitors.

We had a rough over-night crossing and were hove-to for some hours, rolling in the swell until the storm abated and the ship could to get into Ostend Harbour. We had expected a train to be ready for us, but there was nothing and no-one knew anything about us. Luckily there was a PoW camp nearby that provided trucks and took over our charges, leaving us free to concentrate on conjuring-up a train. We went to an Army Transit Mess near the sea at Knokke-le-Zoute. I had not felt seasick on the ship, but now the earth seemed to undulate. Grey wallpaper with red tulips on the dining room walls advanced and receded unnervingly.

This was my first sight of "abroad". I was thrilled with all I saw. Every single little detail seemed different from England. Square pillows instead of oblong, duvets instead of blankets, unfamiliar furniture, sights, smells, food, clothes, hairstyles, make-up, mannerisms, handshakes, the very air we breathed, all were unmistakably foreign. Frank was my mentor. He had been at German and French universities before the war and took endless trouble to show me round and look after me. We still had no news of a train, so we left one person to battle with the shaky telephone system and keep an eye on the station, while the rest of us ventured further afield.

I loved the trams, with their several linked coaches and sing-song bells heralding their arrival. We took one along the coast to Zeebrugge, the scene of a celebrated Naval engagement in the previous war. A bitter December wind blew off the North Sea. All was windswept, the houses shuttered. Still no train, so we went to Bruges. It seemed unscathed by the war. When Belgium fell, it all happened so fast, the Germans sweeping straight through without needing to fight. I was enchanted by the canals, the old buildings, picture galleries, the Béguinage, the foreign picturesqueness of it all.

I had my first introduction to art, looking at paintings with Frank, an informed escort. It was all a brilliant eye-opener, everything seen for the first time. I managed to contact my brother in Brussels, arranging to go over, but word came that our train was on its way and we didn't dare stray far from base. A pity, as a great party had been laid on for us. We located an RAF Equipment Store, where Betty and I got kitted out with battle dress, boots and heavy leather sleeveless jerkins.

It was as well we did, our ordinary uniform would have been inadequate for the rigours ahead.

When our train arrived at last, it was awful. For the men, there were cattle trucks with no heating and a few wisps of straw on the floors. (Identical to the ones used to dispatch loads of Jews to their deaths in concentration camps.) For the women and our party of three RAF officers, one RAF sergeant, two WAAF officers, we had a Belgian third-class carriage, with slatted wooden seats. The coach had a central corridor, was partitioned into two sections and had a single lavatory in the middle. The twenty-seven women went in one end, we set up camp in the other.

We got everyone installed in the coach and trucks, but lacked an engine. We could only move when we found a train going our way and could hitch our carriages to it. Progress was desperately slow. We crawled a few miles, then stopped, crawled a little further, then stopped again, and sometimes even reversed. We hoped we were making for Wiesbaden, but any hope of getting to a particular destination by a certain time quickly evaporated.

We concentrated on survival. The cold was intense. We were living on American tinned rations. Our Polish Sergeant was a magician, getting candles for us. He knew there was a tap on the side of the engine where hot water from the cylinder gushed. He got us a bucket. Not a drop of the precious hot water was wasted. First the food cans were dropped in to be heated, then Betty and I washed in it, then the men washed and shaved. Finally the lavatory was flushed.

This routine went on for three days and nights. We slept as best we could, propped against each other. The train often stopped long enough for the men to be let out of their trucks to urinate, which meant that Betty and I could not get out to stretch our legs, for the sake of their delicate sensitivities. We would not have minded, but the Germans were prudish.

We counted our twenty-seven women regularly, not that they wanted to escape. With us they had food and security. Sometimes our twenty-seven became twenty-eight, as one of the women had a husband who kept nipping in and hiding in the luggage rack.

By the second day, the inevitable scourge of diarrhoea cropped up. We had to take in an Admiral, who was plainly ill. That added one more unwelcome addition to the 33 of us sharing a fetid lavatory with no flushing water.

On the third day, we were stuck in a marshalling yard. Our engine had gone and we could not move again until we located another heading south. Our valiant Pole arranged for Betty and I to have a hot bath. Gathering our sponge bags, we followed him across tracks to a house. A German woman welcomed us in, showing us to a room with an old-fashioned tin bath. Great jugs of steaming hot water were brought, with large towels. Betty, not having experienced communal living, was a bit bashful, so I stripped off first and hopped in. Rupert Brooke's "benison of hot water" indeed. Then Betty's turn. Both clean, glowing and dressed again, we thanked the woman and headed back to the train. Or did we?

In excited anticipation of the bath, we had failed to take bearings to find our way back. After a good deal of panicky rabbitting up and down, we found our coach. Much refreshed, we settled down for another night on the wooden slats, wearing every stitch of clothing we had to keep the bitter cold at bay. No engine meant no heating.

From voices we'd heard, apparently people were living in some of the trucks. One family was alarmed that we had seen them, obviously thinking our uniforms meant trouble. We gave them some cigarettes and they were overjoyed, not to smoke them, but to use as valuable currency.

Next day, an engine appeared. Our Pole stuck his gun in the driver's ribs to encourage him to shunt the train until he could get our coach coupled immediately behind the engine and connected to some heating. The Admiral was very ill, as were some others by then. The heating was necessary if we were to get them home alive.

The railway followed the Rhine, passing vineyards, castles, villages, freight barges and the Lorelei, which we had sung about at school. The terraces of vines surprised me. I had expected them to grow much taller, more like Kentish hops strung from high poles. This stretch of track beside the river was in good condition, so we made better progress and arrived at Wiesbaden.

Germany was divided into four zones, occupied by British, American, French or Russian troops. Wiesbaden was in the British Sector, so we delivered our dishevelled lot to a tented camp. We checked in at the best hotel. Our first priority was a hot bath. Betty went to explore and was away over an hour. I was concerned, not knowing where to search for her. She arrived back to recount that she had asked the way to the baths in her best German and found herself in the clutches of muscular women giving her the full Spa treatment in murky sulphurous tepid water. She had not enjoyed it.

By this time I had enough working German to understand most of what was said, but still used an interpreter to translate my orders, so there would be no misunderstandings. The women were very nervous about their futures. Although they whined and grumbled incessantly, they did not want to leave the British Sector, but our instructions were clear. Each must be released in the Sector she had registered as home.

For some, this meant the Russian Zone. They were terrified, but they had to go. I got them segregated, put into a truck with an armed soldier to see they did not jump out again, and hopped up into the cab with the driver and set off for the Russian Zone. I had learned a lot in a short time from our Polish Sergeant.

After several hours driving on snowy roads, we came to road-blocks marking the border. I handed over a group of scared women, with all their papers, to a fur-hatted Russian Officer. There was nothing more I could do for them, though they wept and pleaded. It was dreadful to leave them like that, but I had to tell the driver and guard I was ready to go. We went.

In the days when I was a part of the organisation raining bombs down on Germany, I gave no thought to the plight of Germans as individuals. The more we killed, the sooner the war ended. I had lived in the Blitz. I had no pangs of conscience. This was different, I had got to know them as individuals. By the time I got back to Wiesbaden, Betty had dispersed the rest of the women to whatever fate awaited.

We could consider our next move. We had been away about ten days, though England and home already seemed dim and distant. I posted off cards home whenever there was an opportunity.

We went to Frankfurt and saw what RAF bombing had done. I had seen London after the Blitz, but this was something else. Streets led through hills of rubble, like masses of spoil tips round a mine. Here and there the gaunt skeleton of a burned-out building still stood, but the overall grey impression was of rubble and total devastation as far as the eye could see. Narrow railway tracks snaked along the roads, carrying small trucks loaded by buckets passed hand-to-hand by a chain of figures clad in clothes of no shape, no colour, matching the rubble itself. There seemed to be no human faces under the scarves tied over their heads.

The scale of task they were tackling rendered their efforts puny by comparison. Leave it, for goodness sake, walk away and start afresh somewhere else. Where did all the trucks go to empty their pitiful cargoes? I had never before felt self-conscious in my uniform. Now I wanted to pass by on the other side.

The five of us, for our sergeant had gone, were directed to an address, but it looked like another mountain of rubble. There was a doorway. We went in and down a long staircase, emerging into warmth, light and the music of a swanky nightclub. The shock of it had us reeling in disbelief. The dreadful sights and conditions of the past ten days had become our reality.

How fast one adapts, how quickly we relaxed. There was plenty of food, drink, cabaret and dancing. I was stunned, but the beat of the dance band got to me. I thought of nothing but the present moment. We were swept along by the atmosphere, even down-to-earth Betty was mesmerised. A lonely USAF officer joined us. As the evening wore on he became our dearest buddy. Next day, he was driving by jeep to Salzburg. What more natural than to accept his invitation to join him? We arranged that Frank, Ron and I would be picked up by jeep early the next morning. Betty and Jack would go to the airfield, hitch a ride and fly down to join us. We would spend Christmas in Salzburg, conveniently forgotten by London, and get back straight after the holiday. Excellent plans are so easily fixed at the end of an evening in a night-club.

Next morning, we felt less sure, but the jeep arrived on the dot and off we went. Our papers were a little unorthodox, but we were going to the U.S. Sector. We talked our way successfully past roadblocks, sentries and guards. We drove all day, stopping to eat and stretch occasionally, then driving on through the night. My only fear was of driving into a wire stretched across the road at neck height as we went through endless dark forests, but nothing sinister occurred. Each village we passed appeared deserted, all its inhabitants abed, leaving a Christmas tree ablaze with lights. It was still dark when we drove into Salzburg, with a huge tree shining from the centre of the bridge, reflecting in the black water below. The cold had numbed me so deeply that I had to be lifted out of the jeep and helped to get moving again. Our luggage was frozen through, clothing rigid, toothpaste iced.

Salzburg under snow was straight off a Christmas card. Mildly surprised, we found it was Christmas Eve. We'd lost track of dates. Before midnight, the sound of bells drew us towards the Cathedral, the sonorous note of the deepest bell tingling down my spine. A procession of clergy was entering the West Door, resplendent in snowy white, crimson, purple and gold, carrying candles and jewelled crosses. We managed to squeeze in and stand at the back of the packed congregation, becoming caught up in the surge of music from the organ and voices that rang to the roof in ocean waves of sound.

Next morning, we climbed the snow-covered hills above the city, with the broadcast voice of Bing Crosby singing "I'm Dreaming of a White Christmas" echoing off the surrounding mountains. Too tired to go any further, I was welcomed into a farm chalet, while Frank and Ron went higher. My sparse German had to express my appreciation for their spontaneous hospitality to a stranger.

The little room was their sitting room and kitchen. Home-made wooden benches and chairs softened by bright cushions, cheerful curtains and rugs on the plain plank floor made a cosy interior. A tabby cat slept by the fire and young chickens had a box under a settle. Outside, small boys skied with bits of wood lashed to their boots with twine. They skied with natural ease, taking jumps from an improvised ramp with perfect poise.

There was no sign of the others coming from Frankfurt to join us. After checking several planes in, we reckoned they were not coming. We heard of a ski lodge run as a Leave Centre for the US military at Igls, high up in the mountains above Zell-am-See. We were made welcome. I was given an alpine attic, all scrubbed pine and a bed with a plump square duvet. If I lay under it, I was so hot that sweat trickled. If I stuck a toe out, I risked frostbite. It was my first serious conflict with a duvet and I have never mastered adjusting it to the climate outside. Frank knocked on my door at dawn, when the valleys below us were full of cotton wool clouds, turned flamingo-pink by the sunrise. The sky turned to brilliant blue in the sparkling air. Straight down through a pine forest were glimpses of the lake, but we were well above the tree-line.

Ron and I had never skied before. As the place normally only catered for men, all the boots and skis were big and heavy. I took the smallest, but found them cumbersome and hard to control. There were no nursery slopes and I could only stop by sitting down. Skiing looked so easy, but I fell and laughed, laughed and fell all morning. We stopped for lunch, then, rested and fortified, went out again. Thinking I had got the hang of it, I was over-confident, went crashing and severely sprained my left ankle. It blew up into a purple, green and yellow mess, but nothing seemed broken and anyway it was time to make our way homewards.

Innocently, I thought we would not be missed. In fact, the Old Man was in a terrible fuss, ringing his network of contacts without success. If Betty had only stuck to our plan, we would all have arrived back together, with some convincing account of the delay. "Last seen heading South in a jeep with an American", did little to mollify him. Mother did not receive the cards I had posted, and was getting anxious until Betty phoned to reassure her that all was well. We were oblivious, having a wonderful time.

The Arlberg-Orient Express was due in Innsbruck the next day, so we got tickets to Paris. Frank, ever solicitous, booked two compartments so that we could stretch out on the over-night journey. I settled and fell asleep immediately. Waking in the morning, I found I had a companion, a French Army Officer of exquisite manners, who had taken it upon himself to cover me with his greatcoat in the night. Such gallantry, such chivalry. Frank's face when he came to see how I had slept was, as they say, a study.

Paris! We had a problem when we arrived. We were flat broke. Not expecting to be away so long, we had made no arrangements for money. Ron found his pocket had been picked and his wallet was gone and all the banks were closed. However, we had acquired masses of cigarettes from the Americans and they were good currency. Now was the time to cash them, but how? Poor Frank, an honest Quaker, spoke French, but was ill-cast as a spiv. I stiffened his backbone as best I might and he went off to sell them on the black market. I never asked how or where he did the dastardly deed, but he came back with enough francs to tide us over.

We checked that Betty had passed through the RAF Transit Mess before Christmas, so I knew Mother would have heard I had been a little delayed. Frank knew the city well, having been at the university, and was an excellent guide. My ankle was still painful, but I wanted to see the sights. I took plenty of aspirin and hobbled along, too excited to care.

My art education started in Bruges, extended in Salzburg, blossomed in Paris. We went to the Louvre, Les Invalides, Montmartre, Right Bank, Left Bank, we went everywhere. Reluctantly, we enquired about getting home and got a promise of a flight if we went to Orly Airport two days later. Flying in an old Dakota with no seats, we sat on the floor among the gear and had a bumpy ride back to England. We had been away over two weeks. I had been "abroad". Ostend, Bruges, Wiesbaden, Frankfurt, Salzburg, Igls, Innsbruck, Paris.

Limping back to the office next day, I found there had been quite a little flutter over my exploits and Betty was a trifle upset at being deemed responsible for mislaying me.

But it was all small beer compared with the real news. The unthinkable had happened. The Old Man had been demobbed. Briefly; (a) There had been a stylish farewell party for him, which I had missed. (b) I was to go to tea with him and his wife. I took (b) to be a feeble leg-pull, but right on cue, in he swept in a city suit and bowler hat. Though demobbed, he could not keep away. No criticism was made of my trip and yes, I was to go to tea that very afternoon.

They lived in a tall thin town house, just like him, with its steeply sloping roof mirroring his shoulders. His charming wife had been suddenly faced with a husband fretting at home all day, so had bought cans of paint and set him to redecorate the house from attic to cellar. It was strange to see him in this domestic role. A warhorse pulling a milk-cart.

ADI(K) was being disbanded, so I went to work in an office where all the WAAF Intelligence Officers' files were kept in a filing cabinet. I had a lovely nosy time surreptitiously reading them and finding all manner of comments on the confidential reports of old chums who had, or had not, passed Selection Boards. The pithy comments were shrewd. I nervously sneaked a look at my own file. In 1941, the C.O. at Waterbeach had put my name forward. I was rated as "a pleasant stooge, but immature." That let me off kindly. I was eighteen years old, very green and had not even remembered to call the officers "Sir".

I was expecting my demob papers daily, still with no idea what to do next, when a lucky chance cropped up. Offices were operating in Brussels, Paris, Rome and Athens to sort out recompense for those who had, at appalling risk, formed escape-lines through which soldiers and aircrew shot down over enemy-occupied territory could be returned to England. There was a vacancy in Athens and I was willing to sign on for a further six months in order to go. Just as it seemed fixed, news came of riots in Greece, due to over-excitement during elections. A few people had got themselves shot. The Athens posting was switched to an RAF Officer.

I was offered Paris instead. School French was on my records, but no one thought to test me. Panicky visits to the Berlitz language school only confirmed my ineptitude. They only taught by the spoken word, I could only learn from the written word. I borrowed a 3in thick French dictionary, dating from my eldest aunt's schooldays.

Leaving the Berlitz, close to tears after a frustrating lesson, I chanced to meet Gay, not seen since Pershore days. I was invited to meet her husband, Spencer, for supper at their flat in Holbein Court. Spencer had been the youngest Colonel in the Tank Corps and was now trying to make his way as a barrister. Gay, now called Grizelda, (a prescient move), was training as a florist at the Savoy Hotel, a wickedly heavy, cold, underpaid job.

I received my Movement Order to report to Victoria Station to catch the boat train for Paris. Faithful Frank, now a civilian, came to see me off, bearing an enormous bouquet. The platform barrier slammed shut as we reached it. I watched in disbelief as the tail of the boat-train vanished out of sight. It seemed that my Movement Order had confused my reporting time with that of departure. With luggage, dictionary and bouquet, I returned to Chislehurst and set off again the next day. The flowers were left with Mother.

CHAPTER
TWENTY-SEVEN

Final fling

During the Occupation, the Hotel Commodore, Boulevard Haussmann, was commandeered by the German Military. Now it was our turn. I lived there, in a double room with a private bathroom, maid and valet service. The office was in the Hotel du Palais Royale, a pleasant twenty minutes walk four times a day, as I went back for lunch. Instead of groping in German at ADI(K), I now floundered in French at MI9. The staff was a mix of RAF and Army, with a few French civilians, most of whom had been in the perilous business of running escape-lines.

Earlier in the war, when telling aircrew what to do if shot down, I said: "Make for Marseilles and ask for Pat." Pat was real and he was there, a Belgian doctor who, as Pat O'Leary, became an R.N.V.R. Officer who put the Scarlet Pimpernel's legendary exploits in shadow. He was betrayed by "Roger le Légionnaire", and imprisoned, so colleagues shot Roger. Pat made a seemingly impossible escape and continued his underground work.

Like Leonard Cheshire, he was not physically impressive, but had the same well-earned heroic

296

charisma. He was leaving soon after I arrived, but his aura lingered. When he came in from time to time, there was an immediate buzz. "Pat's here."

I took over Wendy's desk, while she was away on wedding leave. Her area was Brittany and the task was to evaluate claims, recommending appropriate rewards for those who had assisted allied personnel to return to England. Wendy, a Channel Islander, spoke excellent French and knew Brittany well. She knew what she was about. It would have been far better if her section had been left alone while she was away, as my meddling did nothing but harm. The cases she'd left unresolved were not straightforward.

Questionnaires had been widely circulated. Bretons wrote quaint French. Names were complicated by women tacking-on their own names when they married and changing again when widowed. Under "Occupation", many entered "Entrepreneur", not a term in common English usage then. I puzzled over the number of "Undertakers" in rural areas.

I took my weighty dictionary to the office every day, hiding it in the cloakroom. When I'd amassed a list of unknown words, I nipped out to consult the tome. The others in the office must have thought my frequent visits did not square with my apparent good health.

We were only concerned with the escape réseaux, not with the French Resistance or S.O.E. (Special Operations Executive). It was not always easy to make the distinction. All who had helped evaders in any way were to be given a certificate. In addition, specially-minted gallantry medals were awarded. Widows of men killed by the Germans for the part they played were awarded pensions. Replacements for donated clothing and bicycles were arranged.

I shuffled papers endlessly, searching for something positive to do. I painstakingly translated a questionnaire indicating that a farmer had given a pair of boots to an airman. That seemed straightforward. I thought he'd like new boots. Unfortunately the letter asking him his boot size provoked a furious response, as the unfortunate man had had both feet amputated. Abashed, I was even more timid and left Wendy's files as nearly as possible as she had left them.

The British Officers' Club was in the Rothschild mansion, next to the British Embassy. It had a big dining room, good food at affordable prices, several comfortable sitting rooms, a long Long Bar, dancing nightly to a top-rate band and a lovely garden, with lawns and shady trees. One evening I was asked to dance by a Clark Gable look-alike, in the uniform of the Scots Greys. Straightaway, it was as if we had practised together for years. Bliss. I had missed good dancing since I was commissioned. Jock was an ex-Chindit, a Regular Army Captain, at present stationed with two other officers and some men at a château in central France. They had the gruesome job of locating British servicemen buried in France, digging them up and re-burying them in official War Cemeteries.

Jock's C.O. was also in the club, with an English girl-friend in Red Cross uniform. The third officer was another Scotsman, a bit older, married and not interested in Paris life. Following our dancing rapport,

Jock asked me to lunch the next day. We met in the Long Bar for a pre-lunch drink. I had some Dutch gin which went straight to my head and legs, making the walls and floor tip alarmingly. I negotiated the long sweeping staircase down to the Dining-Room with meticulous care and got through lunch by dint of intense concentration. Gradually the world steadied.

An invitation to the château for a weekend followed. I was a bit dubious, but the Red Cross redhead, Christine, was going, so we went together by train to Argenton-sur-Creuse, where Jock met us with a truck. The Château de Chabenet was pure Walt Disney, with round towers, battlements, dry moat and drawbridge. The owner still lived in part of it and the army had the rest. A letter came during the day, inviting the three British Officers to a dinner party at Prunget. Jock and I took a jeep and went off to find the place and meet the host, Louis.

At Prunget, two pepper-pot towers supported an archway over wooden entrance gates leading into a square grassy courtyard. Along the southern side ran a low single storey farmhouse, with stone walls a yard thick, set on an escarpment overlooking a river and millstream. Louis came out to greet us and the invitation was extended to Christine and me, probably to the annoyance of his girl cousins from further along the valley.

The main door led into a sitting-room, with an open fireplace taking up most of one wall. An archway led into a dining area, with the kitchen beyond. Bedrooms were at each end of the building. Rugs on the stone floors and comfortable furniture were simple and well-chosen. Clearly this was a fairly upper-class set-up and the informal country ambience did not disguise the fact that it was a wealthier strata than I was accustomed to. On this first evening, my four British fellow-guests were way out of their social depth. All went reasonably well, if a bit strained. The cousins were shy of speaking English, although they had all been well-taught by English nannies when they were small.

Louis was an excellent host, his English fluent. He was an army officer at the start of the war, returning to Paris when France fell. He worked for the Resistance until betrayed by a well-known English socialite who wined and dined with high-ranking German officers. The Gestapo came for him at their customary hour of 2a.m. and he spent the rest of the war in Mauthausen concentration camp. The British army eventually liberated him and tenderly nursed him back to health. He helped them track down some of his tormentors and now was glad of a chance to offer hospitality to the British in the area.

At the end of the evening, he asked if he might telephone me in Paris, where he lived and worked at the Treasury. Back in the office on Monday morning, he called to invite me to a lunch party at the Jockey Club, mentioning that the English wife of a friend would be there. The Jockey Club; I was impressed. The boon of uniform was not having to fret over what to wear. Just see buttons shone and stocking seams were straight.

Anxious to do the right thing, since my life up to that point had been deficient in the social graces, I worked out a carefully timed arrival. I found too late that I'd muddled two streets with similar names. I was in the wrong one. Instead of arriving at least superficially cool and poised, I arrived late and flustered.

The hall porter took my cap, ushered me into a lift, pressed the button and closed the door. It ascended but, between floors, it stopped. Pressing buttons moved nothing. Peering through the grille door, I could see an outer door not properly shut. I was alone, with no one to rescue me, so I got down on the floor and by reaching to the limit, closed the offending door. Dusting myself off, I got out as the lift levelled at next floor. No sign of Louis, just a long lounge full of men. I walked through, praying for Louis to come and claim me. Instead, the chatter died away to silence, all eyes on me. With rising panic, I turned tail and fled down a staircase. A waiter coming up, with a laden tray borne aloft, nearly dropped it at the shock of seeing me. I regained the ground floor, to the surprise of the Hall Porter, but he re-inserted me in the lift and pressed the button again. This time I sailed straight up to the top floor, passing the main lounge into which I had unwittingly blundered, where no woman was ever permitted to tread.

By this time, I was seriously late, embarrassed and my first effort at soigné Parisian society life in total disarray. Louis greeted me and introduced me to the group, including a snooty English Comtesse, whose appraising look summed me up with deadly accuracy.

To rub it in, she embarked on a rigmarole as though she thought I might be the daughter of a fellow-member of her father's London club, who had a daughter in Paris blah-blah-name-drop, name-drop. Having no defences, no ammunition and wishing no further humiliation at her hands, I silenced her the only way I could. "I'm from Bromley." Now I had finally turned up, the meal proceeded, course after course, wine after wine. Everyone else drank, so I followed suit. They were used to it; I was not. Finally it was coffee and brandy. Still I went doggedly on, too fuddled to spot in time that only the men ordered brandies. Yet one more glass appeared in front of me, but I left it.

The ordeal over, Louis suggested strolling down the Champs Elysées, through the Tivoli Gardens to the Louvre, to show me his favourite Rénoir. He must have seen me struggling and, kind and considerate, thought I would appreciate a little fresh air, but was too gallant to ever admit he'd noticed anything amiss.

Out of a narrowly averted disaster, I gained friendship with a darling elderly lady, Madame du Breuil de St. Germain. She loved being asked to tea at the Officers' Club, where their coffee éclairs delighted her. Paris had lived on the brink of starvation throughout the German occupation. Rats were eaten.

In Paris, Louis and his cousins had apartments round the same courtyard, guarded by a concierge in her cubby-hole. On my first visit I did not know I had only to press the bell, wait for the click, push the door and walk in. I rang several times before the concierge came grumbling out to see who was plaguing her.

For the next six months, Louis was a good friend and I saw a side of French life which would otherwise have been closed to me. Longchamps for the racing, private dinner parties, the 200 Club, couture fashion shows, week-end parties down at Prunget. There was still no petrol for civilians. Perhaps just as well, as Louis' photograph album recorded the powerful sports cars he had wrecked. Twice captain of the French Olympic 4-man bobsleigh team, he loved speed.

At Prunget, he had converted stables on the west side of the square into living quarters for Pierre and his wife, who looked after the place. When he came for a weekend, his luggage a rucksack, Pierre met him at Argenton station with a tandem and they pedalled back up the hills together. To cook for him, Mme. Marandon came up from her cottage by the Mill. She was an ample smiling woman with crinkled brown face, brightest of blue eyes and her white hair in a bun on top. She produced excellent meals, often finished with mounds of freshly-picked wild strawberries with goats' cream cheese.

A wide sunny terrace ran the length of the cottage, bounded by a low stone wall where the land dropped sheer to the level of the river below. The stone-built privy was sited on the edge, the hole in its wooden seat the draughtiest place I ever sat. A medieval dungeon tower, resembling a high square church tower, stood at the northeast corner. Le Donjon must have been an efficient gaol, with only one door to guard at ground level. The prisoners, confined to the upper floors, were too high to escape by jumping out. A use for our

303

redundant high-rise blocks? Louis lent it to parties of needy children from Paris every year.

One weekend I was invited down, bringing a friend from the office, Rosemary, and swimsuits. Not having a swimsuit with me, I tried to buy one, but the shops were still bare. I found one in a boutique. Initially I spurned it as too brief, but there was nothing else. Hand-knitted in navy blue wool, it had a miniscule bra top and skimpy briefs. Not the thing for Eastbourne beach, but I didn't want to appear dowdy alongside the sophisticated French. I bought it. We went down by train and took the local taxi, an ancient Citröen with a coke-burning stove mounted on the running-board. A chimney-pipe went up and along the roof. Before starting, the driver raked the stove with a poker, topped it up from a sack and in a swirl of sparks and smoke, we proceeded, slowly, jerkily, up to Prunget.

The river had been cleared of weed and a diving board constructed. There was to be swimming, followed by lunch in the Mill. When time came to change, I donned my little number and sauntered to the river, with studied nonchalance. Most of the men were already by the diving board, but the French girls not yet arrived. They emerged, wearing old-fashioned pre-war demure one-piece swimsuits. One glance and I dived in to cool my blushes.

Reluctant to come out, I turned on my back to paddle about a bit and saw that the wool had stretched in the water and lost all elasticity. The pants were drooping but, held by a drawstring at the top, they should not fall right off. The tiny bra triangles were floating free. The water was cold, I could not stay submerged indefinitely. Clambering back on the bank, wrapping myself in a towel, I found inky dye streaming down me.

Mme. Marandon rose to the occasion, giving us a fine lunch party, all sitting at a long table in the mill. In the afternoon we went up the valley to the cousins' family house. We only had Jock's jeep, so Rosemary and I elected to go on the tandem. Her arms were not long enough to reach the dropped handlebars, so I went on the front. Our first few attempts were wild uncontrolled zigzags, then we got the hang of it.

To encouraging cheers, we were away at a great rate down the lane, round the corner and slap into a flock of sheep. In a whirl of arms, legs, sheep and metal, we collapsed. No harm done. After a few more lurching zigzags, we continued our journey and still arrived ahead of Jock's jeepload.

Three of the girls, Françoise, Elisabet and Simone became my friends. When France fell, they had all left Paris and lived in the country for the next four years, quite cut off. The occupying Germans were never in the vicinity, nor were the later British or Americans, until the three gravediggers arrived.

At first glance, I had taken them to be schoolgirls, then found they were older than me, well educated and knowledgeable in music, art, history, all things I sadly lacked from my woefully narrow schooling.

Simone was a qualified engineer, Françoise in her last year at the Sorbonne. Elisabet was too shy to speak English to me, and I to speak French to her.

One evening in the 200 Club, under the beneficent influence of champagne, our tongues were loosened and we chatted like two long-parted sisters, pledging never to be so tongue-tied again.

My social life was getting mildly complicated by the parallel and very different friendships with Louis and Jock. Much as I enjoyed dancing with Jock, I was not keen on mixing him with my Parisien friends. He had been married to a girl greatly his social superior, whose family made their disapproval clear. When the marriage broke up, it left him sore, with a nasty chip on his shoulder. His time in the jungles of Burma with General Wingate's Chindits had affected his health, but he would not accept that his tolerance of alcohol was impaired. He had been an army boxing champion in his time, and tended to want to settle any little imagined slights with his fists. On the dance floor, he was fine, but socially he made me nervous. Consequently, when I went to Prunget, I kept clear of Chabenet. When he came to Paris, we did not mix with my other friends. I should have dumped him, but the pull of the dancing was too strong.

In the office, I had another set of friends, with Rosemary, Katie and Wendy, who was now married to B. Johnson. At the beginning of the war, B. was working in Brussels as secretary/chauffeur to a wealthy Belgian. When the Germans overran Belgium, he went underground and played a valuable role in setting up a major escape line through France, over the Pyrénées and down to Gibraltar, for return to England. Several times he made the trip himself, accompanying parties, walking all the way to the Spanish border and back. He worked on his own, so was not formally a member of the British Armed Forces. After VE Day, he was made an Honorary Captain in the Intelligence Corps, given only an M.B.E., the same as the Beatles. He deserved better.

He later died of cancer, probably caused by his war service, leaving a widow and three young children penniless after all emigrating to Tasmania. In London, the ex-service charities played pass-the-parcel with the family. The only one I could get help from was the Asylum of St. Annes, who gave what little assistance they could.

John worked in the office. As an RAF pilot, he had been shot down early in the war and spent the rest of it in a German PoW camp, so missing growing up in the mixed community that had moulded the rest of our age group.

To the concern of his friends, he started an affair with a French woman, the C.O's secretary. Her cheap perfume was a knockout at thirty paces. She was a lot older, had a child of about ten, and wanted marriage to an Englishman for her own purposes. He would not listen to anyone's advice and, with a wedding day fixed, drastic action was imperative.

The C.O. gave a friend of John's as much leave as he needed and the use of a jeep. He left and re-appeared a few days before the wedding, with incontrovertible evidence that the woman had been living with German soldiers, making money on the black market, betraying people to the Gestapo and was wanted by the police under her real name. With a British husband and a new name on a British passport, she had hoped to get clear away. Faced with this, poor John was shattered. The wedding was off, the woman sacked, and John went to the Brussels office for a month.

When he returned, everyone seemed determined to throw me at him. He really had an eye for pretty blonde Sylvie, a French typist, who was just what he needed, but all conspired to pair him with me. He was a darling and we enjoyed nightclubs and parties together. I found myself three-quarters in love with him. The remaining quarter knew that now the war was over, weddings were in the air and, fond of him as I was, I really would not have married him. He added another strand to my already overcrowded social life. Too many late nights.

One evening, at the Club, we fell in with an RAF Officer who was passing through Paris on his way back to demob and a wife. Above all, he wanted to go to a nightclub with a floorshow and a Can-Can. We were reluctant, partly because, on our meagre pay, we could not afford to go on paying exorbitant prices for bad champagne. He was most insistent, offering to pay for us all and please would I bring a girlfriend to make up a foursome?

Wrongly, I telephoned Rosemary, who was already in bed, and persuaded her I had a dream man here for her. Poor Rosemary was a bit too serious to enjoy frivolous night-life, but her neuro-surgeon boyfriend was giving her a bad time, so very reluctantly, she agreed. In the time it took to ring Rosemary and organise a taxi, our new chum got drunk.

We walked him up and down in the fresh air in a frantic effort to sober him up.

When we got to the Commodore to pick up Rosemary, she already regretted giving in to my pleading and got grumpily into the car. My conscience was in overdrive. John and I tried to keep her blind-date quiet, playing for time. The evening was not a success and I got my just desserts when our tipsy friend knocked a full glass of wine into my lap. My favourite dress, made of maize coloured crepe, shrunk when wetted. The whole front of the skirt shot way above my knees and never came down again. Rosemary was magnanimous in accepting my abject apologies next day. I was contrite.

John, with his pleasant affable manner, got on well when introduced to Louis. They had both been prisoners of the Germans, but an Offlag and a Concentration Camp had little in common beyond an absence of women. They agreed they had felt too weak for that to bother them.

Louis had survived because he was mentally and physically tough. Younger and older men quickly succumbed; very few came out of Mauthausen alive. Louis worked in the kitchen where the German Officers' food was cooked, so keeping above starvation level. His family had no idea of his fate until an Austrian guard photographed him, standing in the snow, wearing prisoners' striped pyjama uniform. The print arrived anonymously through the post in Paris.

Jock was becoming a liability and tended to turn up in Paris unannounced. Beneath the swashbuckling facade, I was glimpsing a petulant small boy. The French seem to love all things Scottish. There was certainly more tartan to be seen on Paris streets than in Edinburgh. Heads turned, drawn by that most flattering headgear, the Glengarry. If he had worn his plaid trews too, he would have started a riot.

One weekend, both he and his C.O. arrived in Paris at the Army Leave Hotel, the Georges V. Jock was ticked off in public for being there without permission. Equally publicly, Jock knocked his C.O. down and blacked his eye. He turned out to be an unpleasant worm, who was later court-martialled and jailed for flogging the blankets meant for wrapping the dis-interred dead. After the war, I saw him hanging about outside Earls Court station, looking very seedy.

Louis invited Rosemary, John and me for a weekend at Prunget. We went by jeep, but had trouble getting petrol to return. There was plenty over at Chabenet, so we went over. I crossed my fingers, hoping that Jock would be in Paris looking for me. Unluckily he was there, scowling blackly when he saw me with John.

With understandable ill grace, he gave us the petrol, while I skulked guiltily in the jeep.

Our work in the office completed, the last task before the office disbanded was to arrange ceremonial presentations of the certificates. We hired the biggest cinema in Paris and sent out invitations, each allowing two guests. On the day, the cinema was packed. A band played the National Anthems and lengthy felicitous speeches were made by the British Ambassador and numerous other worthies.

For the presentations, we set up six distribution points in the aisles. Seats were allocated alphabetically and we had the appropriate certificates ready. It was all well thought-out, but failed to allow for the emotion of the occasion. I expected just to shake hands and present the large envelope, with the name inscribed by a calligrapher. But not only the recipients stepped forward. So did their proud relatives. Each was introduced, each shook my hand, embraced me and kissed me on both cheeks and made speeches of gratitude for this, the proudest day of their lives. There were smiles, tears and bouquets. And we were supposed to be thanking them! It was very moving, but it slowed down the ceremony.

Louis was among the recipients. He prized his certificate highly, had it framed and hung it with his Olympic trophies. He had walked two Scottish soldiers right through France into the unoccupied zone. They were sandy-haired and un-French looking. Having been hiding in a loft for so long, they were out of training for the hard night-walking they had to do.

Louis arranged the whole exploit in a smart café in the Champs Elysées, under the noses of German officers. The colonel of a Scottish regiment had a number of his men hidden in northern France, trapped after Dunkirk. Finding escape by the Channel ports impossible, he took the bold step of coming right into Paris to get help.

Further ceremonies were arranged in provincial cities. John and I were in charge of Lille. We hired their little rococo opera house, with its faded opulence of red plush and flaking gilt. We engaged the local firemen's band.

On the day, an unreliable army major came with us, detailed to make the main speech from the platform. We went first to the Mairie, to drink a Vin d'Honneur with the Mayor and civic and military dignitaries. In our turn, we received them all in the upstairs salon of the Opera House, gave them wine and circulated, trying to speak to everyone.

By now the Major was far from sober. After a hasty whisper to John, I whipped downstairs, found the Major's car and instructed the driver to wait till the Major fell asleep, then return him to Paris. Johnny manoeuvred the unsteady culprit out and into the car. While John was doing this, I was left single-handed to struggle with small talk in my rickety French.

After an agreed interval, I was to lead them all onto the stage. I led the party out of the salon into a warren of passages and stairs and got hopelessly lost. After some scuttling up and down, I saw an emergency exit, crashed open the doors, led the procession out into the street, round the corner, swept them in again through the main doors, down the aisle and up on to the stage. Our ceremonial entrance was greeted with a standing ovation.

Les Pompiers played the National Anthems with more panache than skill. Johnny improvised a splendidly flowery speech, which was followed by several more from the French. I had a table on the side of the stage, with a box of envelopes ready. Seasoned by my Paris experience, I was well practiced in the art of making the presentation, accepting their appreciation, shaking hands, embracing and kissing each twice. Finally, everyone dispersed, radiating cordiality.

At the end, I was left with one indignant man without an envelope. When I returned to Paris, I found he did not qualify as, after helping slightly once, he became an informer for the Germans. He had a nerve to even show his face in such company.

We never saw the Major again.

CHAPTER
TWENTY-EIGHT

Under false papers

Our work in Paris done, I could return to England for demobilisation, but I was in no hurry. After six months at the pace I'd been living, I needed a little holiday. I coaxed Rosemary to come with me. She was older, had lived in France and Italy before the war, so her French was fluent, if a trifle elderly in style. She could do our talking. I fixed a return date three weeks ahead. With the office typewriter and an assortment of the rubber stamps so beloved by French officials, we composed some "official" papers, quoting our passports: "His Britannic Majesty's Secretary of State requests and requires in the name of His Majesty all those whom it may concern to allow the bearer to pass freely without let or hindrance and to afford the bearer such assistance and protection as may be necessary." It is impressive in English, it was imperious in French.

We took a train to Marseilles and found a ferry going to Corsica next day. Permits were necessary, so we flourished our "papers", bought 2nd. class tickets and went on board for an overnight trip. (In Paris, Rosemary had tut-tutted; not now.) We were led down and down to a cramped four-berth cabin, next to the galley manned by leery Lascars.

314

Before the full extent of our penny-pinching sank in, a sailor summoned us to see the Captain. Were our bogus papers rumbled so soon? Sheepish, we presented ourselves on the bridge. "Bon jour. I was in England with the Free French Navy. I saw your uniforms. How can I be of service to you? Have you good cabins?" "I'm afraid we did not get 1st Class tickets . . . ." A sailor was despatched to fetch our luggage and install us in a 1st Class cabin at no extra charge.

Next morning, the boat's arrival at the busy little port of Ajaccio drew crowds to the quayside. The recent end of the war broke four years of Corsican isolation from mainland France. In the bustle of docking and unloading, Rosemary and I did not pass unnoticed. The locals were short, dark and swarthy, the workmen mostly in faded blue, the older women in unrelieved black. They spoke the local equivalent of broadest Geordie.

We booked into the only hotel, overlooking the harbour. From our bedroom windows, we gazed out over a jumble of terracotta pantiled roofs. The colour-washed buildings were faded to infinitely subtle shades of bleached ochre, apricot, blue and non-colours whose origins were uncertain. Here was my first sight of the Mediterranean, everything a fresh wonder to me.

We were soon sought out by the British Consul, an elderly Englishman, known as "The Major". To impress us, he wore a regimental tie, frayed blazer and grey flannels crumpled from long storage in a musty suitcase. He was pathetically glad to see us. He claimed to have been an officer in the army, pre-war. When war came, he was apparently living cheaply on the island, maybe with a remittance from home, if he did not return to pose an embarrassment to his family. His pre-war Sandhurst voice chimed incongruously with his seedy looks, nicotine-stained, with discoloured teeth. His only redeeming feature was that he had one of the few cars still running.

"I am delighted to welcome you both to Corsica. Have you any plans? I would be pleased to drive you to the beach tomorrow." Rosemary looked doubtful, but I was dying for my first swim in the Mediterranean, sparkling sapphire and emerald, so remote from the cold grey of the Channel seen from a Bexhill beach. It seemed churlish to refuse, so we agreed.

A touch dubiously, we set off with him in his dilapidated Citröen, its health no more robust than its owner's. The beach, when we finally reached it after driving through the factory area and past the cemetery, was a grubby strip of grey shingle, scarcely worth the penalty of his company. I was not going to change into my brief swimsuit, so we only paddled in the edge of the rather disappointing water. The cemetery might have been more worth exploring, each grave celebrated with a statue, cross or flight of religious fancy, carried out in wrought-iron or marble. Curled faded photographs and garish artificial flowers adorned every grave.

Next day, we packed a meal of rough bread, goats' cheese and fruit and went up into the mountains behind the town. We climbed through olive groves up to the herb-laden air of the shrubby maquis. The mountains stretched away, each valley filled-in with another peak behind, like a child's drawing. Glancing back, the turquoise sea was dotted with fishing boats, as it stretched shimmering to the horizon. We met only one shepherd as we walked all day. When we made our way down to Ajaccio in the evening, the flank of the opposite hillside seemed to be shifting. Blink, blink, and we could pick out herds of goats, the bells on their collars tinkling or clonking as they moved.

There were no bus services, but a single-track railway ran from Ajaccio, in the south-west, diagonally across the island to Bastia at the north-eastern tip. Two trains a week. The toy train climbed doggedly up from the fertile coast, with many loops, to Vizzavona in the mountainous centre, where we got off. The village hotel was straight off a Swiss alpine postcard, with deep eaves, polished wood floors and pine logs burning in open grates. The mountain air was still, sound carrying miles.

Nearby Corté castle perched on a pinnacle, surrounded by a jumble of buildings cascading down the hill. With no vehicles, the narrow streets teemed with people, children, dogs, chickens, goats, donkeys and mules. Rosemary and I were an astonishing sight for them. Their curiosity almost overcame their shyness, but even Rosemary could not understand their patois. Hamlets clung to precipitous mountainsides, with no apparent access, except by mule or donkey track. How did they survive up there, with thin soil and the deep snows of winter? We spent another day in the mountains, feeling on the very top of a fabulous world until a blanket of cold mist

317

engulfed us. We had no warm clothes, no compass. Luckily it went as fast as it had come and we were warm again.

Reluctantly, we had to move on when the next train came through. In Bastia, the weekly ferry to Nice went the following day. Again, our "papers" got us tickets, 1st class this time. Half the population seemed to have converged to catch the boat. The town's hotel had been destroyed by a wartime bomb. Whose? We looked at the only other hotel, but dismissed it as too isolated and dilapidated.

Walking back into the town, we tried again. After several fruitless enquiries, we were directed to a house with an outside staircase. Up we went and were admitted uncertainly by a matronly woman, dyed auburn hair, much make-up, raddled. As Rosemary courteously repeated our request for a night's lodging, I noticed sniggering girls in cotton dressing-gowns peeping out of cubicles. Rosemary ignored my nudge and went on talking graciously to Madame. I took her by the elbow, drew her to the door and down the steps. "It's a brothel", I hissed.

There was nothing for it, but back to the hotel, through rusty gates, up a gritty drive, under rattling palm trees to what had once been a place of considerable elegance. A brass bell in the hall echoed forlornly. We were about to leave, when a porter/manager shuffled out, viewing us unpleasantly. It was mutual. We acted haughty, booking a double room as we were not going to risk being separated. A brass double bed dominated the dingy room. "Look at this!

The mattress is slashed down the middle as if a dagger has been plunged in. When it's dark, armies of bed-bugs will troop out and devour us," quavered Rosemary. "It's that or the floor. I'll risk it".

We locked our door, put a couple of chairs against it, had a good night's sleep, and woke refreshed and unbitten in the morning. After a meagre breakfast of thin coffee and dry rolls, the only occupants of the palatial marble-floored dining room, we paid our bill and left. We sat in the sun on a grassy bank by the roadside. "We've got all day, what shall we do?"

"Hi there!" A jeep pulled up and two U.S. Army Sergeants jumped out. We were amazed; we'd no idea there were troops on the island. They drove us to their Base. With the Yanks' usual friendly hospitality, we were treated to a fine lunch, with the novelty of peanut butter and pumpkin pie. They would accept no payment, they just wanted us to listen to their talk of home and admire their family photographs. In the evening, they escorted us to the ferry in great style. It didn't strike me as strange but such a casual attitude was new to Rosemary; she was dumbfounded.

Despite our 1st class tickets, we could not get a cabin. The little steamer was packed, probably grossly overloaded. Passengers with all their belongings thronged the lounges, the passages, deck. "What's it to be? A chilly night on deck or take our chance below?" Before we could decide, the Captain called us. Again the insistence that only the best would do for two British Air Force Officers. "I greatly regret not having a cabin with bunks available for you, but I would be

pleased if you would accept the use of my day-cabin."
We settled in for a rough night, making ourselves
reasonably comfortable in two yellow deck chairs, as
the boat put out into an increasingly stormy sea. A pea-
green Polish Officer joined us. He wrapped himself in
his greatcoat and sat immobile in a corner all night,
waiting to die.

Our cabin did not include a lavatory. Rosemary went
in search below, but was soon back, reporting every
inch of floor was covered with huddled bodies, crying
children, chickens and a stench of vomit that even the
smell of Gaulloise cigarettes could not mask. Waves of
the Equinoctial storm broke over the deck outside our
cabin. It served us well, with no chain to pull for ample
flushing.

By morning, the sea was pearly calm again and the
sun shining as we docked in Nice. After agreeing a date
to meet again in London, Rosemary took a train along
to Genoa to visit relatives. I fancied a few days at the
British Officers' Leave Hotel in Nice, still reluctant to
go home. To my dismay, it had closed, taken over by
the Poles. I was wondering what to do, less confident
on my own, when a Polish WAAF came down the
steps and recognised me from our Officers' training
course together at Windermere. "You were all so kind
to me when I was shy and lonely there. It would be fine
if you would stay in our club. I am so happy to see you
again". I was showered with free hospitality, all offers
of payment waved aside. It was good to see her among
her compatriots. It must have been hard with no one
who spoke her language.

I caught the bus to Grenoble, via the Route Napoléon, soon to close for the winter. It climbed upwards, from the soft Riviera to the harsher mountains above, stopping at tiny villages on the way. Sumac trees blazed against a gentian-blue sky. As they stirred in the breeze, the mountainside seemed ablaze.

Luggage was strapped on the roof, so all the lashing and untying at stops gave time for passengers to get out and stretch their legs. Very welcome as the seats were hard and cramped. My fellow passengers were a mixture of local schoolchildren and villagers getting on and off, sometimes where there was no sign of habitation for miles around. Cheerful students, returning for the new term at Grenoble University, sang as we went along, encouraging me to join in. We all shared food we had with us.

When we reached the pass at the top, and started to drop down the northern side of the Alps, we left summer behind. The temperature plummeted and we were into chilly autumn. I was quickly back into discarded tie, jacket and stockings, but still shivered. In Grenoble, I stayed one night in the best hotel, assured that I was in the very room used by Napoléon. I could almost believe it. The bed was very short and in need of a new mattress.

Grenoble was famous for its glove-making industry. Every other shop sold them. A Frenchwoman did not consider herself properly dressed if out without gloves.

I returned by overnight train to Paris, to collect my belongings and make my way back to London. I spent my last evening with Louis, quite unable to thank him adequately for all his kindness, hospitality and friendship. He still maintained he was forever in debt to the British for rescuing him from Mauthausen. Rosemary had spent six months in Paris, craving marriage with her neuro-surgeon, who had no intention of leaving his wife. It was galling for her to see me walk away from a proposal. I would never have fitted into French society life.

We met in London to go through the demobilisation process, having to go all the way to Warrington, complete the formalities and return again, still in uniform. Unlike other ranks, Officers had purchased their own uniforms, which remained their property.

With a final round-up of petrol coupons, though I could not drive, a rail-pass to the furthest destination I could think of (to visit my Grandmother in N.Ireland), some coupons to buy clothes, and a food ration book, I went home to where I had started out, nearly five years earlier. I put away my uniform. I felt bereft and hollow.

CHAPTER
TWENTY-NINE

Call me madam!

I was lucky in the year of my birth. It gave me a childhood in the uncomplicated world of the 1930's. Feminists may recoil in horror, but there was plenty of scope within the well-defined social structures of the period. Total freedom to do just about anything can be intimidating to all but the bold. In the WAAF, whatever our backgrounds or class, we were all pitched into the same uniforms, bound by the same regulations. I had five wonderful years of hard work, long hours, inadequate sleep, mostly living in damp Nissen huts, but enjoying myself, having fun. The strength of the friendship and comradeship would not be understood by the later generations who followed us.

Those not living at the time have a problem understanding the overwhelming relief we felt when the atom bombs dropped on Hiroshima and Nagasaki, bringing the war to an abrupt end. Without them, it would have dragged on endlessly, with infinitely more death and destruction than the wiping out of two cities and their hapless inhabitants. As news of the treatment of prisoners-of-war in Japanese camps came through, any sympathy we might have felt was cancelled. That may not be how later generations see it. I speak for myself.

Now it was 1946, I was 22 and had no idea what to do next. We were all thankful the war was over, but the radical readjustments necessary were difficult. Nothing could have lowered my spirits faster than finding myself a civilian again in Bromley. Life was dreary, I was lonely, everything seemed pointless. I could raise little enthusiasm for anything. Rather than run a few steps to catch a bus, I would apathetically let it go and wait for another. Everything was worn, tired and shabby. Food was still in short supply, and so was fuel. If there was a rumour of coke available at the gasworks, we wheeled down an old pram and brought back a baby-sized load. I was grumpy and disconsolate.

After six hectic months in Paris, juggling work, French social life with Louis, English with John, Jock getting stroppy, too many nightclubs, too little sleep, too many long-distance weekend trips, I was not in good shape. Mother was shocked at how haggard I looked on my return. A good thing she didn't see me before my remedial holiday with Rosemary in Corsica.

Grannie lived to see us all safely home from the war. When she died, it was found that a bomb had hit the Cemetery, wrecking our family graves, leaving jumbled relics. It was hurriedly set to rights in time for her funeral, but whose bones were where, we'll never know.

Things at home were fraught. Peter had married Pina in Sicily and brought her home. Poor girl, she spoke no English, she couldn't cook, the English climate was at its worst. They lived in a horrid rented bungalow in West Mersea, on the muddy shores of Essex. She was pregnant and sickly. If my life was grey, hers was coal-black. Back in sunny Sicily, it must have seemed a great idea to marry an English Officer and escape the narrow primitive life of Catania. Post-war reality was a cruel let-down for her.

Mother elected to go and live with them, to teach her how to run the house. I thought they would do better to work it out on their own. Rashly, I said so in a letter to Peter. He showed it to Mother and fur flew. I suppose I was jealous, harking back to our childhood, when he got all the attention.

Meanwhile, I was sulking at "Hurst", feeling forlorn. Mother had the admirable foresight to see that I wouldn't want to live with the three aunts, so the morning-room became our sitting-room and the downstairs pantry turned into a little kitchen. This worked well and I was grateful to her for thinking of it. The aunts had no shortage of kindly-meant suggestions for my future career, but I spurned them gracelessly. BBC/TV pressed me to "star" in a programme about a WAAF returning to civilian life . . . "Thanks, but no thanks." I had once narrowly escaped getting stuck on a WAAF recruiting poster.

The first spark of hope came when I found I qualified for a training grant, having had my education cut short by the war. The Good Housekeeping Institute ran a Cookery School, conveniently near Victoria Station. It seemed a good idea to learn to cook; there would be no servants for my generation.

I got the grant and enrolled for a course of three months domestic cooking and three months catering. I was happy to be doing something positive, after hanging about for two weary months, and glad to be back with a group of my own age. I did not look at it as a start to a career, but it pushed that problem aside for the moment. Something would turn up.

It was a bitter winter. The first job in the morning was to turn on all the ovens, leaving doors open to warm the kitchen. We worked in pairs. My partner had cooked for her family since she was twelve when her mother died, so she was astonished that someone of my age could be so totally ignorant. I learned as much from her as I did from our tutor. Later she became a TV cookery demonstrator and the author of many cookery books. I like to think that it was my incompetence that sparked her realisation that there were many more like me, needing guidance.

We could take home some of what we cooked, but as the staff got first pick for their own lunch, it did not pay to be the best. Mother had never learned to cook. During her married life, she had cook/generals, Ivy, then Myrtle. After her divorce, living at her parents' home again, the family only went into the kitchen on Boxing Day. Using her good common sense, she started cooking during the war, but it was a boon when I was taught the proper techniques and could pass them on to her. We reversed the usual "learning at Mother's knee"; more "daughter's elbow".

Being a cookery school seemed to ensure generous rations of food and getting a good midday meal was an asset. Much attention was paid to the presentation of dishes, with the ubiquitous garnish of parsley. If parsley supplies had failed, the school would have collapsed.

For the catering training, we cooked for local office staff who belonged to a lunch club. It was popular, always with a waiting list. They got a good meal cheap, with only the slight risk of something going wrong, like when I started to make a gallon of custard, mistaking ground ginger for custard powder. Cooking on a large scale was a change of gear. Vegetables were cooked in vats, puddings made with huge mixers, soup in cauldrons. We used remarkably few implements, pitching in with bare hands, up to our elbows as necessary. I got ticked off for decorating a tray of mashed potato with my fingernails, instead of a fork.

Towards the end of the course, all the lifting of heavy pans upset my spine, which had been damaged when a hoyden at school pulled away a chair I was about to sit on. Luckily the course was almost finished, so I did not forfeit my first-class certificate. I was glad to have had the training, but adamant I would never go into catering as a career.

Treatment for my back by an osteopath followed. Another of his patients was the Manager of the Mayfair Hotel. I went for an interview and was offered a post as Holiday Relief Housekeeper at the Grosvenor Hotel, over Victoria Station. Having no better idea, I accepted, bought the requisite black dress and moved in, glad to be independent again.

The hotel had grown shabby through the war years, but was well-run by a formidable white-haired Head

Housekeeper. Her function was to supervise the chambermaids who looked after the bedrooms and the daily cleaners who came in early to clean the public rooms. Although apparently so superior, she gave me some surprises. She asked if I knew how to clean a lavatory and showed me I didn't. She brandished a lavatory brush and plunged it rhythmically in and out of the water, setting up waves to carry water away over the S-bend. When the pan was nearly empty, she attacked it with Vim. "It should be pure and white as a lily."

She accompanied me on an evening round, checking that the maids had tidied the rooms, emptied ashtrays and bins, turned down the beds and laid out nighties and pyjamas. She casually tried on guests' hats and sampled their perfume!

My main mentor and friend was Pam, the First Assistant. Her private life was not good. For years she had been dangled on a string by Raymond. He ignored her for long spells, then turned up expecting her to go out with him at a moment's notice. She always did. Obviously he was a married man, just amusing himself with her when it suited him, but she could see no flaw in him. Her parents confided their worries to me, but I could think of nothing that would help. The affair dragged on. Ultimately, when she found herself pregnant, he dumped her.

A housekeeper's job is a bit ghostly, as she sees so little of the guests. It is her business to see the maids clean the rooms while guests are out and to prepare rooms for new occupants between lettings. One came to judge the guests more by their possessions than by their presence. Most were reasonably tidy. A few left the contents of their suitcases strewn over the bed, chairs and floors and the bathroom awash with wet towels and spilt cosmetics. They expected everything tidied up for them and usually left without a tip.

Most of the chambermaids had been there many years and were pleasant and reliable. There was one terror, Norah, on my floor. She was a tyrant to staff and guests. I did not appreciate her apparent power, just taking her to be an unpleasant woman and an indifferent worker. Many rooms had no private bathroom and I pulled her up for leaving an unemptied pot in a bedside cupboard. Angry at being caught out, she was excessively rude to me. I had her up in front of the Head Housekeeper on the spot who, while scandalized at my temerity, now had a cast-iron reason to sack her. To her chagrin, the union did not back her. She went. All were astounded at my "bravery" in dealing with her, but I had just been the fool that rushed in where angels had feared for years to tread. Had there been a strike, I would have been the one to pack my bags.

Two turrets at the top of the hotel housed the maids' dormitories. Bare lino on the floor, iron bedsteads, hard mattresses, minimal furniture, no central heating and electric stoves forbidden. Hardened as I was to WAAF huts, I found these conditions a disgrace. No wonder they could not get young girls to stay. The older ones were used to it and probably had nowhere better to go; it was their only home. Some years later, a fire broke out in one of the turrets, perhaps caused by an illicit heater, but the fire brigade arrived too promptly and put it out before the wretched place could be destroyed. All hotels housed their staff shamefully badly.

I moved to the Mayfair, as Fifth Assistant. I was soon Third Assistant, leap-frogging the permanent Fourth, who was a fixture. This little sinecure hid some episode in her past, leaving her devoted to, and scared of, Mrs Medway, the Head Housekeeper. Life seemed to have stopped for her at some early point in her life and she clung to the hair styles, clothes and speech of film stars in early movies. She was probably into her sixties, but still saw herself as a blond blue-eyed little girl. Some man must once have said: "Darling, never change!" As a housekeeper, she was useless. Some years later, I saw a newspaper account of a murder at the Ritz. The duty housekeeper, when asked what action she took said: "I'm afwaid I wan away." Yes, it was little Miss Begbie.

The Mayfair was far more congenial than the Grosvenor, though I missed Pam. Off duty, I could cross Piccadilly to use Green Park as my garden. In the evenings, I got to recognise the local prostitutes, operating from bases in Shepherds' Market, each with her own stretch of Piccadilly. I felt their eyes watching me, ever wary of a lone female. One evening as I turned into Stratton Street, a well-spoken gentleman raised his hat and started walking beside me. As we reached the Mayfair, I suggested he had made a silly mistake, leaving him seriously embarrassed under the amused eye of the doorman.

We had four residents. The Duke of Devonshire was courteous and aloof. Carole Browne, leading actress in West End theatres, kept a room during runs of plays. She was always ebullient and glamorous in public, but perhaps a little lonely in private. Carroll Levis was at the height of his TV fame, with a long-running series of "Discoveries" programmes for budding TV stars. He and his wife had an alarming brown dog. I usually get on well with dogs, but no one got near this one. I was told to stand still while this brute leapt up at me, like waves lashing the Eddystone Lighthouse. I was never bitten, just scared. One evening, Mr. Levis returned from the Palladium in a very strange state. He claimed to have "Seen the Light", rambled incoherently, alarmed the floor waiter, who sent for the Assistant Manager, who sent for the doctor, who sent for the men in white coats and he was taken away. We didn't see him again.

Our fourth resident was Lady C., a Director's protégée. She was mad, but harmless, forever insisting sinister men were following her. She particularly craved to become acquainted with the Duke. Despite her raddled appearance, one could judge she had probably been a pretty socialite in her long-passed heyday, now reduced to existing in a bed-sitting room. She liked to telephone the Duty Housekeeper for an evening chat. When she got me, she was upset to find someone new. "What is your name?" "Miss Ford-Hutchinson." "Nonsense, housekeepers don't have names like that. What is your name?" When she got to know me, she liked to give me little presents, usually old stockings with holes in them.

One evening, she called me, with John, one of the Assistant Managers, to give us champagne. Unfortunately she poured it into toothmugs from her bathroom, where we reckoned she parked her false teeth at night. We improvised a charade to divert her, while I nipped into the bathroom, poured the wasted champagne down the sink then washed and refilled the glasses.

We occasionally got weird visitors. Late one evening, I returned to the hotel, wearing a long evening dress. Reception were unhappy about the man who had booked into the bedroom next to mine. When the maid had gone in to turn down the bed, she found pornographic posters stuck round the walls. A porter with a truncheon escorted me to my room. When he had gone I found I could not unzip my dress. I had pulled it up with a long button-hook, but it would not work in reverse. Such are the problems of the single girl. The porter came back, unzipped me, and stood guard while I went across the corridor to the bathroom.

Being used to working with men, I liked their company and found friends in the Assistant Managers' office. John was a bachelor, Scottish, rather shy and thoroughly nice. He asked me out a few times, but we had to be discreet as Assistant Managers were one up from Housekeepers in the pecking-order. Mrs Medway might not approve.

My friendship with John had started with a rat hunt. The hotel had recently switched from solid fuel to oil.

When the surplus coal was removed from the basement, rats were flushed out and ran riot. One of the maids came to me in a panic, there was a rat in her bedroom. I went to the Assistant Managers for help. John armed himself with a shovel and went in pursuit. I hate rats, so retreated to the safety of my office. Later, John came to tell me he had slain it, and stayed chatting for the rest of the evening. Thank you, rat.

Endlessly checking bedrooms was tedious, so any change was welcome. The Metropole Hotel at Folkestone was part of the same hotel group. The Manager expected a big influx for the weekend of an Air Show, so asked to borrow two housekeepers. Two of us quickly volunteered and went off like excited kids on a seaside outing. The Manager was flustered by all the extra activity. This invasion of hearty young men, many newly discharged from the RAF, upset the normal genteel decorum of the hotel. He was probably near to fainting when his protest that all rooms were booked was swept aside. Beds were not important, mattresses on the Ballroom floor would do very well.

The order was passed to us. Exploring attic store-rooms, we found plenty of spare mattresses. How to get them to the Ballroom? They were heavy and awkward to carry, but we reckoned they would be manageable if rolled and tied. I went down the stairs, counting the landings and turns. From the packed Bar, I recruited a gang of volunteers. With one stationed at each junction, we started the mattresses rolling, all the way from the attic to the Front Hall. My crew were efficient, if a touch boisterous. The unfamiliar sound of

333

laughter wafted to the Manager's ears. I looked over the bannisters to see him standing aghast, as the stream of mattresses bowled past him, to be laid out in neat rows in the Ballroom. The operation was a big success and done so quickly that I could go off duty in time for a party with my new-found friends.

A few weeks later, greatly to my surprise, I was summoned by Mrs Medway, all gush and charm. There was a vacancy for a Head Housekeeper at the Great Eastern Hotel, Liverpool Street. She would like to recommend me. Incredible. On the face of it, it was ridiculous. Head Housekeepers are middle-aged women with total authority over a large staff. I was twenty-three years old. Clearly she had a motive; I suspect she feared my eyes were sharp and I might observe things she would rather keep private. She had no cause to sack me, but saw a way to shift me by fulsome praise.

It seemed silly, but I went for an interview with Mr Howe, the Manager. He was a gentle little white-haired man and I found it impossible to stick to my resolve to add three years to my age. The thought of it made me blush. I was offered the post and Mrs Medway was happy to release me at the end of the week. I never quite knew what she was so anxious to hide, but she was very friendly with one of the Directors.

During my last week, John took me to a party at a friend's flat. Leaving there with a group, we found it hilariously funny to topple plump plastic sacks, put out for refuse collection next morning, down steps into basement areas, like Humpty Dumpties. Mindless vandalism in Mayfair.

We went on to another friend's flat, out at Chalk Farm. Time passed and it was too late to get the tube back. Telephoning failed to raise a taxi. That left us with just our host in a one-bedroomed flat. He pitched a single mattress into the sitting room, wished us "goodnight" and shut the door. I was chivalrously awarded the mattress; he would make do with chairs. I had gone out for a summer evening wearing a silk dress. I peeled that off, keeping bra and pants. John settled for shirt and pants. We tried to sleep but the night became cold and we had no blankets. I invited him to share my mattress and his jacket as a covering. Thus passed the remainder of a chaste, chilly and uncomfortable night.

Next morning, I set off first, with John to follow in half an hour, to ensure we did not return together. By the time I had taken a train in the wrong direction, then slept past the station where I should have changed, I had used up my half-hour start. I wanted to avoid going into the hotel by the front door, passing the Hall Porter and Reception, so sneaked in by the staff entrance. John and I arrived together. The doorkeeper was suspicious of who I was, but I shot up some back stairs, changed into my boring black dress and went on duty.

Tut-tut, such behaviour from one so soon to be a Head Housekeeper, to be addressed as "Madam" by all her staff.

CHAPTER
THIRTY

Barking mad

Before moving to the Great Eastern, I bought some false hair, fashioned it into a bun, hoping it might make me look older. It didn't make much difference, but was a gesture towards trying to adopt a less frivolous mien. I soon threw it away. Mr Howes thought my youth could be compensated for by the presence of his wife. She was of delicate health, had no children and nothing to do all day but arrange flowers. My predecessor had been a disaster. Now Mrs Howes envisaged being in charge, with me to do all the hard work. That would not work. The staff system needed radical reorganisation. I had a major job on my hands and I could not work with interference and my authority being undermined.

I gritted my teeth and smiled as long as I could, but it became so impossible I had to tell Mr Howes, as gently as possible, that I must either be allowed to do my job, or leave. I was sorry for him, but bless him, he knew I was right. He had the unenviable task of telling his wife to mind her own business. She and I had an emotional session, but she accepted that I was no threat to her position. I suggested that she busied herself choosing fabrics and wallpapers for the rolling programme of redecorating the bedrooms. That sorted out, I had no problems and they both treated me most kindly.

I had a big bed-sitting room with a bathroom, high up, overlooking Bishopsgate. I would dearly have liked a suite, with a separate sitting room to entertain my friends, but it was an old hotel and there wasn't one. The first night, I was startled awake by the clamour of fire-engines. In the morning, I saw I was opposite the fire station and learned to recognise the crash of the big doors opening, so the ensuing bells did not make me jump.

I was lovingly looked after by Tilly, an elderly chambermaid. She called me in the morning, pulled back the curtains, commented on the weather and brought me a tray of tea. Half an hour later, the floor waiter came to ask what I wanted for breakfast. Five minutes later, he was back with it. Later he returned for the tray.

In the evenings too, I was smothered with kindness. The duty chambermaid came to turn down my bed; the floor waiter came to light the fire; Tilly looked in to be sure my bed had been turned down properly; the waiter came with the menu; the duty housekeeper popped in for a chat; the waiter brought my supper, course by course; he came to collect the tray; he returned to see if I needed more coal; Tilly came to see if I would like a cup of tea. All had to be thanked, though I was inwardly screaming for a little solitude. I hardly got a chance even to wash my hair.

My job as Head Housekeeper was the toughest, least rewarding job I ever did. The hotel then was high quality, patronised by the City but, owned by the railways, it was union-ridden. The Manager was liable to get a shop steward, still in his greasy overalls, coming into his office to thump the desk over some imagined grievance.

A new Catering Wages Act had just come in, laying down stringent rules for hours to be worked. My chambermaids worked some split-shifts, as staff were needed in the evenings. This entailed complex new rosters to ensure that each maid worked the prescribed hours while still maintaining a high standard of service. I made a bad blunder. Drawing on my own service experience, where we were adept at accumulating time off, to maximise time at home, I assumed my staff would appreciate the odd long weekend off. I laboured late into the nights to work out how this could be done. Satisfied I had done them proud, I issued the new rosters.

I wanted to speak to one of the maids, but when I went to her floor, she was not there. Thinking she might be in the service room where maids kept their things, I went there. I walked in to find all the maids assembled, being harangued by Olga, their communist shop steward. They were surprised to see me. I was stunned to see them. Anything could have happened. I had no time to think. "All go back to your floors immediately. Olga, come with me." It came out with authority but it might have come out as a squeak. With eyes down, they all trooped out. Olga truculently demanded another maid to come as witness. The three of us returned to my office in silence. I was glad to get behind my desk to hide my shaking legs. I took the wind out of Olga's sails with a speech I heard myself making. Her expression changed from aggression to amazement, as she realised she was being told that I was on her side and intended my staff to have the best possible deal. From then on, she was my valuable ally.

I had brought it on myself by not appreciating that experience had taught them to expect any change to be for the worse. I failed to realise they did not want long weekends off, for two reasons. Firstly, they liked to be around to collect tips when good clients were leaving. Secondly, rather sadly, few of them had homes to go to. They took hotel jobs mainly because it provided bed and board. They were agreeably surprised when I had improvements made in their bleak shared bedrooms and a new sitting-room provided. After more long hours, I re-hashed the rosters to everyone's satisfaction.

I had three Assistant Housekeepers, but the ones I inherited were not good enough. I needed a competent First Assistant who would use some common sense if I was away. Pam, at the Grosvenor, would be ideal, but I could not ask her to come to work under me, since she had trained me in the first place. It did not cross my mind that that was precisely what she wanted to do, but was too shy to ask. Luckily, we resolved the misunderstanding. She came and we worked happily together.

I took on another assistant, an amiable soul with a pleasant manner. For no good reason, there was a little question mark about her in my mind. After a while, it got back to my ears that when she was on weekend duty, she was apt to be too amiable and hopped into bed with some of our male visitors. She had to be sacked, but I did not know how to tell her. Knowing she had been found out, she made it easy for me. She resigned and departed, still happy, still smiling.

Not all staff problems were as easily resolved. I took on a most respectable middle-aged chambermaid. On her first day-off, I was called to the Manager's office. He took me to the window to see an astonishing scene on the pavement below. There stood my new chambermaid, looking well-dressed and normal, but at intervals she emitted a sound like the bark of a sea-lion. Heads turned. Some, unable to believe their ears, stopped and a little crowd started to form. The Hall Porter was sent to bring her in.

I had to talk to her, but what should I say? I called her to my office and gently expressed my concern about her unfortunate "cough". She seemed quite unperturbed, offered no explanation and did not demur when I suggested arranging some treatment for her at our local hospital, St. Bartholomews. I appealed to them for help. On the day of her appointment, I sent one of my housekeepers with her, to help her get to the right place. In the bus en route, she barked twice, causing consternation, no one spotting the source of the sound.

I later heard from the Sister of Barts' Outpatient Department that the appointment coincided with an Arthritis Clinic. When the bark reverberated off the tiled walls, patients who had been locked solid with arthritis for years demonstrated mobility beyond the dreams of the most dedicated physiotherapist. I was really sorry to lose her, but the Manager once heard her bark on a staircase. She had to go. After she left, I recounted the story to my brother, who worked in Kingsway. He phoned me one morning, told me to listen and stuck his telephone out of the window. Above the noise of the traffic, there was no mistaking the tell-tale bark. Poor soul, I wonder what became of her?

The Manager, a kindly man, had a prejudice born of experience, for staff of one nationality. Good staff were hard to come by. In summer, our younger maids tended to drift off to hotels by the sea. When an apparently experienced chambermaid applied, I broke the Manager's rule and took her on. She did not wish to live in, but to come daily. It was unusual, but I saw no objection. Many of our visitors were in London for the Olympic Games and there were reports of missing binoculars and cameras, often the empty case left behind. We had no lead to a possible culprit.

My new chambermaid came to see me, distressed that she had broken her glasses and asking for time off to get new ones. Without them, her sight was poor and led her to steal dollars from a wallet, thinking they were pounds. She tried to use them and was caught. In the closet where she changed out of uniform before she went home, I plunged my hand in among the folded eiderdowns and blankets and found a sizable cache of binoculars and cameras. We attempted to get everything back to its rightful owner, but were left with about fifteen to add to our weird assortment of lost property. People leave amazing things behind. In addition to umbrellas and false teeth, we had an unclaimed false leg.

The Manager chided me for taking on a maid of his least favourite race without a reference, but I was able to assure him that her parish priest had provided a letter of recommendation before I took her on. I heeded his advice more closely after that. Although the Bar staff were not my responsibility, when the overweight Stillroom Manageress broke her leg, I was called to comfort her. She wept noisily. An ambulance pulled up at the front door and a stretcher was brought in. At the same time, several police cars were waiting to pick up senior Police Officers who were attending some lunch function. The combination of vehicles drew a crowd. Emerging with the casualty, still clutching me with a damp hand, I faced a sea of faces and press photographers with flashing cameras.

The worst aspect of hotel management is that it has to function round the clock, every day of the year. As long as I was in the building, I was never really off duty. We were perpetually short of staff, particularly cleaners. The worry of trying to run the place with chronic absenteeism was becoming a nightmare. I started to wake each morning, dreading the day ahead. There was no job-satisfaction in endlessly having to plug the gaps. It upset the good workers, who naturally resented having to cover for absent colleagues. They hated having their shifts upset and I hated having to ask them.

I got a good deal of practice in hiring and firing. Experience taught me to take note of my very first impressions. The camera-thieving maid was an example. I had not liked her as she walked in and sat down, but allowed that instinct to be over-ruled in the course of the interview.

Finally, the stress got to me. I'd been prescribed some Penicillin and came out in an itchy rash all over. I was awake all night, so a doctor was called. He sent me on sick leave and ordered an ambulance to take me home. I instructed it to come to the backdoor and went down in the goods lift.

At home, our old family doctor, Dr Stillwell, came and prescribed strong sleeping pills. I slept for some hours, then half-woke, apparently about to die. I managed to ring a bell, which summoned Mother. I felt semi-paralysed, could hardly breathe and was terrified that if I did not hang on and concentrate frantically, I would die. Although it was around 2a.m., Dr Stillwell came all the way from Beckenham to save me. By the time he arrived, I felt marginally better and the dreadful sensation of imminent death lifted. He was apologetic for over-dosing me, in his anxiety to relieve me from the fiery itching.

Not long after I returned to the hotel, I spent an evening with Betty and Rosemary. They were shocked at my state and reasonably pointed out that I did not have to stay there. I was not still in the WAAF, only moving on when "posted". I had but to give in my notice.

Such a startling thought had not occurred to me. My sense of responsibility to Mr Howes and my staff had blinded me. As the realisation sank in, a crushing weight lifted. I knew exactly what I wanted to do next.

No more hotels. I wanted to work in a shop. I immediately wrote to Harrods and John Lewis. The latter replied that they were no longer taking women for management training, as the bright ones kept leaving to get married.

Harrods offered an interview. I felt a hat was necessary for the interview, but only had one I hated. At the last minute, too late to go out to buy another, I attacked it with scissors, ending up wearing half a hat. I smartened myself up as best I could and went West. Harrods' Personnel Manager was puzzled that I should want to give up what was, on the face of it, a very good job. I explained to her satisfaction that I was not about to be sacked, but wanted a change of career. That understood, she offered me a place on their "Contingent". It was then May, so I fixed to start in September.

I gave in my notice to Mr Howes. He kissed me fondly and gave me his blessing. Pam did not want to take over my job, so a successor had to be sought. Mr Howes gave me a pile of applications from a previous advertisement that had not been looked at, because I was appointed. Among them I found one from my predecessor, who had been sacked for utter incompetence. Not realising she was applying for her own post, she said rude things about her employer and presented herself as a paragon.

The staff gave me the kindest send-off. Poor Tilly had been crying for days. And so, with a final jangle of my weighty bunch of keys, I left. No need to try to look older now. The mirror told me that. I needed a rest.

CHAPTER
THIRTY-ONE

Sun, sea & parsimony

I needed a break, preferably with sea and sunshine. Rosemary introduced me to a family wanting an au pair for the summer in their villa at Pilat Plage, south of Arcachon on the west coast of France. Joining them in Paris before the great exodus, I got off to a bad start. I was told to take five-year-old Georges to school, then go on to the park with three-year-old Christian in a pushchair, plus Dinah the dachshund. After three hours, I was to collect Georges and all return to the apartment for lunch. We set off in good order. Georges chatted away, I understood little. I deposited him, with his rain cape, at the school. So far, so good.

Christian was too young to consult on where to find the park. I asked passers-by. Heads were scratched. My destination scarcely merited the description of a park. It was just the area in the centre of a residential square, with a few trees, some benches and a great deal of dusty gravel.

When busy, three hours pass in a flash. Three hours with Christian were an eternity. The hands of my watch seemed stuck. I wound it, I shook it, I put it to my ear. I had allowed twenty minutes for our return trip. All would have been well, if only (those fatal words) I had taken proper note of the name of the street where the school was. I had taken so many twists and turns to find the park that I could not find the way back.

The school itself did not have a name, it was just a terraced house like a hundred others in the vicinity and all the streets looked the same. Christian was no help. Without Georges, I could not even find my way back to the apartment.

A lady tapped my shoulder and pointed to my dog-lead with an empty collar dangling from it. "Please, God, help me. I have lost the school, the boy, and the dog." Retracing my steps, I found Dinah and put her collar on a tighter hole. Blessings on her. When I looked up again, we were outside the school. All the other children had gone. Mademoiselle was not pleased. Georges led us home and I hoped Christian would not relate to Maman anything of our disastrous morning. In the middle of lunch, Mademoiselle phoned to complain that not only had I been late, but had left Georges' raincape behind. As it was the last day of term, a furious Maman had to get the car and go to fetch it immediately.

The next day was pandemonium with preparations to go to Pilat Plage. Numerous other relatives and several big dogs lived in the adjoining apartment and kept popping in through a communicating door to add to the confusion. It was a noisy melée of people shouting each other down. We finally got away, the car packed to capacity. The household was to comprise the two boys, their mother and grandmother, the dog, and me. My job was total care of the boys. Their mother, Nicole, took no interest in them. She wanted them out of the way, while she sat knitting little pink garments for the daughter she was expecting. She got another boy.

The surly cook, already at the villa, Aïnhara, had a large brown mongrel. To the children, it was as big as a cow, so they called it Mimi Vache. Mimi was an ugly brute and got into a fight with the cook's dog from a neighbouring villa. The owners joined in, wielding broomsticks. All were finally separated by Nicole throwing a bucket of water over them. Mimi came out of it with a broken leg. It was splinted and she skulked most of her time in her owner's bedroom.

I took the boys down to the beach in the mornings, returning for lunch. After the boys had a rest, we returned to the beach for the rest of the afternoon. Nicole was too stingy to hire a tent where I could leave things. Twice a day I had to struggle back up steep paths, in blazing heat, with boys, pushchair, buckets, spades, balls, wet towels, swimsuits and dog.

The magnificent beach of Pilat Plage stretches away south, out of sight. The shallow sea is calm, sheltered from the Atlantic breakers by the thin spit of land that encloses the Bassin d'Arcachon.

I taught the boys to swim. For small children, the beach was boring. No Cornish rocks to climb, no pools teeming with marine life, no streams to dam. The silver sand was too dry and slippery to make a decent sandcastle. There was no shade, not even a puff of cloud for protection from the relentless midsummer sun. We lacked a parasol.

I had been promised a tiny weekly wage and half a day off a week. Instead of just paying me the agreed amount, Nicole always consulted the newspaper to see if the rate of exchange had shifted, in case she could pay me a few centimes less.

On my half day, I was free after I had put the boys down to rest, so long as I was back in time to bath them and put them to bed. I just had time to catch a bus into Arcachon, buy a copy of "Elle" and sit under a shady tree outside a café to enjoy a café liègeois. My wages just covered the cost.

Georges was never a problem at bedtime, but Christian would call me back again and again. I would line up all the things he might ask for, the drink of water, the favourite toy, etc. It taxed his ingenuity to think up new excuses. "I've got smoke up my nose". I think he wanted a cuddle from his mother; no chance.

One day, it was apparent Georges was not well. I asked for a thermometer to take his temperature. After some delay, Nicole said she had "broken it". The scorching heat of the beach was out of the question, so we trudged into the pine forest, where we could sit in shade while I read to them. I read Beatrix Potter and Mickey Mouse to the boys until I knew them by heart. (Jeremy Pêche-a-la-Ligne and Le Roi Mickey.) I learned a lesson in "Be Prepared". Pine needles do not mop-up well. Georges had mumps. Two weeks later, Christian swelled up too. Although I had mumps at school, I was not immune. Nicole chose to ignore my swollen face, expressing surprise when I lay on my bed instead of going to Arcachon on my weekly "day off".

There was some debate about the origin of the mumps. As it has a long quarantine period, it seemed obvious to me that Georges had picked it up at the end of the last school term. Nicole would not accept that. She blamed me for consorting with the only other people on the beach, a Belgian family with two children a little older than my two charges. Nicole only came to the beach once, to inspect the Belgians. She pronounced them socially inferior, but I found them friendly and pleasant. I was glad to have someone to talk to and for the boys to have some playmates. I missed them when their two-week holiday ended.

Dinah was an English-bred long-haired dachshund, owned by the grandmother and greatly prized on account of its impeccable pedigree. That mattered. Herself the daughter and widow of generals, she was a prize snob. Dinah had been in the habit of sleeping on her owner's bed. One morning, Grandmère woke to find her missing. She had slipped quietly down to my basement room in the night.

The catch on the door was faulty and she pushed it open with her nose. I awoke to find her stretched out beside me on my narrow bed, her head beside mine on the pillow. Grandmère was mortally offended at this show of disloyalty, hinting that I must have lured her down. My bed was so narrow I had no wish to share it.

As both children and dog spent most of their time with me, it was natural, but awkward, that they came to look to me for affection. The boys were too young to be tactful. I was not letting Nicole's mean ways upset me. I was getting the remedial seaside and early nights I sought. At meals I hoped to improve my French. I was fluent within the limited vocabulary of a five-year old, but got lost in adult conversations.

When I had been there about three weeks, an elderly English family friend arrived. I fancy she had invited herself. Her execrable French was intolerable, so English was spoken at meals. Nicole's English was worse than my French. The boys did not like feeling excluded, so played up to get their mother's attention. They were ignored until fretful, went too far and got cuffed a bit too hard, often about the head. I could not intervene to head-off trouble; I had no authority at mealtimes.

Georges was a sweet-natured child, plain with mousy hair and protruding ears. Christian was beautiful, with golden wavy hair and lustrous dark brown eyes. He was indulged and spoiled, at the expense of his older brother.

The visitor upset things, fanning seeds of discontent. To me, she harped on about Nicole's ingrained parsimony. The food was poor because Nicole would not buy decent provisions. The cook was bad because Nicole would not pay enough to get a good one. I did not want to hear, I preferred to ignore what I could not change and didn't wish to be made to feel exploited. In the evenings, I went down to my room soon after dinner. From the drone of conversation in the room above, I could catch my name, so presumably she was then criticising me. The wretched woman soured the atmosphere. She stayed six weeks.

When she left, Nicole's seventeen year-old brother, Henri, came to stay. There were no companions of his own age around. The family did not speak to any of their neighbours. He wanted some tennis coaching, but it was ruled out on account of the cost of hiring a court and paying the coach. There was not much else for the boy to do. I felt so sorry for him I offered to coach him, thinking we could go late in the day, when it was cooler. My offer of free coaching was accepted, but we had to go straight after lunch, in the hour while the boys were resting. He made good progress. Although taciturn with the family, once away, he lightened up.

Pilat Plage was not a real village, just a number of villas dotted among the pines. There was one restaurant, a small épicerie and a boutique. To the south, a range of high sand-dunes ran behind the beach. Before I knew how hard they were to climb, I promised the boys I would take them to the top. With Henri to help, carrying Christian much of the way, we succeeded.

The white sand was so fine and dry that every footstep sank deep, like walking in a hot snowdrift. From the top, we could see over the top of the pine forest below and along the endless beach that ran to distant Biarritz and the Spanish border. The powdery sand later made the dunes popular for skiing.

After I left, Henri was to have a young Englishman to stay, for mutual language practice. I found his father was the head of the prep school my brother had attended and who used to join us on Christmas Day.

The son, Colin, had been a horrid little boy. When Mother used to drive the school car, he was one of her passengers. He liked sticking a penknife into the other children. I had not seen him for many years. I hope he grew up to be delightful.

The boys' father, François, was to arrive on the 14th July and stay for August. Grandmère looked down on her son-in-law, as he was a business man and came from Alsace, both cardinal sins in her eyes. I found him an exceptionally nice man, who deserved their respect and affection. He was big, fair and friendly. We enjoyed each other's company, but I had to be circumspect. Neither Nicole nor her mother had a glimmer of understanding that a simple friendship could exist.

In England, the war had made a huge difference to the easy way men and women could get along together. In France, the war had put them into a time warp. I'd noticed this with Louis' cousins who had spent the war isolated in central France.

It was proposed that a grand excursion be made "to the ocean". This meant driving north to Arcachon, then doubling back down the long spit of land between the lagoon and the Atlantic. It was to be a great day out, with other relatives joining us, taking three cars. There were hints, often expressed before, that English scones would be nice, but I did not nibble. By the appointed day, all the grand plans had evaporated in fussing and aggravation. There seemed little prospect of getting away at all. Picnic plans were abandoned with general bad temper all round.

After lunch, the convoy finally rolled and we eventually got to where we could admire the mighty breakers rolling in and crashing on the beach. The party was re-assembled to sit round a table and oysters were ordered. Once these were despatched, we all got back in the cars and went home again.

It was nearly time for me to leave. As a treat, François, Nicole, Henri and I went to the local nightclub. It was romantically situated, looking out through pines to the sea below. With the band, the dance floor and tables outside, it was idyllic on a fine summer night. Nicole would not dance. Certainly she was showing her pregnancy by this time, but she could have danced if she wanted to. Henri sloped off, presumably in search of local talent.

So François and I danced, rather close. Nicole sat looking very sour but I had scant sympathy for her. I did not like the way she treated her children and she showed no affection or gratitude to her husband, who did all he could to please her. I enjoyed the brief evening and, as the song says: "I could have danced all night . . . " If only . . .

It was August, and time for me to go. I had come to recover from the stresses of hotel housekeeping and had a fine convalescence. Three months of fresh air, sunshine and the company of small children had made me fit and brown. On the last day, with my small luggage packed, I was ready to catch the bus to Arcachon station. We were all out on the terrace and Henri was chasing the children, getting them over-excited. Christian, running full tilt, glanced back over his shoulder and ran smack into a jutting brick wall with an awesome thump. With both hands clapped over his eye, he ran howling straight past his mother to my lap. I was terrified of what I might find when I calmed him down enough to let me look. Mercifully his eye seemed undamaged, but he was brewing up a mighty shiner. I gently handed him over to his father and went down the hill to catch the bus.

When my daughter was about sixteen, she was invited to join some school-friends who had rented a part of a villa somewhere in France. It was the same villa, Aïnhara, where I had spent those months so many years before. The bedroom door-catch was still not fixed.

CHAPTER
THIRTY-TWO

First Floor, Ladies' Lingerie

Time for another scene-shift and to exchange the Ambre Solaire, the beach clothes, espadrilles for sombre black. I joined Harrods' "Contingent", a group of about 20, either University graduates or those whose previous experience marked them out for early promotion. We were to learn by going to any department suddenly short of staff. Two of us went to Toys and found it wasn't child's play. Frank (ex-LSE) took on boxed games, needing a hasty squint inside the lid to see what it was about. I tackled dolls, thinking it would be safer territory. Each morning, I faced a pile of naked dolls and tried to dress them. I'd assemble a fetching outfit, only to find the openings too small to go over the doll's head. Each time one sold, it fell to me to replace it.

Customers often wanted advice on a suitable choice for a certain age, the child always "of above average intelligence". Georges and Christian were my only benchmarks. For fun, Frank and I shunted awkward customers between us. "Perhaps a game would be more suitable for such an intelligent child?" If Frank saw me coming in time, he side-stepped, leaving me in the mire.

Next stop, the Ladies' Coat Department. The room had windows across one end and showcases down each side, so customers were funnelled in. Seniors in the front row sized-up the approaching victim, either stepping forward with a smarmy smile or melting away, letting the next row take their pick. Temporaries like me hovered at the back, to pick up their leavings. Their judgement was fallible and I could see shafts of annoyance if I picked up a sale that had slipped through their fingers. Winter coats in the mass are heavy to handle. After a day getting them in and out of showcases, shoulders and arms ached, as well as legs and feet. We couldn't sit, except at coffee or lunch break.

The average Department had a Buyer, responsible for buying the merchandise within a budget agreed with the Management. Setting the selling prices was the hard part. They should also spend time out on the floor, learning what customers wanted. This is where many buyers fail, preferring to impose their own taste on the public. Sir Richard walked the floors regularly and wanted to see his Buyers out on the front.

The Assistant Buyer saw to the daily running of the department, organised staff, dealt with problems and difficult customers. The Buyer's Clerk processed orders, invoices and sales records, liaising with the Marking-Off Room Clerk, who unpacked and checked incoming goods, put on price tickets and sent them up to the department. A Packer put sold clothes in a box with layers of tissue-paper and strung it with a carrying handle. No slinging in a plastic bag. Harrods Box Factory was on the premises. A couple of Juniors ran errands, but after a week in the job they got canny and were never around when wanted. Each saleswoman was responsible for a section of the stock, which needed tidying and dusting every morning, with fresh stock brought forward from reserve. A good Buyer can learn a lot from her staff, if she will only listen.

Next was the Linen Department. Here the problem was the varying sizes of sheets, blankets and towels, plus the range of fabrics for each. The safest corner seemed to be among the fancy linens, where I could discuss the rival merits of pink roses versus blue bows. Since one had been sent because they were short of staff, no one wanted to be plagued by daft questions from temporaries, who were liable to rob them of commission anyway. Tact was needed and sweeteners by occasionally writing a sale in an assistant's "book".

Then, a move away from the sales floors to Enquiries, i.e. Complaints. Each morning I started with a batch of letters from customers and had to pursue each query, find a solution and draft a reply. Most were concerned with Accounts or Despatch. I walked miles a day, visiting the departments where the sales originated, up to Accounts at the top of the main building, down to the basement and under the tunnels that led under Brompton Road to Trevor Square, where goods for despatch were handled. Electric trucks pulling wagons careered through the tunnels, clanging their bells. Parcels trundled on overhead conveyor belts, all making a fearful din. Pedestrians scampered through the tunnels at their peril.

I found it galling to see a really bitchy customer get away with a spurious complaint. I dictated a placating letter to a Mrs McVicar, angering her still further as the typist addressed her as Mrs MacNicker. Some knew the customer is always right, if she shouts loud enough. Serious trouble, involving big money, was handled by a rough-diamond cockney character with a plush office and deep comfortable armchairs for those he saw in the store. Often he went to a customer's home, perhaps on a matter concerning interior decorating or furnishing. He had a free hand to negotiate, using tough or tender as he thought fit. I would love to have heard him in action; he could settle anything. For me, it was all valuable training. I got to know key people in the behind-the-scenes departments. I knew who to go to.

I joined the Trimmings Department on the Ground Floor, selling artificial flowers, feathers and baubles, mainly for trimming hats or dresses. A sophisticated lady, older than me, was also on that counter. She had been the very senior WAAF Officer on the selection board when I was a nervous candidate, passed to go to OCTU. I think she came to Harrods hoping to become a Buyer quickly, but she did not stay long and went to a job elsewhere. Harrods' loss. Meanwhile, we had fun. We would amuse ourselves with little charades when we both pretended to be French, going into a double act over whether Madame would be more élégante with the grey feather or the yellow carnation.

I moved on for a spell in Fashion Jewellery, expecting to enjoy it, but strong lights reflecting off the merchandise in glass-topped counters were hard on the eyes. Here, customers were shameless at buying a piece one day and bringing it back, after the party, with the usual "my husband does not like it." This routine was used blatantly with Fashions too. Hats, bought on Friday were worn to a wedding on Saturday and brought back on Monday. Even dresses with sweat-stains or make-up on them were sometimes returned.

On to the Lingerie Department on the first floor. This I enjoyed. The Buyer was first class, a pleasure to work with. She was without an Assistant Buyer at the time, so I was "Acting". We sold dressing gowns, negligées, nightdresses, pyjamas, slips, knickers and combinations. Combinations were a speciality and a steady trade, They could be made from wool, silk/wool, spun silk, sea-island cotton. The tops could be opera-top (ribbon shoulder straps), round-neck, V-neck, sleeveless or short-sleeved. The legs could be short, medium or long. The size could be small, women's, OS or XOS. They could be pink or white. Imagine the possible permutations and problems of what to stock, without using up the department's entire budget. Each garment was beautifully made, fully fashioned and complicated to manufacture. Consequently, they were expensive. Harrods had the best stock in the world and mail orders were received from all round the globe. A dissertation on the subject, suitably embellished, went down rather well at dinner-parties.

A customer brought in several pairs of musty combs, belonging to her late mother. Enquiries established they had been bought some years previously, but not worn as the lady became bedridden. Now the daughter sought to cash them in. She was most surprised when I suggested that she would not like to buy something which had been out of our care, in someone else's house, perhaps attacked by moth . . .

A Hungarian customer, who lived alone with her dachshund in a Sloane Street flat, so appreciated the help I had given her in choosing her combs that she came regularly to the department for a little chat. One day she came in without the dog under her arm, weeping copiously. She'd been crossing Knightsbridge when the dachs was run over, still attached to its lead.

The position of Assistant Buyer for Lingerie was advertised. I and about a dozen others applied for it and were put through I.Q. tests and interviews. I was delighted to be appointed.

One of our suppliers was a Jewish refugee from Central Europe. She had a little group of embroideresses making exquisitely embroidered silk nightdresses and slips, each a work of art. We took all she could make. She always brought them in herself and it was a joy to open the box of rustling tissue paper and admire the beautiful workmanship. The price she was paid was probably pitiful for the skill and time spent on them. The time had not arrived when price-snobbery meant that the more expensive, the more the object was prized. Nor were there so many foreign residents and visitors, to whom price was irrelevant.

Still in the future were credit cards, a prize possession for a mistress. Later, some people even came to like having pricey manufacturers' logos showing.

Friday lunchtime sometimes brought men, looking for a naughty nightie. We kept black and red chiffons in stock for them. Some came bashfully, some brashly on a breeze of alcohol. When asked about size, they looked round the department until they saw a body they thought right. "Same as her."

Taking things to a fitting room for a customer to try on revealed the remarkable underwear, or total lack of it, some people wore. One middle-aged lady from the shires was starkers under her tweed suit and twin-set. Apparently well-dressed ladies wore grubby worn-out underwear long overdue for the dustbin.

I would not have liked to be in the adjacent, but separate, Corset Department, where they had to fit bras, corsets and belts on grotesquely varying figures. I took some lingerie over to a customer already in one of their fitting rooms. Madam was drunk. She swayed so much that she could not stand on one leg to get the other into the garment. One of us had to prop her up while the other guided the errant limbs in the right direction.

Their department backed onto the Zoo, where there was a problem with rats. They were regularly poisoned and died behind the fitting rooms. They reeked. The smell of decaying rat is distinctive, I could recognise it anywhere. I learned a lot at Harrods.

Unfortunately, I did not take to Miss Sowden, Head of Staff Training. There was mighty little training available for anyone above the rank of Junior. Hearing that Harrods sent two people on an annual one-week Summer School at one of the Oxford colleges, my Buyer put my name forward. Miss S. was very sarcastic that I had the temerity to ask to go, mentioning in passing that one of the places was anyway reserved for the person who came top of the textile study course. It was news to me that there was such a course. I got details and enrolled, with Penny, Assistant Buyer of Knitwear.

We learned the properties and treatment of different textiles; wool, linen, cotton and synthetics, which was basic for anyone in the rag trade. The tutor was unused to having females on his courses, and made coy jibes at our expense, so it was doubly satisfying when Penny and I took the first two places in the little exam at the end of the course. Now I qualified for the next Summer School? Miss S. flatly denied that being top of the class gave entrée to such a treat.

My contentment in the Lingerie Department was shattered when Management moved me to Girls' Wear. Miss Betts had been Buyer there many years, with a reputation for being an autocrat with a sharp tongue. Her faithful old Assistant Buyer had cracked and been sent on indefinite leave. I was to take over. There was much to learn. Some sizing systems were by age, some by length, some by chest measurement, some bearing no apparent relation to anything, least of all a child.

Miss Betts' office organisation was first-class and I was grateful to her for taking the trouble to teach me

363

how her system worked. As a Buyer, the snag was that she was happiest running an efficient office, but took less interest in the merchandise and none whatever in what the mothers and daughters wanted to buy. The party dresses were hopelessly old-fashioned, the styles had not been changed for years.

A fundamental weakness lay in the conflict between the general policy of the store and the particular needs of a clientèle tied to school terms. The store's financial year was divided into two "halves", from 1st February to 31st July and from 1st August to 31st January. Each "half" had a rigid budget. The official policy was to run stocks down at the end of each "half", prior to the Sale.

At Christmas, when the girls came off the school trains for the holiday, there was nothing much left on the rails. The same happened at the end of the summer term.

The Management were not silly and a better arrangement to meet the needs of that particular department could have been arranged, but they were never asked.

With the Christmas holidays in sight, I begged for more party dresses. I had a chat with one of our suppliers and he made me a sample of just what I wanted. It was dark tartan taffeta, quite "grown-up" and suitable for 12 to 16 year-olds, who had left frilly pastel net behind. Surprisingly, Miss Betts gave me carte-blanche to get as many as I needed. The supplier co-operated and I had daily deliveries arriving by taxi and brought up main stairs straight into the department, in plain wrappers. This broke all the rules, but the staff and customers were delighted. Perhaps at some of the Christmas parties half the girls were wearing identical dresses.

My main job, as I stood out in the middle of the department, was to direct customers to the Ladies' Cloakroom, in the adjacent Baby Shop. The range of euphemisms for "lavatory" seemed infinite, through Powder Room, Rest Room, Bathroom, Toilets to whimsical flights of fancy.

Talking to the rep. from Tootals, I found they ran a little course for retailers at their Head Office in Manchester. This sounded like a good idea, but I knew better than to mention it to Staff Training. Miss Betts was reasonably amenable. Despite her fierce reputation, she treated me very well. Next time Mr Leathes, a Director, came round, I asked diplomatically and got his instant approval. Miss Sowden was told to arrange for me to attend the course.

While there, I stayed with Mollie, my WAAF friend from RAF Holme-upon-Spalding-Moor. She and Kim were now married and living in nearby Lymm. The week in Manchester was instructive. We were taken through all the processes at the cotton mills. I was struck by the appalling noise in the weaving sheds, which must surely have led to deafness, and by the numbing boredom of the jobs. Imagine all day watching looms to spot broken threads, or watching cloth moving rapidly over a light-table looking for flaws.

On the course, I met a girl who worked at the Head Office of Marks and Spencer, in Baker Street. She invited me to lunch in her staff dining-room and showed me round. I was impressed. The money was good and a five-day-week was appealing. Harrods closed at 1 o'clock on Saturdays. By the time I travelled home, had lunch and changed, there was not much of the day left. I arranged an interview and was offered a job as a Trainee Buyer. I could not even envisage any promotion at Harrods, so I accepted. I told the Staff Office I would be leaving.

Within 20 minutes of returning to the department, Mr Leathes appeared, huffing and puffing, saying that under no circumstances was I to take any action. Within the hour, Sir Richard sent for me. He asked me one question: "Do you understand the value of money?" He offered me the job of Buyer of the Gift Department on the Ground Floor. I was amazed and delighted. It was good-bye to a five-day week, but no-one turned down a Buyership at Harrods.

CHAPTER
THIRTY-THREE

Buying time

The Gift Department was in a sorry mess. The Buyer had been sacked. He'd thought he was not being allowed enough money to finance the volume of trade he believed he could do. He gambled. He spent to the hilt very early in the "half", placing further verbal orders for later confirmation, by which time he reckoned he would have increased sales sufficiently to justify an additional spending allocation. He had tried this before, on a small scale, and been reprimanded. This time, he had plunged deep. One of the suppliers was unhappy at being asked to keep stock aside without a confirming order and enquiries were made. The Buyer was away, his desk was searched and a drawer full of unsigned orders found. On his return, he was up before Sir Richard, and out.

Harrods were fair with the suppliers involved. Accepting responsibility, they honoured any verbal orders where to cancel would have been damaging. The result was an unbalanced stock, with a glut of some things and a dearth of others. The Department had to be left to run through Christmas and the January sale used to clear the decks for a new Buyer, moi, to make a fresh start on 1st February.

I had to kick my heels in the Girls' Department for a couple of months, too shy even to walk through Gifts, and nervous of what I had taken on, knowing absolutely nothing about the job. I had no training, beyond what I had picked up in the Contingent.

I knew I would need a Really Good Suit, so boldly went to the French Room, where top-class clothes were made-to-measure in their own workrooms. As a Buyer, I could purchase anything in the store at Cost + 5%; even at that, it was expensive, but I knew I needed it for my own self-confidence. It was a beautiful suit, of finest cloth, excellent style and cut, but I was disappointed with it, without knowing why. Although as a Buyer, I could wear any colour, I figured that a black suit was sure-fire smart. Only much later did I learn that black is only good on people of certain colouring; not me.

Although still not actually "there", I was invited to the annual Buyers' Cocktail Party in January, when all the fashion buyers twittered about what they would wear to impress their peers and the Management. I bought a mustard-yellow hat to wear with my new posh suit. I was looked over critically, passed muster, and accepted into the ranks of the blessed.

The atmosphere on the Ground Floor was more relaxed and friendly than up among the Fashion Queens, who took themselves seriously and put on airs and graces, some carefully modulating their vowels to obscure humble origins. In summer, the annual Ascot Week saw their finest flowering. Sir Richard always had a box for them, so they could observe what potential customers were wearing. It never dawned on them that they were there for educational purposes. The flutter over what each would wear was a delight to witness. At coffee one morning, the Handbag Buyer let slip I was going to Ascot. She knew because she was lending me a handbag. Shock! Me? A Ground Floor Buyer? Surely not. I had to explain I was going as myself, not a Harrods Buyer. Though not running in the Fashion Stakes, I did have the one smart accessory they lacked, a top-hatted escort squiring me in the Cavalry Club tent.

On February 1st I took a deep breath and walked in to face my new staff. The Assistant Buyer, Lucy, naturally resented having a novice brought in over her head, but generously got over her disappointment and I couldn't have had a more loyal devoted Assistant. My clerk seemed bright and the sales staff were good and knew their stock well. They would be my tutors. I spent time with each, asking her opinion on the section of stock she looked after, encouraging them to tell me if they did not have what customers asked for. When new stock arrived, I invited them all to have a look and tell them about it. This seemed plain common sense. I was amazed by their surprise and pleasure at being included as part of a team.

From the day I started, the pressing urgency was to get in new stock, as no forward orders had been placed. I had to dive in and get on with it. I did not know what would be new and fresh and what had been running for years. I had to work out what I should buy from an unbalanced stock, from which the best had already gone. I had only the unloved and unsold to learn from. I took Lucy's advice about which suppliers to visit first and was frank with them about my lack of experience. That way they would be foolish to be anything but genuinely helpful, and so it turned out.

I found I was blessed with the invaluable knack of "feeling" how much to order from a collection. Without consciously totting up as I went along, the total would come out remarkably near the figure I'd budgeted for.

I seldom had to vary a confirmation order. Broadly, we covered leather goods — jewel cases, make-up cases, writing cases, needlework cases, desk sets and photo frames; decorated table mats and trays; ornaments, pottery, glass, waste-paper bins, linen bins, dressing table sets. In fact anything decorative that might be given as a present. "Gifts" was a dreadful name, but no one could think of anything better. At least it was better than its old name, "The Foreign Fancy".

An early priority was to improve the display, getting ankle-high platforms raised to waist height. We had two main platforms, each forming a large island round a pillar, plus sundry tables, showcases and shelves round the walls. We changed the main displays frequently. If Lucy and I decided, say, to have a main show of pigskin and scarlet, to show off our innovation of having cases lined with interesting colours, we raided the whole room for colours to make up a striking show. This would look great, but having denuded other displays, we ended up having to re-do most of the room and it was a scramble to be ready by the time we got busy.

Dazzled by our display, customers bought from it. That was the object of the operation, but it was hard not to feel almost peeved that our artistic endeavours had been promptly diminished. Any event could supply a theme. The day of the Boat Race was an exercise in light and dark blue. Long-handled shoehorns, thoughtfully bought for the occasion, were crossed as oars.

From the point of view of the staff, it was easier to have similar merchandise grouped together, but to have impact and catch a customer's eye, some colour grouping was needed to save the place being a visual muddle. We were well-located, with one of the main arteries of the store running through the department, taking customers past our main displays. Our other axis was good too, running through Silver to the Food Halls. Lifts were close.

Position is of crucial importance. A department tucked away off a main thoroughfare has a crippling handicap.

It is probably easier to buy for a big London store, where many customers are visitors, than a provincial shop whose locals soon know the stock and need the constant titillation of the new. But it is more complicated than that. Staff get bored with familiar stock. Something fresh will engage their interest and be passed on unconsciously to the customer. Older stock, even though it might be better value, can become boring, and hard to shift. If at that point, a new assistant arrives, the chances are that the old warriors will soon get sold.

Harrods price tickets neatly told a story. Each "half" had a serial letter. When we were in, say, "F half", a ticket with "E2" would have dated from the second month of the previous "half". The cost of the item was shown in code. It had to be changed from time to time, as it became known to busy little journalists seeking to make mischief.

At stocktaking or with a Sale looming, it was easy to see what had been hanging around too long. I did not put much in our Sales, after learning a sharp lesson early on. A slightly chipped pot was sold at a much reduced price, with the bill marked that it was damaged. The purchaser gave it to a friend as a wedding present. She brought it back, demanding a refund. Should I have told her that her friend got it cheap? I didn't, but sold no more damaged goods. I wrote them off and offered them free to my staff.

The suppliers, of course, were agog to have a go at me. Every morning they were in the department, all wanting to establish themselves with the new Buyer. I blessed Lucy for weeding them out.

What Harrods bought had a trickle-down influence through the Gift Trade in hideous manifestations. I could see it at work when I went to the annual Gift Trade Fair, held in Harrogate's biggest hotel. I did not go to buy, but to see what to avoid. On my first visit, I had no idea the impact my arrival would have. There were stands in the Ballroom, where I could get round reasonably easily, but upstairs bedrooms had been cleared to make individual showrooms. As soon as I set foot in the corridor, heads popped out of every doorway, anxious to inveigle me in. I was glad I'd had the forethought to be booked into a different hotel, where I could eat in peace.

The important thing was to avoid buying products that would be offered in shops with lower overheads and therefore able to sell at lower prices. Harrods' overheads are massive, but customers still expect them to sell at the same price as elsewhere. Few appreciate the difference between a bare, cash-only, self-service shop and a store offering a plush ambience, free credit, free delivery and a high ratio of staff to customer. These things are not free but part of the price.

Setting selling prices is the hardest part of the job. Any fool can stock nationally advertised lines, turn in high sales figures, but with inadequate mark-up. I sought lines exclusive to Harrods, providing a good margin for the store, but were still good value to the customer.

With the co-operation of the best table-mat supplier, I developed a Harrods' set of London prints. The originals were reproduced in black/white, then hand-coloured. To know them from others, we privately called them the "Mansford" Series. (Half Lucy's name+ half mine.) I'm waiting to see them come up on a TV antiques show, and see what the "Experts" make of the name.

We also brought out three new exclusive colours for mats, nick-naming them "Haze, Blaze and Maze." Some months later another supplier came to show me his new colours. Wow! I'd been robbed. Apparently the Colour Council had pinched "my" colours and promoted them to the paint trade as Princess Margaret Blue, etc., especially for the forthcoming Coronation.

Some suppliers wanted to sell something to me and then trot round other shops, saying "Harrods have bought this". One supplier was particularly bothersome. I turned down a nasty cigarette box, got up like a park bench. He had it advertised in a magazine, quoted a price, adding "Available at Harrods." To teach him a lesson, I took twenty on "Sale or Return", kept them in a cupboard for a month, then told him to come and take them away. No one had asked for one.

An elderly gentleman wanted to sell me velvet-covered wastepaper baskets, for which I already had a reliable source. Seeing my name, he had rightly deduced I must be a relative of his fellow-officer in the Connaught Rangers, Great Uncle George, of Rangerford, Stranocum. He wore the regimental tie, and was disappointed I didn't recognise it. It was humiliating for him to be reduced to flogging bins, so I bought a few. His glue wasn't up to the job and the fabric fell off.

Our main leather suppliers were clustered in the Islington area. Walking through once-elegant squares, it was sad to see them so near to dereliction. If I'd had more foresight and money, I could have bought myself a nice little nest-egg. Many samples were sent in by post, usually wrapped in newspaper in a shoe-box. The accompanying letter, on headed paper, would be along the lines of: "I have been an Account Customer at Harrods for many years. I have made these crinoline ladies/galleons from sea shells/barbola work/pressed flowers for our local sales of work. All my friends tell me they are so lovely that I should sell them to Harrods." All had to be properly repacked and returned with a letter firm enough to dissuade further advances, without being hurtful. An occasional variant was: "I have sent these as presents to the Royal Family."

One day, I told Lucy I was too busy to see any suppliers, not even to make an appointment. A Mr Freeman asked to see me. Lucy did as I'd asked, but he was reluctant to go. I saw him, and he saw me, but I did not register. I finally went over to him and found he was the father of Diana, a friend at school with me at Ancaster House. Several times they had included me when they came down to take Diana out for the day. His firm had been supplying the Gift Department with expensive leather desk sets and onyx cigarette boxes, ash trays, etc. I went to his showroom in Regent Street and placed an order. Onyx, more aptly known as soapstone, scratched and bruised very easily and I had to give up stocking it.

There was a tricky conflict between what I should stock and allied departments. Turnery sold plain table-mats and trays, ours had prints on. The Silver Department sold silver frames, ours were leather, and so it went on. When I turned down inferior quality mass-produced cocktail mats and saw them turn up in the adjoining Stationery Department, I was round to my Section Manager in a trice. Sir Richard helped me if he spotted anything impinging on "my" territory. The Buyers of other departments were very good-humoured. We all coffeed and lunched together in the Buyers' Dining Room, helping to ensure feathers were not too ruffled.

A Section Manager's role was to oversee a group of departments and keep a strict eye on the money. Buyers are prone to get carried away with enthusiasm for some merchandise that has caught their fancy, but when their coffers are empty. To wheedle out any more, they had to be very persuasive. The closing figure for the "half" was the crunch. If it was too high, the amount got docked from the next "half". In a perfect store, the buyers would be so self-disciplined that this framework would be unnecessary.

My Section Manager, Miss Sloan, was the very best. She had a crisp sense of humour, expressed with keenest wit. Her lightning grasp of finance had answers on the tip of her tongue while I was still scribbling sums. No calculators then. She never interfered with the running of my department, but was always there for help and advice. That a lady with so much of value to say and such power of articulate expression should be struck down with throat cancer, lose the power of speech and gallantly learn to speak again with an artificial voice-box, was a bitter swipe of fate.

By April, the Christmas catalogue needed settling. I sought about fifteen items, from which perhaps a dozen were picked. Points to consider:

1. Not to repeat anything shown in previous years.

2. Neither too expensive nor too cheap.

3. Not breakable, as most items were posted or delivered.

4. Not too hard to describe or illustrate.

The Advertising Department dictated presentation. They could make an ordinary object look fabulous, or kill something good stone dead. They would not say if they would be sketching or photographing and it would be August before I saw a proof, by which time it was too late to vary an order. It was a gamble. Customers would be furious if an advertised item was sold out by Christmas Eve, but it was depressing to have unsold catalogue things in January.

To be placing an order in Italy in April, with so many unknown factors, meant trusting my hunch and crossing my fingers. Frankly, I was very lucky not to have disasters. Once the catalogue went out, we could judge very quickly from the first batches of mail orders. A prompt response meant not displaying in the department, unless specifically asked. If demand was sluggish, we put out a major display.

I would have liked to have bought more from individual British artists and craftsmen, but I found them impossible. Promises to deliver by a given date were seldom honoured. The matter of price was a minefield. The costing of a handmade article in terms of materials, labour, overheads and profit was possible, but evaded. I did not haggle. They were free to state their price. If I could add an adequate mark-up and arrive at an acceptable selling price, I was happy to place an order. They were obsessed with the final selling price. They sent in friends to peek at the price tickets and then felt aggrieved if it was more than they had been paid. If they could, they would then act as retailers, quoting Harrods' price and offering to undercut for a direct sale. Taken as a group, I was shocked to find them unreliable, amoral and self-righteous. Such a pity.

I went to an exhibition to promote Scottish craftsmen. I found enough to be worth flying to Scotland to meet some of the individuals whose work I liked. I made so little headway against bland indifference that I was unable to order enough to justify my plane ticket and hotel bills. What few items trickled through were late and many damaged by inadequate packing.

My first buying trip abroad was to Paris. Harrods belonged to the Associated Merchandising Corporation, an American organisation with offices in main capital cities. Their job was to arrange itineraries for visiting buyers, to act as interpreters and then to handle the paperwork translating orders into goods delivered. The system was wide open to abuse, "minders" being bribed to bring buyers to their showrooms, so I was cagey.

Luckily my contact man was new, honest and helpful. Before starting, I asked him to come with me round some Paris shops. He then traced the sources of things that caught my eye. One new find was "Porcelaine de Paris", who made dishes/ashtrays of fine bone china, decorated with coloured transfer prints of vintage cars, hot-air balloons and old railway engines. I placed a big order, earmarking the cars for the Christmas catalogue. They were a sell-out. What a vintage car industry sprouted from that, throughout the English gift trade! I had twinges of regret, as tidal waves of vintage cars and hot-air balloons, getting ever nastier, washed over any object not moved out of the way in time.

By chance, there were seven other Buyers in Paris at the time. We all stayed at the Hotel Continental, Place Vendôme. It was Harrods' policy to put their Buyers into the most expensive hotel, regardless of its inconvenient location. I was amazed at the naïveté of our apparently sophisticated Buyers, who'd been visiting Paris regularly for years, but acted like timid tourists. They moved only by taxi, never venturing on the Métro, let alone a bus. They consulted tourist guide-books for 5-star restaurants for every meal and then wondered why their generous expense allowances did not go far.

I had a lot of ground to cover, nipped around on the Métro and ate at the nearest promising-looking little place. One day, I was just leaving the AMC office for lunch, when I encountered three women Buyers twittering over finding a taxi to take them all the way to a rip-off place in the Champs Elysées. Greatly daring, they decided to come with me. You would have thought I was taking them to a white-slave dive. They enjoyed a good meal, at modest expense, but begged me not to let-on where we'd been.

The Toy Buyer, an enterprising fellow, was keen that we should all go out for the evening. We counted our money and thanks to my thrifty ways, I had enough to lend to those who were skint. We went to a nightclub I knew, where we would get a good meal plus a floor show and good-humoured entertainment. We had a great evening. Most of the waiters were also entertainers and a fair bit of audience-participation was called for.

As a party of eight English we had a little Union Jack stuck on our table. I was pushed forward to "volunteer for England" as one of four nationalities. Sitting on a chair on the dance floor, I had to drink wine spewing from a long-spouted carafe held high above by a waiter. Glug, glug, glug, it poured down my gullet. Two dropped out, leaving me versus a French girl. I cracked first, but was thought to have done well. I spent the next twenty minutes with my head in my hands, recovering. Our sweet elderly spinster Needlework Buyer sat glued to her chair all evening, with the wide-eyed wonder of a small child gazing at a Christmas tree. She loved it. Most of the others were returning to London the next day, but I was staying on.

By the time I got back, tales of our evening had grown with the telling. Some of the Fashion Buyers, who had not been there, were a touch sniffy, but the men were keen to know dates of my future trips.

My next was to Milan and Florence. Mrs Gaunce, the Lampshade Buyer, was going at the same time, so we travelled together by train, as she didn't want to fly. Even in the comfort of First Class, it was a long journey, rewarded near the end by the run along the Riviera, with the brilliant Mediterranean so near the track. I had started the trip a touch under par, having dined at The White Tower, in Soho, the previous evening and not got to bed till 2a.m. I must have reeked of garlic. Arriving in Milan early next morning, we couldn't get into our rooms before noon. The ultra-modern hotel had no lounge, not even comfortable armchairs to relax in.

I went to a supplier with a spectacular showroom in the country. A wall of glass overlooked a wide river and gentle countryside. Glass shelves spanned the windows, so I was looking at green glassware with a glorious view beyond. It all looked lovely, but I had to remember the environment at the point of sale. Delicious though it all looked, I only bought a few tall jugs and carafes. When the consignment arrived in the department some months later, I was glad I had been restrained. It was all right, but its magic had remained in Tuscany.

Mrs Gaunce and I sometimes shared the AMC interpreter, so it was often convenient for me to go along and sit quietly while she did her buying. It was surprising and instructive. She found a lot of Art Nouveau and Art Deco type lamps, which excited her. These styles had been out of fashion for so long that they struck my eye very oddly at first, but by the end she had broadened my limited vision considerably.

In Florence, we were booked into an expensive hotel, but the weir on the Arno thundered right under our windows. I can usually sleep through anything, but even with cotton wool and a pillow over my ears, the roar of the water got into my head. It rained relentlessly for three days, but there was no time for sight-seeing anyway. I started at about eight in the morning and finished after at eight at night. I was mainly looking for Florentine leatherwork. The workshops were dotted around the oldest part of the city. I was led down winding alleys, up twisting stairs into little workshops, seemingly unchanged since the days of the Medicis. I hoped to buy for the Christmas catalogue, but each workshop was too small to have the capacity to make the amount I needed.

We stopped for a couple of days in Paris on the way back. This time there were no others there to party. Most of the suppliers I wanted to see were out in industrial suburbs. Any far off the beat were customarily asked to bring samples in to the AMC office, but I wanted to see the actual place of manufacture, at least on my first visit. It was hard on a salesman to have to work from a suitcase, as though on the pavement in Oxford Street, and I needed to get the feel of the company and see whether what I was being shown was a small part of the whole, or their total range. What they thought I would like could be less interesting than something that caught my eye elsewhere in the showroom.

Mrs Gaunce wanted to go to the Folies Bergères. She was a serious lady, dedicated to her work, and thought the Folies might be a source of inspiration. Surely an original reason for seeing the show? Mrs G. mentally ran a flex up any static object and popped an imaginary shade on the top. I was dining with Louis and, hearing of her wish, he insisted on taking us both, hugely amused at being a tourist in his own city.

Harrods was a great place for celebrity-spotting. Reading my Evening Standard on the way home told me who was arriving on the Queen Mary. Most would be in the store the following day. Although usually instantly recognisable, their size was often a surprise. Great hulking cowboys turned out to be two jampots high and fragile blondes a strapping six-foot. Gregory Peck did not disappoint; he looked almost too like Gregory Peck to be real. On screen, Ingrid Bergman was an icon of beauty. Without make-up, wearing a drab raincoat, she went unrecognised, not commanding a second glance. Walt Disney was pleasant and chatty. Perhaps it had something to do with having his stars under control, with no tantrums, scandals, alcohol or casting couches to bother about. Stage and film stars, public figures, politicians and the Royal Family all came.

When the Queen came shopping, she came early, before the store got crowded. Usually the Buyers fell over themselves to serve her personally, but I felt the regular assistants had many awkward customers to deal with, so it was only fair they should get the plums too. Anyway, they could do it far better than me.

I had a message that the Queen wanted a big set of table mats for her Ascot Week house party at Windsor. We sorted some out, with original hand-coloured prints of Thames views and London scenes. I went out to get a taxi. The Green Man on the door called one up for me, but a vulgarly overdressed woman tried to push in front of me. The Green Man waved her aside. To me: "Where to, madam?". Me, loudly: "Buckingham

Palace please." That fixed her. Out of her hearing, I added: "The Mews Entrance please." I was seen by a member of the Household, who was sure I had brought exactly what H.M. wanted. I was treated with the utmost courtesy and given a glass of excellent sherry.

When one of my assistants, eyes popping, put her head round my office door, with "I think you'd better come!", I went out to find Lady Churchill there. "I would like a jewel case big enough to take all these things. They are such a nuisance in separate boxes when I travel. I would rather have them all in one case." Out of her shopping bag showered velvet-lined boxes of all sizes and shapes, which she rapidly opened one after another, spilling out necklaces, rings, bracelets in a glittering torrent of diamonds, sapphires, emeralds and rubies, on to a table in full view of the public. If I'd kept my head, I could have shepherded her into the adjacent Jewellery Department, where there were private cubicles. Instead, my assistant swiftly put suitably large jewel cases out and we tried various arrangements as casually as if we were packing for a picnic. "This one will do splendidly. Thank you very much, it will be much better having everything together."

The discarded boxes went back in her shopping bag and the new case, with its priceless cargo, wrapped and put in as well. I walked out of the store, chatting with her, handing her over to the care of a Green Man, who summoned a taxi to take her safely home.

One elderly gentleman only came to the store on rainy days, as he liked to wear a lady's rubberised silk raincape. As he was over six feet tall, and liked his capes long, they were specially made for him. He also spent liberally in the Perfumery Department, being very particular about his choice of lipstick and eye-shadow. Not all customers were as courteous as he was.

One woman had the gall to try to return an expensive seal-skin beauty case, bought three weeks earlier. It had plainly been used and the leather was water-spotted. She was blatantly lying. I tried: "Perhaps your maid has . . .", but I could do nothing with her and had to take her up to the Query Department on the Fourth Floor. She berated me all the way, continuing in the lift, to the surprise of other customers. I said not a word. I was furious to hear she was given a credit and protested so vigorously that the amount was not charged against my department.

We had to cope with the odd drunk or nutter, but on the whole our customers were pleasant and appreciative. Among the locals was Joyce Grenfell, then at the peak of her career as an acute impersonator, not of individual people, but of characters we could all recognise, such as the kindergarten teacher. "Don't do that, George." She bought quantities of blouses, for the pleasure of listening to an elderly assistant, who claimed to be a Russian Princess, speaking a theatrical mixture of broken English and French. She crept into the Grenfell repertoire.

I was happy in my work, enjoying the friendly atmosphere, liking being part of the big enterprise. There were none of the petty grievances that could sour a union-ridden workplace. Representatives attended meetings with the management and a regular newsheet circulated. The hours were still long, with travelling time added, plus working Saturdays till 1p.m., but for me it was luxury to have to stop daily at 5p.m., after the round-the-clock everlasting routine of a hotel. When the store closed, we were promptly shooed out, as steel shutters came down between departments. I once ran back to get something and got a fright, scared I was being shut-in for the night.

Buyers had three weeks annual holiday, which Sir Richard would not allow split. He reckoned we needed a week to unwind and two to enjoy. In addition we had a week of "spring" holiday, which had to be taken before the end of February.

Of six free Saturday mornings, I always had to reserve one to help Mother cook lunch for sixteen before the Bromley Conservative Fête. Harold Macmillan was our M.P. As well as the Macmillans and his Agent, we had various local tom-noddies and a VIP to add lustre to the platform party. Churchill's daughter, Mary Soames, was a delightful guest, with the happy knack of making you feel you had been friends for years.

The dining-room table was made even longer than at Christmas, leaving no space to pass round the end. By seating my brother Peter on one side, and Pam's husband Harry on the other, they could slip out between courses to act as waiters and change the plates.

Macmillan was a witty mimic, with a brilliant account of Churchill being very cross with General de

Gaulle. The lunches always broke-up with reluctance, in order to be punctual for opening the fête.

In the afternoon, Peter and Harry doubled as bouncers, preventing undesirables from gate-crashing the platform. One old duck wanted to clamber up to embrace Mary Soames. I was happy to stay at home, do the washing-up, and put my feet up for half an hour before going along to put in an appearance.

On top of work, I was getting all the social life I needed. I was not pining for immediate matrimony. It was beginning to look as though being so picky would leave me on the shelf, but I would not marry until I found a man I liked, respected and loved. Rating two out of three was not enough. Frank had been around since our trip with the German prisoners. He was good, faithful and affectionate, but his idea of an evening out was a meeting of the embryonic United Nations or a visit to sandals/beards/dirndls in Belsize Park.

I'd known John since we were children and I went to some local dances with him. Galoshes. When I was invited to a party, "and do bring John," it was dumping time. I met Harold at a party, mistaking his sister for his wife. It was not until he asked for my telephone number that I realised my mistake. A pity he was a wimp. He picked me up from Harrods for lunch one Saturday. Driving to Hyde Park Corner, he wanted to go down Constitution Hill, but his driving was not assertive enough to cross the lines of traffic, so he was forced to go round again. I visualised spending the afternoon circulating. The second time round, I stuck my arm out of the window and we were let through. Dennis squired me to Ascot and dined me at his club, but was not taken seriously. Divorced, he had a beautiful daughter about to leave boarding school. He didn't know what to do with her, so I suggested Universal Aunts agency. They arranged for her to go "au pair" to a wealthy French family's château. She married the son, becoming a Vicomtesse.

As my Harrods' department had no windows, we lived with artificial light and breathed umpteenth-lung air. In winter, we were like pit-ponies, for it was dark when we came in and dark when we went home. I craved fresh air by the weekend, so joined the golf club. I had not played since I was an eleven-year-old, partnering Grandaddy. Mother no longer played, so I had her clubs. My putting was still erratic, but my swing was soon back in its groove.

I caught my daily train to work from Shortlands. If I was a little later than I should have been, I chatted with an ex-boyfriend of Pam's. He was one of a group waiting for a City train that left from the other side of the same platform. Peter was among the City group. I "missed" my early train several times. Soon after we were introduced, we chanced to meet at the golf club. He asked me out to dinner. On the sixth time we went out together, he said: "Marry me soon." He richly met my rule of three. I liked him, I respected him, I loved him. It was the end of August. I couldn't decently leave Harrods until end of the current "half", on 31st January, so I went on a long-planned holiday to

Switzerland with Brenda, a friend since hotel days. On my return, Peter and I announced our engagement.

We found a cottage in Kent and planned an April wedding, but Peter became gravely ill with Rheumatic Fever. He was too ill even to sign his name, so I got Power of Attorney to complete the purchase of the house. I had already made my wedding dress and those for my three bridesmaids. They had almost grown out of theirs by the time we were married in June. We lived happily ever after, until, soon after his retirement, he started slipping away, little by little, trapped in the strangling tentacles of Alzheimer's Disease.

For several years, the onset had been so insidious I failed to recognise it. I thought he'd only had a slight stroke. I was mercifully blind. We were in mid-ocean, en route to Martinique and Guadeloupe on a French container ship, when I realised the ghastly truth.

The illness accelerated over the next five years. He died four days after our Ruby Wedding Anniversary.

CHAPTER
THIRTY-FOUR

Back to Padstow

Now I am a widow, my son and daughter both married, enriching me with a daughter-in-law, a son-in-law and five lovely grandchildren. I've craved to return to Padstow, but now I'm nervous of what I may find. What changes have been forced on the town? With its ancient role as a port gone, has the need for a tourist industry turned it into a Theme Park? Should I just remember it as I had known it?

After Wadebridge, I start seeing signs to the "Camel Trail". I pass one or two before the penny drops. I know the old railway track by the river is now for walkers and cyclists, but do not at once make the connection. "The Camel Trail"! Was some member of the Heritage Industry rewarded with a prize for coming up with the cute name? Or shot? I pull into a lay-by to reconsider the wisdom of going on. It's too late to retreat, I must take my chance.

I drive into Padstow in the soft sunshine of a perfect May evening. Wondering where to stay, I'd spotted an advertisement for the Dower House, Fentonluna Lane. That puzzled me. I knew nothing of that name and didn't recognise the illustration of a handsome double-fronted house with bay-windows. Following signs, I drive in and park. No wonder I didn't recognise it. It's the Nook, one-time Vicarage. The only facade I remember is the forbidding one on the top corner of Fentonluna Lane, the elegant back hidden by a high stone wall. Now the opening for cars reveals what has been out of sight for so long.

Taken up to my room, I go straight to the window. Overlooking the town, to the Estuary beyond, I see only solid golden sand. I look over to Rock and up towards Wadebridge, but there's not a drop of blue water in sight. Before the surprise of this sinks in, a slight movement to the left catches my eye. There, grazing quietly, is the Prideaux Place herd of deer, the direct descendants of those so memorable in my childhood. I'm moved that they should be there, at this moment, on that small visible patch of the many acres of the Paddock.

After my drive from Hampshire, I want to stretch my legs, so walk the few hundred yards to stand in front of Prideaux Place. I prepare myself in case it is run-down and dilapidated, but it looks splendid. My spirits lift. Freed from its old dark creepers, it looks in fine shape. A notice by the gate shows it is open to the public. I can go tomorrow.

I do not even know who the present owner is. After old Col. Prideaux-Brune died, it did not pass to Major Dennis. Although he and his family lived there, he was not the eldest son. I'd heard of another brother, who was not quite approved of. His main crime seemed to be that he belonged to something called "The Dress Reform League"; he wore corduroy trousers.

The family are still at lunch, so I leave a message and my maiden-name with the guide. As I start to stroll away, the sound of running feet on the gravel makes me turn. A young man says "Do please come in. Father wants to meet you." I am greeted by Peter Prideaux-Brune, introduced to his wife, Elizabeth, and his two sons. We talk non-stop, each able to tell the other of past events, filling in gaps. He tells me who accidentally shot the Windsor stag, the gift of the King. I'm astonished. Poor man, how he must have suffered for having squeezed the trigger at the wrong moment, at the wrong animal. I hope his identity was not common knowledge in his lifetime. I will not repeat it even now.

I join a guided tour round the house and am invited to wander where I please and to come tomorrow, when the house is closed to the public. Old family photograph albums are laid out in the library for me. During World War II, the U.S Army had the whole place and the gardens got completely overgrown. The flower gardens lie behind the house. The ground rises steeply and grass paths lead to the Italian garden, now happily restored, laid-out with formal beds round a central fountain.

The Dutch garden I remember as being square, with several stone-flagged levels down to a central pool. Massed irises and tulips contrasted with grey paving, reflecting in the water when the light was right. There is no sign yet of its existence, but I think I know where it might be. I would like time to explore; the bones of it must be somewhere under all the bushes and choking ivy. The estate archives may prove me wrong. The gardens are not seen from the main rooms; they look out over the Paddock to a glimpse of the Estuary beyond.

Sitting in the sunshine on the steps outside the library, my mind a jumble of impressions, I notice a few scaffolding poles, left behind by a crew, after filming "As You Like It". There's also a large stone finial on a square base, lying tipped on its side. My eye is drawn back to it, because the house is adorned with right-angled battlements, not large stone balls. Something white glints in the sun. Looking closer, I see the underside of the base is polystyrene. The weathered old "stone" looks authentic, but I could pick it up with one hand.

There have been no cattle in the Paddock for many years, so the Yard lost its original purpose. The bull's little yard now stores white china pipes and lavatory pans. The splendid dairy building has recently been restored and re-roofed. Instead of being used for milking cows, it now houses the carpenter's shop. Peering in, it looks very different from the well-ordered neat place I remembered in its previous location, in the coach-house block. It occurs to me that before the cows were milked there, it might originally have been stables, with the dairy as the tack room.

I skirt the shed where I had seen the doe skinned. Parked cars stand where the row of heads had stood, or I might fancy the stones still blood-stained. The whole Yard is scruffy. Rusty old farm machinery litters one barn, blue plastic sacks move in the breeze, some rusting corrugated iron creaks against a wall and weeds grow unchecked. On a grassy patch in the middle, a pile of mixed rubbish looks as though it's been there some time, with bent metal, white plastic, crumpled chicken-wire and an orange parking cone.

On my way out, I see one entrance pillar still has its urn, but the other has lost its top. One thing that had been insignificant in my childhood is now a glorious sight. A copper beech in its prime soars above the lichen-covered slate roofs. As I walk back to the Dower House, I look for the gate to the Shrubbery path, but after we left, it must have become disused and overgrown. I glance at the spiked railings and hope no other deer tried to leap them and got impaled. Now that the main road into Padstow no longer passes the twin-towered entrance gates, many visitors to the town leave again, ignorant of the treasure they have missed.

So far, so good. My welcome at Place has heartened me and made me glad I've come and not turned tail and fled for home. Now I have the keys to Fentonluna in my pocket, but not yet the courage to use them. Neither am I quite ready to tackle the town. That is where I fear to find the worst changes. Instead, I walk down past my old home and left along St. Saviours Lane. I still treasure the small wooden stool, with my name carved in the top, made for me by Mr LeBlanc Smith, the elderly gentleman who lived in the house next to Fentonluna, now called St. Saviours. I wish he could have known how much I valued such an unexpected present from a virtual stranger. Mother always used it to stand on to wind the clocks at

"Hurst". It is a bit battered now, but with me still and often used.

Going through the iron gate at the end of St Saviours Lane, the full view of the Estuary starts to unfold. Along the top path, wooden seats have been installed, with their backs against the stone wall bounding the edge of the Estate. Each bears a plate in memory of a local resident.

The War Memorial is as I remember it, but another thirty-five names have been added since the Second World War. Sadly, the same family names are there again. Some women lost their husbands and brothers in one war and their sons in the next.

Whatever may be the fate of the town, nothing mars the panorama from the War Memorial and Stile. The tide is in, the water brilliant blue like the sky above, with a few puffy white clouds drifting across. The panorama sweeps from the headlands, back past Greenaway and Brea Hill, the dunes of Rock and on to where the Camel turns away up to Wadebridge. Then the eye travels round to the Iron Bridge, the Jubilee Obelisk, the New Harbour and finally to the jumble of slate roofs in the town below.

I have an old photo of myself as a child, sitting on top of Stile. I want to take the same view again, looking through Stile to Stepper, Newland and Pentire beyond. But there is a blot. The Council has erected a metal sign slap in the way. I am staggered at the insensitive siting of the ugly object. There's a lady there, so I ask her to stand blocking the obtrusive object, mentioning my reason for wanting that particular view.

"May I ask your name then?" she asks. "Ford-Hutchinson." "I have your "Wind in the Willows'!"

When we had to leave Padstow, most of our toys and books were not forwarded to us and were given to children in the town. This lady, then a child, got my book. She read it herself, read it to her daughter, then read it to her grandchildren. She's very kindly returned it to me, so I can read it to my grandchildren. It is inscribed: "B. Ford-Hutchinson from Mrs Dennis, 1932."

I make my way down the lower path of St. Saviours to the town, passing Chiddley Pumps. Because of the silting of the Estuary, the Rock Ferry now comes in there at low tide. The steps down to it are now well-cut and have a handrail, instead of the rough descent that had caused Grandaddy to slip and nearly crush Granny, as Cynthia Prideaux-Brune had crushed my kitten.

Now there are lock-gates at the entrance to the old harbour, keeping water in at all times. Boats no longer flop onto their sides in the mud and the town benefits from being spared the flooding that so often came with the spring tides. Houses round the quay now have no need of the slots each side of the front door, where a board was dropped in and then sand-bagged to keep the water at bay. The flood-water sometimes ran right through to the Square. The Harbourmaster has been ousted by the Tourist Office. He now has a pre-fabricated hut on the quay between the two harbours. Not so grand, but he is in a better position to keep an eye on the comings and goings in both.

The Station House still stands and the Fish Auction Shed is a Wreck Museum. The tall Smoke House smoked its last kipper many years ago and now has other occupants. In the Square, the shop where Mrs May piled-up our ice-cream cornets is now a pasty shop. "Traditional Cornish Pasties", "Traditional Cornish Fudge" and postcards seem to be the staple stock for the tourists. "Tourists" are a modern innovation. They were known as "Summer Visitors" in our day.

How long does it take to become "traditional"? The fudge must have come in to replace the Cornish clotted cream trade. Shops used to display pyramids of round tins in a range of sizes. They packed and posted cream, certain that it would arrive fresh the next morning. The deterioration of the postal service combined, no doubt, with pages of Food Safety Regulations, seem to have killed the business. The toy shop, where I gazed so longingly at Anna May Wong, is now a newsagent, plus fudge and postcards. I fear she did not survive like "Wind in the Willows", her china head smashed long ago. My only souvenir of her is in a Studio Portrait, by Gordon Chase of Bromley. It shows her sitting on my lap. Although the photograph is not in colour, I know my party dress was lavender moiré silk, with tiny pink and blue rosebuds round the neck and edging the puff sleeves. Anna May Wong wore a black kimono patterned with exotic red and gold flowers, with a scarlet obi.

The old Padstow Institute is now a museum, but although it is not yet open for the summer season, I'm told where to find the curator. Much to my surprise, the Ford-Hutchinson name is still remembered, seeming to open all doors. At the time it must have been a major scandal, discussed by everyone and as much of a surprise to Padstow as it was to me.

The museum is packed with relics from old ships, old posters, newspaper cuttings and a wealth of interesting material, far more than I can study in my brief visit. A glass case containing the 'Obby 'Oss commands my full attention. It is a ferocious-looking beast. No wonder I'd been scared. With the glass between us, I examine it properly. The white and red-ringed glaring eyes, the beaky nose, the sinister scarlet mouth, the straggling grey hair and beard are nightmare-fodder. The predatory snapper protruding from the front looks alert to nip the unwary.

Luckily, Padstow is still not big enough to draw in the chain shops, so each still has its individuality. It remains in scale, nothing is glaringly modern, nothing too bogus-quaint, with one awful exception. In the corner of the Square, where Godfrey May's Jeweller's shop had been, Barclays Bank have erected a pair of gross white pillars, supporting a portico. I think it best I do not describe it more, but turn my back and walk round towards the Golden Lion, with the stable of the Red 'Oss in its yard.

Opposite, the Capitol Cinema is still there, saved from closure by the influx of visitors each season. It's shut. I would like to go in, just to complete a scene from my past. I grew up in Padstow unable to grasp the concept of projecting a moving picture onto a screen.

Either I was dense or Mother did not explain well, but I could not grasp the idea. Mr Pope, the owner, kindly opened the cinema, so that I could go and see for myself. Unfortunately I was taken in the morning, when no film was running. Rows of musty seats faced a blank white screen. If only the projector had been turned on for a brief moment, all would have been clear. I left none the wiser.

I go back to the Square, up Duke Street and see again the Estate Agent, whose poetic name I have treasured all my life. Just where I remember, stands an estate agent's office, but under a name so bland I forget it instantly. I'm asking for trouble, but I go in. I ask the girl what had become of the previous firm. She looks blank. I spell it out. I write it down. She scurries to the back office to get reinforcements to deal with this cranky woman asking a weird question. How can a commercial firm abandon such a memorable name?

I sigh. I face the truth. "Button, Menhennit and Mutton" have gone.

And so must I be.

CHAPTER
THIRTY-FIVE

The End of the Beginning

When I left Fentonluna, aged ten, I had no inkling of how long it would be before I returned. The front door had always stood open. Now it is implacably locked. The old dark green paint has vanished under coats of dull white. My hands are shaking. Fumbling with three keys, I need three tries before I can open it.

Smell registers first. Rotten wood. Before anything else, I dash to the back door, grapple with the lock and open up to let sweet fresh air rush right through the house. It feels vitally important to do this quickly, as though I am only just in time to give it the kiss of life.

Outside the back door is the empty garage, where the dark blue war-horse Renault used to stand. The door is in sections, so that it can run round a track against the wall, leaving a clear way out to the road. There was never a door onto the yard. The car was rolled forward to be hosed down, removing the layers of salt and mud picked up from the farms my father visited. Now, not so much as a drop of oil sullies the stone floor. On the spot in the yard where my angora rabbits' hutch had been, there is a green rotary clothes-line standing gauntly askew.

Back in the house, the kitchen, now clinically correct, is the shape I remember, but nothing else is familiar. Thinking of the scrubbed pine table where I helped Myrtle pluck the pheasants, the dresser with the blue and white cups hanging in rows, the massive range heating the flat-irons, I scarcely notice the smart black laminate work-tops, the white stove and the fridge.

The dining-room, now connected to the kitchen by a serving-hatch, still has the alcoves each side of the fireplace — or has the fireplace gone? Now the walls, table and chairs are hospital-white, on a black and white chequered floor. The alcoves are blood red. This is the room where I angered Father when I bounced the little red ball plop into the stew.

The drawing-room puzzles me. Our walls were palest grey, patterned with slender daffodils. I feel so certain that the alcoves were arched, like those in the dining room. Now they are plain rectangles, so I must be wrong. Since I don't remember how it was furnished, what is there is now irrelevant. It looks very small. I don't even step inside.

Halfway up the stairs is the little half-landing, with a few steps leading up to the nursery. Now it is a bedroom, with net curtains blocking the view of the garden. This is where I grew from a baby to a girl with a governess. As long as Miss Webb was with me, lessons were no hardship. Only one book stands out clearly in my vision. Quite big and heavy, with a red cover, it had drawings, with descriptions below in French. A horse, "cheval, chevaux". I must have had a struggle to grasp why it wasn't "chevals", since it sticks in my mind.

Back up the remaining stairs to the landing. On the right, a few steps down, Miss Webb's room overlooks the yard. Next to it the bathroom. The room over the kitchen was mine, looking over the road, where heavy rushing feet passed when the maroon called the lifeboat out. The deep cupboard still runs back under the attic stairs. The shelves on the left were for my folded clothes, a rail for hangers and my shoes lined up neatly on the floor.

My parents' room seems smaller than I remember. Where did my brother, Peter, sleep? Was he in the attic? No. The new second bathroom has confused me. Of course! That used to be his room. I haven't a key for the door to the attic. The uncarpeted stairs ran straight up.

The spare-room looks the same, used when Pam and her mother, or Granny and Grandaddy came to stay. Grey Grannie, Father's mother, came all the way from Stranocum to try to dissuade him from leaving. I'd once heard raised voices through the closed door, but the significance passed over my head.

The garden looks barren. The ivy has been ripped from the cliff along one side, showing the bare rock beneath. The unclimbable bay tree in the corner has gone, with its leaves that smelled so pungently when I bruised them as I climbed. The wide herbaceous border which ran alongside the wall by the road has vanished. No trace of the clump of montbretia which had hidden my doomed grey and white kitten, flattened when Cynthia P-B jumped on it.

The flame japonica by the conservatory has gone, so has the conservatory, leaving only its tiled floor to be termed a patio, edged by a flowerbed with an incongruous crimson hybrid rose. The lawn is tidily mown, a forgotten plastic football the only sign of life.

The original solid garden gate is still in place, its hinges strong. The paint is chipped and peeling, exposing the wood beneath. Under its deathly pallor, I can still see a scrap of the old faded green. A board naming it "Fentonluna House" is nailed to cover a rotting board. We needed no name-board. It was simply known as "Fentonluna".

My small right foot went into the latch-hole, the left swung up to the top. With a heave I gained the summit, the slab of slate topping the wall adjoining the house. There I used to sit, knees drawn up, arms round knees, safe even when the bull was led past.

My tour is swiftly finished, I will not linger. There are no ghosts. No pheasants hang in the larder, no eel fights for its life on the slate slab.

The net-curtained windows and closed front door stare blankly back at me. The graceful façade is scarred by a white down-comer from the new bathroom. All stands immaculately neat and impersonal, ready for the next family to rent it for a Padstow holiday.

All is still, all is quiet. Nothing moves in the house, nothing lives but the woodworms, who stealthily devour my past. I hope I have left no shadow. I think I shall not come again.

The End

ISIS publish a wide range of books in large print, from fiction to biography. Any suggestions for books you would like to see in large print or audio are always welcome. Please send to the Editorial Department at:

ISIS Publishing Ltd.
7 Centremead
Osney Mead
Oxford OX2 0ES
(01865) 250 333

A full list of titles is available free of charge from:
Ulverscroft Large Print Books

(UK)
The Green
Bradgate Road, Anstey
Leicester LE7 7FU
Tel: (0116) 236 4325

(Australia)
P.O Box 953
Crows Nest
NSW 1585
Tel: (02) 9436 2622

(USA)
1881 Ridge Road
P.O Box 1230, West Seneca,
N.Y. 14224-1230
Tel: (716) 674 4270

(Canada)
P.O Box 80038
Burlington
Ontario L7L 6B1
Tel: (905) 637 8734

(New Zealand)
P.O Box 456
Feilding
Tel: (06) 323 6828

Details of **ISIS** complete and unabridged audio books are also available from these offices. Alternatively, contact your local library for details of their collection of **ISIS** large print and unabridged audio books.

The Salt of the Earth
Diary of a poor family in Woodstock, 1900
Dorothy Calcutt

Life in a poor family in 1900 was a precarious balance, weighted on one side with the pleasures of alcohol and on the other by the influence of John Wesley and General Booth.

This is the story of one year in the life of a large family living on the edge of the Blenheim estate in Woodstock, Oxfordshire. Unemployment was their biggest enemy, but Ma could always be positive and George is lucky enough to find employment at the Palace. It was an eventful year, four deaths and other tragic events temper moments of good fortune, all of them are shared in these delightful memoirs.

A Double Thread
A Childhood in Mile End — and beyond
John Gross

John Gross is the son of a Jewish doctor who practised in the East End from the 1920s through the Second World War and beyond. His parents were steeped in the customs and traditions of Eastern Europe, yet outside the home, he grew up in a very English world of comics and corner shops, sandbags and bombsites, battered school desks and addictive, dusty cinemas.

Looking back on his childhood, he traces this double inheritance. The customs that underpinned family life — Yiddish stories and jokes, the rituals and mysteries of the synagogue — is set against the life of the streets, where gangsters are heroes and patients turn up on the door-step at all hours.